SIL[illegible]

CLOTS

Life's Biggest Killers

Lockstep Medicine's Conspiracy to Suppress the Test That Should Be Done in Emergency Rooms Throughout the World

by
James R. Privitera, M.D.
and
Alan Stang, M.A.

THE CATACOMBS PRESS™
105 N. Grandview
Covina, California 91723
(818) 966-1618

105 North Grandview
Covina, CA, 91723
(818) 966-1618
Fax: (818) 966-7226

First Edition

ISBN: 0-9656313-0-3
Library of Congress Catalog Card Number: 96-72237

TABLE OF CONTENTS

Part Three: Organized Quackery

Preface

This book answers the many questions patients and practitioners have been asking about a life-saving technique: live cell analysis via darkfield technology. *Clots* explains the dangers of abnormalities found in the bloodstream through this important yet largely ignored technique; the part they play in so many disorders and diseases; how darkfield technology detects them; how Dr. Privitera treats them; the vitamins, minerals and enzymes that are a crucial part of that treatment, along with proven methods like chelation; and the diets essential to lifestyle change without which both patient and practitioner are fooling themselves. Dr. Privitera has taught these techniques in his Covina, California clinic to many medical practitioners from around the world. This book is in considerable part the answer to their many requests to "put it on paper," because the people need to know. You will find in it considerable practical information and knowledge gained over many years of clinical experience by Dr. Privitera that both physicians and patients will be able to apply in their efforts to prevent and treat illness as well as to optimize health.

This knowledge, unfortunately, is not taught in medical schools--at least, not in this country. The reason is because it involves methods that are relatively inexpensive. In addition, for many years a small, but influential coterie of medical totalitarians-for-profit has connived to suppress them.

This book is also about the critical battle for freedom of choice in medicine and the orchestrated attempt to destroy it. The authors take no joy in hanging the medical profession's sleazy linen out to dry, but it's a dirty job that someone has to do.

Along these lines, a word should be said about the word "quack." A quack in medicine is someone who refuses to accept the evidence, refuses in order to protect a lucrative scam, an antiquated product, a redundant procedure. In the old days, a quack was someone who was content to peddle 180 proof elixir or blood-sucking leeches. Today, a quack routinely calls a real doctor a quack; indeed, today's quacks have developed quackery into a fine art, complete with front groups that defend it, and that use government to give them monopoly control of American medicine. In *Clots* we call the quacks what they are, and show what true quackery is, mainly by copious reference to their own publications.

This book is about many issues and practices involving Dr. Privitera., the founder of NutriScreen, Inc., a leading provider of darkfield technology and expertise, and a holistic practitioner specializing in allergy and nutrition for almost 25 years. During this time Dr. Privitera has been tormented, penalized and even jailed because he chose to exert his conscience and freedom of choice in providing health care services to his patients. The harassment that he and other like-minded physicians suffer is a result of their desire to use what they sincerely consider to be the most effective and safe means available to help patients and not just practice a limited form of medicine dictated by an economic-political-medical hierarchy. The issues described in the book are in many cases personal but also go to the heart of the disease disaster that grows like a runaway cancer in this country because of our medical dictatorship.

Clots is intended for patients who want to know more about alternative and effective ways to improve their health, and the truth about why many of these “other” ways are stifled. The book also endeavors to help guide health care practitioners who want to use these techniques in their practices.

Dr. Privitera's many years of experience have been translated into book form by Alan Stang, a prize-winning journalist, novelist, lecturer, talk show host and foreign correspondent for more than thirty five years.

If you would like to know more about darkfield, about chelation or other methods described here, please write to Dr. Privitera at 105 North Grandview, Covina, California, 91723, call him at (818) 966-1618, or simply visit the clinic. If it resembles a social club, you are in the right place. Chelation treatment, which is conducted in the clinic, requires a few hours per session in the company of other patients. Thus you'll often encounter lively discussions on the latest political and medical events, with an emphasis on liberty, assisted by the latest videos and punctuated by Dr. Privitera's pithy comments.

Part One

Darkfield

and

Live Cell Analysis

Chapter One
Clots Kill

Last year, 1995, a close friend suffered a severe, paralyzing stroke and was hospitalized. He was a 58-year-old lawyer and a highly productive individual. When I learned what had happened, I called my friend's doctor and asked if I could take a drop of blood to examine under darkfield microscopy. I was given permission. The head intensive care unit nurse, the chief lab tech, and I all viewed the blood under the hospital's darkfield microscope and saw a huge clot some fifteen to twenty times the size of a red blood cell. This indicated the presence of similar clots throughout the entire blood stream--the probable cause of the stroke.

I called the internist and the attending neurologist to tell them what I had discovered and suggested they might want to administer heparin. This is a potent, natural and commonly used blood-thinning preparation that would have broken up the clots and helped improve circulation. Both physicians turned down the suggestion because, they claimed, "It is not standard protocol to rely on darkfield examination for the presence of clots."

The heparin at that point may or may not have extended life or increased the slim possibility of recovery. I felt, however, there was nothing to lose.

Without any effective treatment, my friend's condition deteriorated. Deep inside the brain, cells were suffocating from lack of oxygen caused by clots blocking blood vessels. He could not speak, and could hardly move. After a week, he no longer had any eye movement. At this point, his doctors gave him a small dose of heparin, but it was too little and too late and he died a short time later.

Why the doctors didn't give him heparin earlier than this I don't know. It is common knowledge that the vast majority of strokes are caused by blood clots. Heparin is frequently given in the treatment of heart attacks, where clots are also a major factor. Could they have been upset that an outside physician was suggesting something that was not in common practice?

Could it have been a bias against darkfield microscopy, which is an excellent method to determine the presence of clots, yet is limited in usage by some twisted attitude of the medical establishment to detecting *treponema pallidum,* the microorganism that causes syphilis? You'll find a darkfield microscope used for this limited purpose in every hospital, but not to determine something more common, such as the presence of life-threatening clots. I talk more of this--and other--warped establishment policies in Part Three of this book.

The point is that here was a patient hospitalized with a stroke. Most strokes are caused by clots. We demonstrated the presence of clots. The attending physicians did not accept this proof, nor, apparently, attempt to confirm it through other means and thus start anti-clotting treatment earlier.

The reaction by these physicians was typical. Over the years, I have been largely unsuccessful in attracting hematologists, neurologists and cardiologists to look at this exceptionally effective, rapid and inexpensive method of demonstrating the presence of clots. Is it an ego thing? Maybe they don't want to be enlightened by a general practitioner, especially one involved in preventive medicine. Meanwhile, people continue to die without getting timely evaluation.

I would really like to see every emergency room using darkfield microscopy to evaluate patients who have chest pain and strokes, and other acute medical conditions, to determine the presence of excess clotting.

The reality is that blood clots are the leading cause of death. They are silent, potent killers. When a clot occurs in the brain, interrupting the blood flow, the resulting stroke often kills part of the brain. A stroke is either major or minor depending on the blood vessel where the clotting and blockage occurs. Ninety per cent of strokes are caused by clots. The same percentage applies to heart attacks, in which a clot stops blood flow to the heart in a narrowed artery. More than half the deaths in America today are caused by heart attacks and strokes.

Stroke magazine of August, 1991, reported that infections commonly precede strokes and may in fact trigger strokes by changing the body's "blood clotting system." In one study described by the magazine, infections were present in 17 out of 50 patients (34%), and ranged from mild, upper respiratory problems to urinary tract infections and pneumonia.

Clots also play a role in many of today's major degenerative diseases. For instance, with few exceptions, clots are involved in metastatic cancer. Clots restrict oxygen, which encourages cancer cells to thrive. Clots also produce a substance called "platelet derived growth factor" that suppresses the immune system, thus promoting the spread of cancer in the body.

Do you experience chronic headaches? You probably would never guess that clots are involved in your suffering. But indeed they are. In 1977, Drs. Deshmuch and Mayer won the Harold G. Wolff Award of the American Association for the Study of Headaches by confirming that clots cause migraine headaches. In our clinic, we conducted a study on 41 migraine patients and found 95% of them with significant clotting.

The cell that makes your blood clot is the thrombocyte, more commonly called the platelet, a very small disc about 2 microns in diameter. Platelets originate as megakaryocytes, very large cells that form in the bone marrow. Megakaryocytes fragment into platelets, which then are released into the blood. If you are interested in such statistics, normal blood contains between 200,000 and 400,000 platelets per cubic millimeter.

All clotting isn't bad, of course. If your blood doesn't clot at all, you have a problem called hemophilia. When you cut yourself, you want a clot to stop the bleeding. You want what is called normal platelet aggregation. The trouble starts when your platelets stick together more than they should, which happens in sugar diabetes and viral infections.

Are clots more of a problem today than at other times in history? We don't know but we know about some of the reasons why dangerous clots form. One reason is stress. And for sure we are a highly-stressed society. Stress increases the release of adrenaline into the bloodstream which causes platelets to stick together abnormally. Smoking, alcohol and caffeine can also stimulate abnormal platelet aggregation. So can deficiencies of niacin and magnesium. That is why magnesium is said to be a miraculous defense against heart attacks.

In recent years, research cardiologists have become excited over the discovery of anti-clotting properties in many naturally-occurring chemical compounds found in vegetables and fruits. It is possible that diets low in these foods may very well be a prime factor in abnormal clotting activity. Since abnormal clotting is so dangerous, it is supremely important for the doctor to know whether it is present.

We have experimented in clinical practice for many years in search of the best test. For instance, we used the platelet aggregometer for years. We found it impractical, because so many substances--pethidine, morphine, septra, EDTA, theophyllin, warfarin, aspirin and heparin, among others--interfere with the test. It is also cumbersome, time-consuming and expensive. The best and quickest test we have found is the darkfield. The test begins with a drop of blood taken from the patient's fingertip or earlobe. The blood is placed on a slide and put under a darkfield microscope which projects the patient's live blood onto a television monitor. You see blood cells as white circles against a black background--hence the term darkfield. On the screen, both doctor and patient can see what the blood in the circulatory system actually looks like at the moment. The doctor explains the activity of the different cells, and gives the patient a Polaroid picture of his blood to reexamine at home.

After many years of using this method, I believe the experience of a patient seeing a picture of his or her own blood on a television screen makes a powerful impact both for understanding the nature of illness and for subsequent compliance with the physician's recommendation. Later in the book, we will show pictures of the different darkfield patterns and activity that appear on the screen and explain their significance. Neither the platelet aggregometer nor any other test offers this advantage. With the latter, the patient gives the blood and it goes off to a lab which comes up with some abstract numerical value at a later date. With darkfield, the patient sees the very nature of the problem, along with the doctor. It's visual, it's eminently educational and understandable, and it's immediate. And it's accurate.

An independent laboratory was used to analyze the blood of 15 patients for the presence of beta thromboglobulin, a protein secreted by abnormally sticky platelets. We compared the results of the laboratory test to our own darkfield results and found 100 percent correlation. The presence of significant clots, as seen by the darkfield, was indeed confirmed by an accompanying increase of beta thromboglobulin secretion.

By means of darkfield technology, the doctor can immediately determine the degree of danger and take appropriate action. That action routinely includes a change in diet, and a regimen of vitamins, minerals, enzymes and other nutritionals, to replace what is missing and correct imbalances. Sometimes, the remedial program includes other procedures like chelation.

The reason diet is so important is that clots are a vital part of the cholesterol problem we hear so much about. Cholesterol is the fatty substance in the blood that is generally related to diseases of the heart and the blood vessels. HDL, or High Density Lipoprotein, is a type of cholesterol that appears to protect people from those diseases. The other type of cholesterol is LDL, Low Density Lipoprotein, which is dangerous. By dividing your LDL by your HDL, your doctor can establish a ratio that strongly indicates your chance of suffering coronary heart disease.

Let's look at a study we did on 45 patients with circulation complaints. All these individuals had clots of 2+ or more under the darkfield microscope, which means a clot the size of two red cells. A clot the size of one red cell would be described as size 1+, etc. The biggest clot in this particular group was a 4+, but clots can be much larger, in which case patients often complain of chest pain. I regard any clot 2+ and above as dangerous, inasmuch as a normal red blood cell may have to alter its shape to squeeze through a minuscule capillary to deliver its oxygen and nutrient cargo. If a clot blocks the way, the blood can't get through.

In our study, 31 out of the 45 (70 percent) patients also showed abnormal cholesterol HDL ratio. This indicates that the darkfield procedure provides a reliable, non-invasive first-level screening tool for determining vascular problems.

We also did a study of 28 patients with angina, another name for chest pain. Twenty seven, or 96% of these patients, showed significant platelet aggregation (clotting) through darkfield microscopy.

Eighty percent of heart attacks involves what is called silent ischemia (decreased oxygenation of tissues). These individuals *do not experience chest pain.* If darkfield microscopy were performed as part of a routine checkup, it seems reasonable to suggest that many cases of significant clotting would be picked up early--and appropriate remedial steps taken--thus potentially saving countless lives of individuals who have no symptoms of a heart condition.

The darkfield microscope method is clearly an extremely powerful tool for determination of heart attack as well as stroke risk. And migraines. And many other serious conditions. I would like to know why this method is not widely used. The fact that it isn't is utterly amazing.

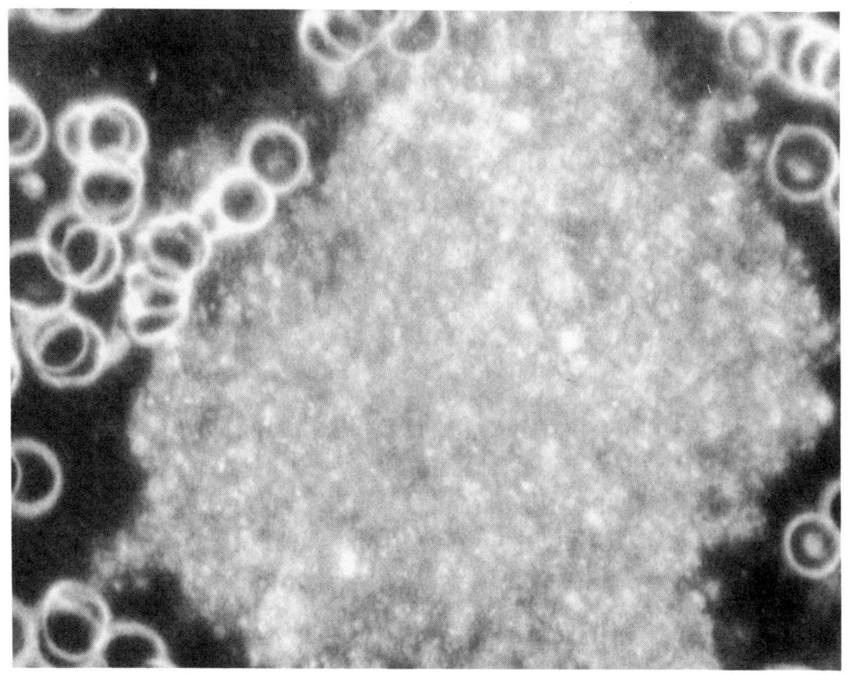

Thrombocyte Aggregation (Clot)

Chapter Two
Clots, Disease and Supplements

Clots prevent the red blood cells from delivering their critical cargo of oxygen and essential nutrients to the trillions of cells throughout the body. When this happens, cells "downstream" from the clot malfunction and die. Thus clots play a key part in many conditions and diseases. Do clots cause those problems? Not totally, but we do know that when we eliminate clots, problems often improve and even disappear.

In this chapter I will describe a number of common conditions that are benefited when clots are reduced. In our clinic, we have found that good nutrition and the use of supplements are extremely helpful to achieve this objective. In the discussion that follows I will discuss how specific supplements promote the anti-clotting process.

First and foremost, eating right is the basis of any successful nutritional program. In my opinion, that means a diet low in saturated fat and high in complex carbohydrates. Refer to Chapter Six for more details. The best results are achieved by patients who eat the freshest and least processed food.

The supplement program starts with a good multi vitamin and mineral formula. We then build on this foundation according to individual needs and severity of clotting. In my practice I recommend a multi in capsule form that provides the following daily nutrients:

Vitamin A (palmitate) 10,000 IU	**Beta carotene 20,000 IU**
Vitamin E (d-alpha tocopherol) 400 IU	**Vitamin D 100 IU**
Vitamin B-1 (thiamine) 75 mg	**Vitamin B-2 (riboflavin) 75 mg**
Vitamin B-3 (niacin) 40 mg	**B-5 (calcium pantothenate)400 mg**
Vitamin B-6 (pyridoxine) 75 mg	**Folic acid 600 mcg**
Biotin 300 mcg	**Vitamin B-12 200 mcg**
Calcium 300 mg	**Magnesium 300 mg**
Potassium 55 mg	**Manganese 20 mg**
Zinc 20 mg	**Copper 2 mg**
Selenium 250 mcg	**Chromium 225 mcg**
Iodine 225 mcg	**Molybdenum 50 mcg**
Bioflavonoids 200 mg	**Betaine/Glutamic HCL 100 mg**
Niacinamide 75 mg	**Choline 75 mg**
Inositol 75 mg	**N-acetyl L-cysteine 30 mg**
L-glutathione 15 mg	**Riboflavin 5-phosphate 10 mg**
Pyridoxal 5 phosphate 10 mg	**Proanthocyanidins 6 mg**
Silicon 100 mcg	**Vanadium 75 mg**

There are, of course, many good formulas on the market. In selecting one for yourself, look for a product that is similar. If you have any questions on supplements, call my office at 1 (818) 966-1618.

The supplements I discuss usually have a substantial effect on clotting as well as many other health benefits. After starting on the program, people typically report feeling healthier and more energized.

I should emphasize that in my clinic I tailor supplements to the status of the individual. The specific supplements and dosages mentioned here represent general daily guidelines that have worked well for many patients as an anti-clotting program. Amounts are designated for mild, moderate and severe degrees of clotting as seen through darkfield microscopy. The term mild refers to the presence of 1+ to 2+ clots; moderate is 2+ to 3+; and severe clotting is 3+ and over.

Supplement	Mild	Moderate	Severe
Vitamin C	**2,000 mg**	**4,000 mg**	**6,000 mg**
Essential Fatty Acids from fish oils: EPA (eicosapentaenoic acid) and DHA (docosaxhexanoic acid) combined 560 mg caps	**3**	**3-5**	**5-9**
Vitamin E (mixed tocopherols)	**400 IU**	**600 IU**	**1,000 IU**
Garlic oil	**2 capsules**	**4**	**6**
Mucopolysaccharides (bovine cartilage)	**300 mg (2 capsules)**	**600 mg**	**900 mg**
Vitamin B-6	**100 mg**	**200 mg**	**300 mg**
Bromelain	**100 mg**	**200 mg**	**300 mg**
Primrose Oil	**3 capsules**	**4**	**6**
Potassium/magnesium aspartate or citrate	**40/40 mg**	**80/80 mg**	**120/120 mg**
Capsicum (cayenne)	**1 capsule**	**2**	**3 or more**
Proanthocyanidins	**30 mg**	**60 mg**	**90-150 mg**

Arthritis

I recommend a combined calcium-magnesium citrate. Research has found calcium citrate to be the best absorbed form of calcium. Other minerals including copper, manganese, and zinc can also be helpful. We measure levels through hair mineral analysis and recommend as needed. Bromelain, an enzyme complex from pineapple, reduces joint inflammation, which is especially useful in rheumatoid arthritis. We recommend 1, 2 or 3 Bromelain enzyme capsules before meals.

We recommend a daily regimen of 2, 4 or 6 alfalfas; and 2, 4 or 6 mucopolysaccharides as bovine cartilage. This has been shown to strengthen cartilage tissue.

French studies have found that a combination of bioflavonoids, Vitamin C and enzymes was 50% more effective than NSAIDS (Non Steroidal Anti-Inflammatory Drugs) in the early inflammation of arthritis.

Glucosamine sulfate and chicken collagen have been helpful. Many studies have shown the former to be of clinical importance in joint maintenance and renewal. Chicken collagen likewise has been shown to give significant relief for joint pain, swelling and stiffness.

Vitamin B-6 is very effective for carpal tunnel syndrome and meralgia paresthetica, a similar type of nerve entrapment condition in the leg. We recommend 100, 200, or as much as 300 mg of B-6 daily.

A relatively new approach in arthritis calls for the suppression of an inflammation-causing fatty acid produced in the body known as prostaglandin two (PgE2). We can suppress it by using plant and fish oils. Primrose oil, for instance, promotes the formation of beneficial prostaglandins known as PgE1 and omega-3 fish oils promote another "good" form called PgE3. These two counteract PgE2 more effectively when combined than when used alone. For this reason we recommend both primrose and fish oils on a daily basis. PgE2 is involved in inflammation, clotting and the pain of arthritis.

In blood studies in England, arthritics were found to be deficient in pantothenic acid, so we suggest 500, 1000 or up to 2000 mg daily.

We also suggest 3 to 5 of a hydroxyapatite--bovine whole bone extract, with a complex of complementary nutrients--that is helpful to bones and cartilage. To head off any confusion, I should point out that I use two types of bovine extracts. One is from cartilage. The other from bone.

Asthma

Anti-yeast therapy may be helpful. In my practice, I have seen many patients improve dramatically on an anti-yeast diet combined with specific anti-yeast substances such as Nystatin. A recent finding indicates that asthmatics have an increased tendency to clot. As in arthritis, the promotion of PgE1 and PgE3 is quite appropriate. Zinc activates the anti-clotting mechanism, and may be helpful if tests show it to be low. Rotation diets may also help.

We also recommend 1, 2 or 3 betaine-hydrochloric acid capsules after meals. Each contains 648 mg.

In addition, we suggest the following supplements: Vitamin B-6 in the range of 100, 200 or 300 mg; Vitamin C at 2,000, 4,000 or 6,000 mg; and Dimethylglycine (DMG), at 50, 100 or up to 200 mg. Molybdenum and magnesium are recommended in amounts depending on hair analysis readings. Glycyrrhizin, a natural agent derived from the licorice root with steroid-like activity, is also helpful. It has a long history of use as an anti-inflammatory and anti-allergy aide, actions which have now been documented by scientific research.

Baldness, Hair Loss (Alopecia)

We recommend the following daily supplements: 250, 500 or 750 mg of cysteine; 5, 10 or 15 mg of biotin; 500, 1,000 or 1,500 mg of inositol; and 100, 200 or 300 mg of silica. The silica should be derived from the horsetail herb, which provides about 18% organic silica. We also suggest tyrosine, 100, 200 or 300 mg daily. Tyrosine is a precursor to thyroid, and one of the hallmarks of hypothyroidism is hair loss.

Bladder Infections

Cranberry juice, available on your supermarket shelves, is a natural source of mandelamine, which is the oldest, most popular and effective solution we know. Try it before you come to see me. We also recommend 3,000, 6,000 or up to 10,000 mg of Vitamin C; and 25,000, 50,000 or up to 100,000 units daily of Vitamin A.

Zinc is supremely important in bladder problems, but many patients who take even as much as 50 mg of zinc daily are still deficient. That's because they don't absorb it. A hair mineral test provides a good idea of your zinc level. Recent studies have shown increased absorption of zinc with picolinate acid, which is a ligand (zinc carrier) naturally found in Pancreatin enzymes. So, we suggest 15, 30 or 45 mg of zinc picolinate daily, and, for the same reason, 1, 2 or 3 Betaine HCL after meals. We have also found other agents such as CLO2 (Chlorine Dioxide) Halox™ quite effective. We use 10 drops, 3 to 4 times a day in 1-2 ounces of liquid. The product is generally available in health food stores.

Burns

Use ice to limit the pain. If possible, immerse the burned area in ice water. A capsule of Vitamin E, squeezed directly on the burn, can be very effective. For many years, patients have told me that raw egg whites have been quite effective applied to new burns. Other patients tell us that vinegar is effective. You could also try aloe vera, another natural substance said to be very effective for burns. PABA cream, as well as aloe vera, is effective for sunburn, and many commercial preparations contain it. DMSO could be helpful. Try these things before you spend money on doctors.

Cancer

In California, a doctor is jailed for treating cancer if he is not Politically Correct, about which more later. I practice in California, and I am Politically Incorrect, so I don't treat cancer. The good news is: I don't have to. In the 21st century, treating cancer will become mostly old-fashioned. Since cancer is almost invariably triggered by nutritional and/or immune deficiency, healers to come will prevent cancer by enhancing nutrition and the immune system. I have no doubt that elementary common sense will one day prevail.

Today, we find that cancer patients seldom have had an immune evaluation. An in-depth evaluation usually finds natural killer cell activity and other aspects of immunity are low. We then work to restore the immune system. The strengthened system can more effectively fight the cancer. The body is rendered more capable of healing itself.

Many patients create fertile ground for cancer by "death styles" that include excessive alcohol, tobacco, junk food (food high in saturated fat, especially hydrogenated fat, or artificial flavoring and coloring), inadequate fruit and vegetables, not enough sleep and too much stress.

Nothing is more important in restoring the immune system than increasing oxygenation. The cancer cell cannot live in a high oxygen environment. Even radiation therapy, which kills the cancer by trying to kill the cancer cells and occasionally killing the patient, is more effective when administered with increased oxygen. Therefore, we use many antioxidants in rather large amounts which force oxygen into the aerobic pathways.

Among them is emulsified Vitamin A, in a range of from 50,000, even up to 200,000 units daily. We use emulsified A because it theoretically bypasses the liver and goes straight into the lymphatics, which means that we can use larger amounts. However, it is important to watch for signs of excessive Vitamin A, which can be harmful. They include hair loss, bone pain and nausea. I have seen Vitamin A toxicity, even with the emulsified version, from 200,000 units up.

In Australia, Biogland has patented a system called "micellar-contained" vitamins, the superiority of which has recently been proved. The Biogland system is especially effective where there is poor bowel absorption, as in colitis or sprue, or in debilitated states where absorption must be assured.

In severe cancer cases we recommend 5, 10, even as much as 50 grams of Vitamin C a day, to the point of bowel tolerance. You can get diarrhea if you take too much vitamin C. But it is at the level just below this point that the tissues become saturated with vitamin C and it has its most powerful healing effect. If diarrhea occurs, you reduce dosage by a quarter. Another point: when taking vitamin C in large doses, it is best to divide the doses. Don't take it all at once.

Vitamin E is also helpful, in dosages of 400, 600 or 1,000 I.U. daily. We recommend the mixed tocopherols rather than the more familiar D-alpha tocopherol version, because the antioxidant capabilities are much higher in the beta, delta, gamma, etc., fractions of the Vitamin E. Again, cancer thrives in an oxygen-deficient environment. Antioxidants increase oxygenation. Without them, oxygen would attack body fat, and bind to it, forming peroxides. Antioxidants prevent this, with beneficial effects on the metabolism.

We also recommend spleen, which is high in the antioxidant glutathione, or glutathione separately in multi gram quantities. There is some evidence that glutathione is poorly absorbed and that the best way to produce it is to take glutamine and N-acetyl cysteine.

We use thymus, another glandular, which contains thymosin, a hormone known to stimulate T-cell formation. T-cells are thymus-derived--immunologically potent lymphocytes, that kill cancer cells. We recommend both B-6 (200 mg to 600 mg daily) and pantothenic acid (500 mg to 2,000 mg daily) because they stimulate immunoglobulin formation. Immunoglobulins are proteins produced in the body that have antibody activity.

As in asthma and arthritis, there is in cancer as well an increased tendency to clot. Clinicians have noted for years that many cancer patients die of heart attacks or strokes. For this reason, we use large amounts of the fish oils (EPA), from 3, to 6, to 9 daily, or other blood thinners such as flaxseed oil, cayenne pepper and cartilage.

Arginine stimulates lymphocyte production, and is helpful (2,000 mg, 4,000 mg or 8,000 mg daily). However, it should be avoided where herpes is present, because it can promote that condition. Arginine is also antagonistic to lysine.

DMG increases immunity and oxygenation. We recommend 50, 100 or 200 mg daily. Selenium works in concert with Vitamin E. Cancer rates are lower in parts of the United States where there is substantial selenium in the soil. We suggest 400, 600 or 800 mcg daily.

We think it is wise to take 2, 3 or 4 enzymes (pancreatin) before meals. Enzymes digest the sialomucin coating on cancer cells, so that the immune system can recognize and attack them. We also suggest 100, 500 or 1,000 mg of germanium, and 5 to 9 shark cartilage (either capsules or tabs) or 5 to 15 teaspoons a day in extremely advanced cases. Some other substances we use in our clinic are iodine, squalene (shark oil), Essiac tea (multiple herbs) and I.V. nutrient solutions in advanced cases. Soybean concentrate, mitake mushroom extracts, astralagus and una de gato are recent additions to this regimen.

For more information about substances in use around the world to combat cancer, call the Cancer Control Society, at (213) 663-7801.

Colds

First, we need to know what kind of cold it is: viral or bacterial, acute or chronic; and where it is: head or chest. Fluids, both water and fruit juices, are highly recommended. For sore throats, chewable Vitamin C or acerola is very soothing; so are Propolis and zinc lozenges. Non-chewable Vitamin C from 5 to 50 grams a day is excellent, especially for severe flu. One or two 500 mg tablets of arginine every hour may help, by stimulating lymphocyte production. Remember to use it carefully in individuals prone to herpes. Also, try B-6 and pantothenic acid, 100 mg of the former to 300 mg of the latter. The combination will stimulate the production of antibodies. Garlic, cloves or concentrate, is very helpful. We also suggest goldenseal, rose hips, and, for a sore throat, slippery elm. Thymus (3 or 4 daily) is beneficial. Silver (colloidal) is a recent and effective addition to our treatment regimen. Many patients with chronic fatigue syndrome have frequent colds.

Colitis

In this disease, it is important to distinguish between the chronic and acute varieties and food allergy. A urine indican should be done for bowel toxemia evaluation. If normalization of bowel toxemia is attempted through inoculation of the colon with lactobacillus and enzymes, the enzymes should contain bile salts, which are known to be anti-amoebic. We have had excellent results with these. Recommended dosage would be two after meals. We also suggest duodenum substance (500 mg, four to six daily), and nutmeg (1/2 to 1 teaspoons three times daily) for diarrhea. Comfrey with pepsin (2-3 before meals) is helpful; so is aloe vera. We recommend 1-3 ounces, 2-3 times daily. Glutamine has recently been found to improve gut integrity, so we've added this exciting amino acid.

Refined carbohydrates should be replaced by high complex carbohydrates and low saturated fats. Oatmeal is excellent. As in many diseases, stress reduction is extremely important.

Cramps

Cramps come in a variety of painful packaging: purely muscular, menstrual, a byproduct of pregnancy.

Sustained exercise can trigger cramps. One common cause is low magnesium. And most nutritional surveys show that Americans are deficient in this key mineral. Stress of any kind, including physical exertion, drains magnesium from the body. Additional magnesium is lost through perspiration. We have all seen long distance runners drop out of races because of leg cramps.

Calcium and potassium are also helpful for individuals with a tendency to cramp. The first thing I do for patients with cramping problems is to put them on a calcium-magnesium-potassium formula. This often eliminates the cramps. Liquid mineral salts are recommended, but beware of products loaded with sugar calories (via corn syrup) which pack enough sweetness to give diabetes to a whale.

Hormones can trigger female cramps and such occurrences are usually associated with a calcium and magnesium deficiency, so we recommend those minerals. If they do not help appreciably, a whole blood potassium level would also be important.

We also attempt to strengthen the liver, and use an anti-inflammatory approach to suppress PgE2. I discussed this earlier in the arthritis section. First and foremost among such treatments is B-6. We have noted that pantothenic acid taken with B-6 tends to reduce the jitters; pantothenic acid is known to affect adrenal function, so this shouldn't be surprising. Other supplements appropriate here would include 1,000 I.U. of Vitamin E (mixed). Thyroid may be helpful, along with primrose oil or, at least, unsaturated fatty acids and iodine (150 mcg, 5-15 drops a day).

Dental Caries

By now, everyone should know that this problem is a by-product of refined food. Children who eat refined sugar get cavities, but children who eat sugar cane, which of course is raw and unrefined, don't. Refined sugar contains next to no B-6 or trace minerals. Studies also link periodontal disease with a deficiency of calcium and magnesium. A mineral analysis can be most helpful in such cases.

The extensive work decades ago of Weston Price, of the Price Pottenger Foundation in San Diego, California, also shows that whole foods properly nourish the whole person, but the refined "foods of commerce" don't. Price traveled to many primitive tribes where dental caries were rare. On the contrary, almost 98% of civilized people have dental caries, which proves that cavities are a disease of refinement. For more fascinating information about the dramatic impact of refined foods on the health of societies not used to eating such food, read Price's *Nutrition And Physical Degeneration*. Since the mouth reflects the condition of the body in general, a complete nutritional evaluation would be helpful if periodontal disease is associated with severe dental caries. Brush your teeth with a 50-50 mix of baking soda and salt at least at night before bed. So recommends my dentist, Frances Wong, in Covina, who says that the problem is acid bacteria.

Diabetes

Commonly viewed as a genetic problem, this epidemic "disease" is rare where food is scarce or whole and unrefined. Overeating and refined foods are the two horsemen of diabetes. The disease was unknown among Eskimo tribes until the white man brought in white flour and sugar, along with cooked foods. Live blood exam frequently shows various degrees of clotting in diabetes.

We recommend HCL, niacin and EPA to suppress the clotting and inflammatory activities of the PgE2 system. For the same purpose, we recommend PgE1 and PgE3 promoters such as primrose oil, linseed oil, flaxseed oil, unsaturated fat (Vitamin F) and fish. Of course, saturated fat should be avoided. I suspect, however, that the soft, saturated fat of young animals, such as calf and lamb, does not have the same negative effects as that of older animals. My suspicion is in part biblical, since the father of the prodigal son said, “Get the fatted calf. My son is coming home.” He didn’t say get the fatted COW. Most feasts in those days were of lamb.

It is especially important in diabetes to determine chromium and zinc levels with mineral testing. Chromium as GTF (Glucose Tolerance Factor) or chromium nicotinate, which is absorbed twice as effectively as chromium picolinate, and zinc as zinc aspartate or picolinate are helpful. Amounts are best determined through a hair mineral analysis.

We recommend a supplement regimen including GTF (200, 400 or 600 mcg daily); zinc picolinate (25, 50 or 100 mg); EPA (4, 6 or 8); enzymes (2, 3 or 4, taken after meals, the amount depending on the size of the meal); primrose oil (4, 6 or 8); pancreas compound (2, 4 or 6 daily); glutamine (2, 4 or 6 before meals); biotin (5, 10 or 15 mg daily); vanadyl sulfate (7 mg a week); garlic oil (4, 6 or 8 daily); and liver (4, 6-8 or 8-12 daily).

Glutamine is an inexpensive amino acid that has the unique ability to regulate sugar. Garlic helps enormously to prevent clots and heart attacks, but you must use the oil, not the dry version. Liver of course strengthens the liver, which animal studies show is more important in stabilizing diabetes than the pancreas. Soskin showed that dogs with their pancreas removed, given insulin along with large quantities of sugar, had normal blood sugar. Yet, when the liver function in such dogs was disturbed, the blood sugar became very high. *Low Blood Sugar And You*, by Carlton Fredericks (New York, Grosset and Dunlap, 1969), is an excellent book, although it is more oriented to hypoglycemia. Sugary complex carbohydrate sources, such as whole bananas, oranges, etc., can be used with careful guidance.

Arteriosclerosis is a common complication of diabetes. Refer to the discussion on circulation in Chapter One.

Diarrhea

This can be caused, of course, by many things. One cause is stress-colitis. Enzymes can help here because they promote digestion, which is impaired by stress. If the enzymes don't work, try duodenum, which studies show is a specific aid for colitis. Nutmeg is an inexpensive and easy folk remedy, a half to one teaspoon, 3 times a day in yogurt. Yogurt helps reintroduce good bacteria, such as lactobacillus, to the colon, especially in antibiotic-induced diarrhea. A urine indican is recommended to show the presence of abnormal bacteria in the colon. In parasite-induced diarrhea, garlic, and PABA in dosages as high as 1,000-2,000 mg, are appropriate, as well as black walnut and cloves.

If you plan to travel to high risk areas like South America, don't leave home without HCL and enzymes for prevention. Spirits of peppermint and golden seal have also proven beneficial.

Diverticulosis

This is a condition of chronic low-grade inflammation in the pockets of the colon. If these pockets are considerably inflamed, the condition is called diverticulitis. The cause is generally agreed to be a "low residue" diet, i.e., not enough bran and complex carbohydrates. Expect the urine indican to be at least moderately abnormal. As in colitis, enzymes and duodenum are helpful, along with such anti-infectious agents as garlic, echinacea, golden seal, high Vitamins C and A, and zinc. It is critical in this condition to prevent constipation.

Eczema

Rough, flaky, itchy skin can become infected when scratched. Again, the prostaglandin system is the key. As in many degenerative diseases, suppression of the (pro-clotting, pro-inflammation) PgE2 system, or arachidonic acid pathway, is crucial. We have had considerable success with topical preparations containing vitamins, as well as cortisone preparations which can be given orally and parenterally for quick relief in severe cases.

Some patients are afflicted with fungal infections such as candida. Biotin, used as part of a total holistic program, has been effective for fungus and other eczematoid conditions. Recently, we've seen success with olive leaf extract. (See Chapter Nine).

If testing confirms, we recommend the following for eczema: zinc picolinate (25, 50 or 50-100 mg daily); Vitamin A (10,000, 25,000 or 50,000 IU); PABA (500, 1,000 or 1,000-2,000 mg); EPA (3, 6 or 6-10); primrose oil (3, 6 or 6-9); and unsaturated fatty acids (3, 3-6 or 6-9).

Edema

A very common problem often caused by heart disease, allergies, kidney failure, etc. The late pathologist Melvin Knisely showed convincingly that red cell clotting caused lack of oxygen in the extremities. Fluids and acids build up ahead of the blockage. Capillary walls increasingly leak. The supply of oxygen decreases. The edema spreads, like water before a dam. If a particular organ, like the heart or kidney, is involved, it is crucial to bring that organ to normal function.

Recently, researchers discovered an anti-diuretic, anti-sodium hormone in the atrium of the heart. Therefore, we should give the same heart substance for diuresis that we give for angina and high triglycerides. Some of the recommendations for edema are: heart (2, 4 or 6 daily); B-6 (pyridoxine) 100 to 300 mg ; bromelain (100, 200 or 300 mg). Bromelain reduces swelling and has been used in standard medicine for years to reduce bruising, i.e., edema of trauma.

We also suggest potassium/magnesium aspartate (1, 2 or 3 after meals). Potassium is antagonistic to sodium and absorbs better when taken with magnesium. The aspartate form absorbs extremely well.

We also suggest arginine (1, 2 or 3 before meals). Arginine is an amino acid which is the key in the urea cycle and can be very helpful in edematous states.

KD formula is helpful. It contains alfalfa, buchu, juniper, parsley, uva ursi, cranberry, corn silk and marshmallow. According to some sources, silica is a natural diuretic. All green juices and carrot juice are high in potassium and very beneficial. Potassium, of course, is antagonistic to sodium. We also suggest Vitamin C (2, 4 or 6 grams daily).

We would like to discuss all the medical conditions we treat, but we have to stop somewhere. If we have not dicussed your condition, please either call us or get a copy of *Alternative Medicine, The Definitive Guide*, compiled by the Burton Goldberg Group (Puyallup, Washington, Future Medicine Pub., Inc., 1993).

Chapter Three
What The Squiggles Mean

ou've probably never thought of yourself in cellular terms. But that's what you are--a collection of trillions of cells. All shapes. All sizes and functions.

When you come for a darkfield microscope analysis, a technician painlessly takes a drop of blood from your finger and puts it under the microscope. A special lens inside the microscope projects the view onto a television screen in front of you. And there you are--a living picture of the cellular you--right before your eyes. TV never gets more personal or dramatic.

You'll see white rings against a black background. Some by themselves. Some linked together. Those are your red blood cells. You'll see puffy, gray shapeless masses--those are white blood cells. You'll see little crystals of fat scintillating in the background. It's a wondrous world. And it's you. A living piece of you extracted from your body and put up on the screen. And to the health professional who knows how to interpret them, the images on the screen reveal a plethora of information not only about your present health but about how you can expect to feel later.

The images have been classified according to cellular patterns and other visual characteristics associated with different health problems. These classifications are discussed in this and the following chapter.

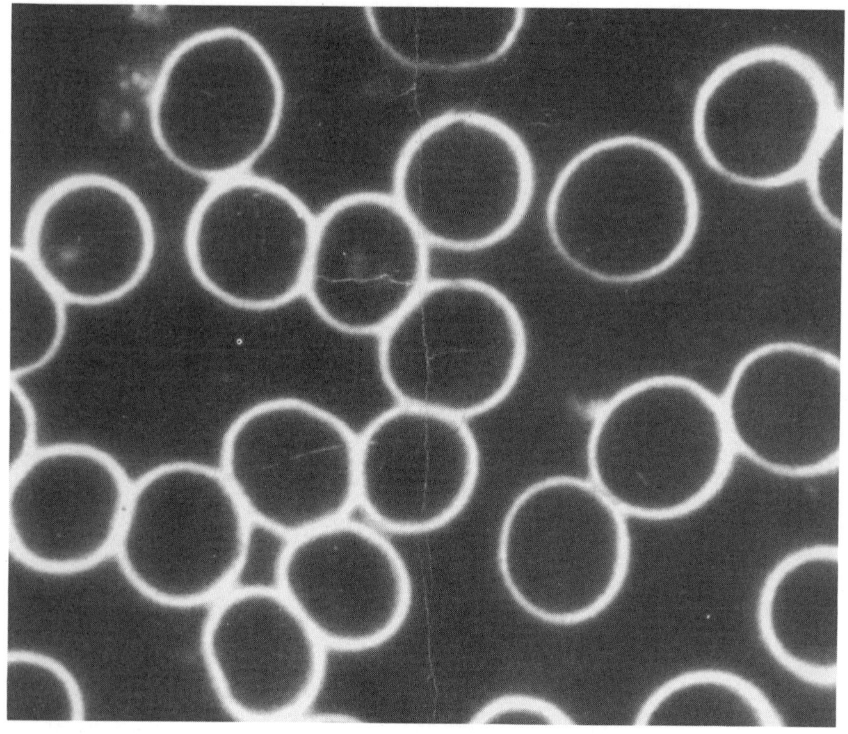

Normal

The dosages indicated here for supplements are daily amounts. The recommended diet for all these conditions is my routine suggestion of low saturated fat, and high complex carbohydrates.

Rouleau

This is the singular of rouleaux in French, and means "a row of red corpuscles," like a pile of coins. A rouleau pattern is indicative of poor oxygenation, which often causes overwhelming fatigue, shortness of breath, bad digestion, edema and low skin temperature. Without rouleau, red cells squeeze through capillaries single file, transferring oxygen to the cell in exchange for carbon dioxide, the spent product of oxidative metabolism. In the patient with rouleau, less oxygen is transferred, and fatigue can result.

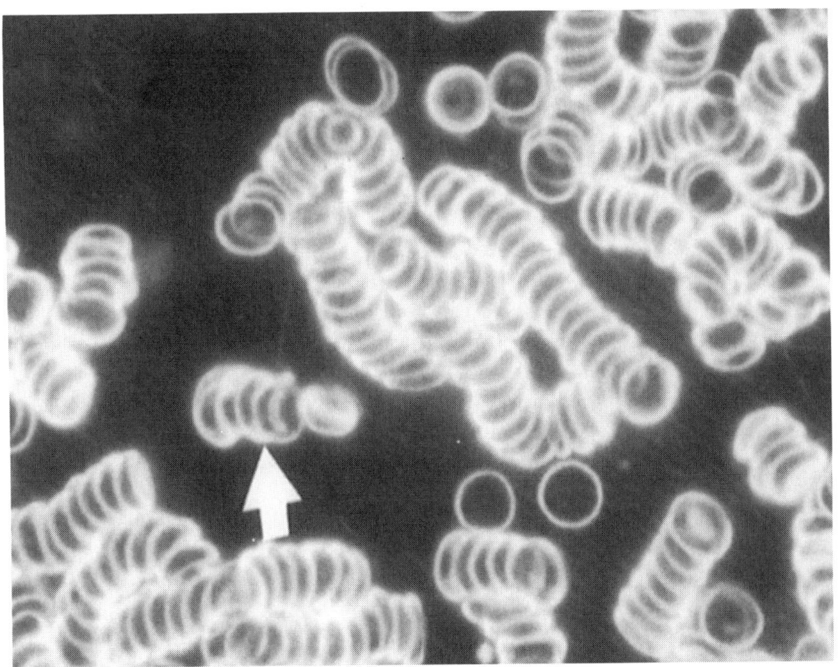

Rouleau

In 1984, a patient study showed excellent response even in severe rouleau to intravenous hydrochloric acid (HCL) at a 1:500 dilution in varying doses from 2 c.c. to 10 c.c. Retesting with the darkfield microscope showed even severe cases ameliorated in 10 minutes. This study proved that rouleau, as described by the late pathologist Dr. Melvin Knisely, of the Medical College of South Carolina, almost 20 years ago, is very treatable. Research as far back as 1831 revealed excellent response to HCL for asthma in the form of an increased white blood cell count.

Rouleau correlates strongly with degenerative diseases and occasionally with high sedimentation (a blood test that provides a non-specific indication of inflammation). Since hydrochloric acid is necessary for the absorption of many minerals, we often find mineral deficiencies when rouleau is present.

We also recommend niacin. Many patients who use niacin experience "niacin flush": burning face and pounding heart. A new product that may reduce or even eliminate the problem has recently become available.

Supplement	Mild	Moderate	Severe
Multi vitamin/mineral formula including:			
Betaine HCL/Pepsin	**1-2 after meals**	**1-2**	**2**
Niacin (non-flush)	**250 mg**	**250-500 mg**	**500-750 mg**

Chylous Material

This is the fat in the blood, which correlates best with what the patient ate before the test. If the patient ate little fat and small portions, but the microscope sees considerable fat, we know he either has high blood fats and/or a weak liver that is unable to clear them.

Chylous material is composed of: 1) chylomicrons which are derived from the intestinal absorption of fatty compounds called triglycerides; 2) VLDL, the very low-density lipoproteins; 3) LDL, the low density lipoproteins; 4) HDL, the high-density lipoproteins; and 5) free fatty acids which consist of long-chain fatty acids attached to serum albumin.

Treatment would include fat emulsifiers such as lecithin, along with the lipotrophic factors, choline, inositol and methionine; essential fatty acids, such as omega-3 oils from fish, lower cholesterol and triglycerides. It is well recognized that Eskimos who generally eat diets high in fish, have low blood fat. Niacin has been shown also to lower cholesterol significantly.

Diet would of course be crucial. It needs to have plenty of good fats, such as are obtained from fish, but low in saturated fat. Complex carbohydrates are emphasized.

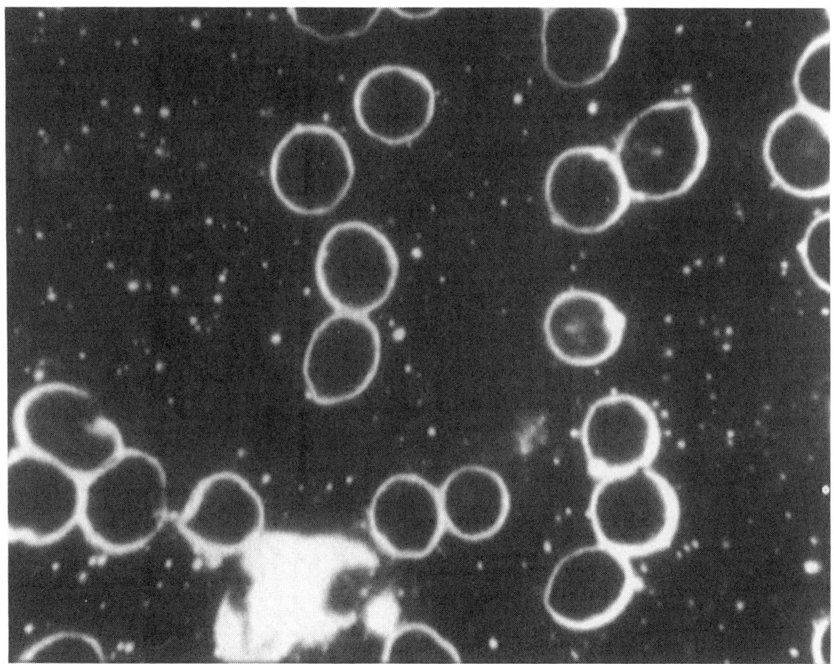

Chylous

Testing would include a urine indican, a test for bowel toxemia, SMA 24 including a sed rate, and a glycolated hemoglobin (percentage of sugar in the red cells) to detect possible diabetic tendencies. We also recommend a hair mineral analysis.

Supplement	Mild	Moderate	Severe
Multi vitamin/mineral formula including:			
Niacin (non-flush)	250 mg	500 mg	750 mg

Liver	2/day	4/day	6/day
Enzymes	1 after meals	2	2-3
Vitamin C	1,000 mg	2,000 mg	3,000 mg
Choline/inositol/ methionine (3 tabs provide 1000 mg choline, 100 mg inositol and 300 mg methionine)	1 after meals	2	2-3
EPA (omega 3)	2	4	6

Neutrophils

Neutrophils, also known as "polymorphonuclear neutrophils" or "PMNs," are a type of nucleated white blood cell attracted to areas of inflammation and proliferating bacteria. These cellular cops literally eat up (phagocytize) the bad guys they encounter, along with any other foreign particles. With the darkfield microscope, we have seen them attack plaque-like particles in the blood and bacteria. For this reason, we want to see active neutrophils. When the neutrophils are active, there is considerable ameboid movement with pseudopod (false foot) formation. Neutrophils comprise about 40 to 60 per cent of the total white blood count.

Impaired neutrophilic viability is often accompanied by low hydrochloric acid. In this situation, the cells remain small, inactive and poorly defined. Such images show up in cancer patients treated with chemotherapy. In fact, in about 80% of cases of impaired neutrophilic viability, there is low hydrochloric acid associated with chronic degenerative disease. Poor immunity, infectious conditions and malabsorption frequently are found with faulty neutrophils.

Neutrophils are fairly uniform in size (12 to 15 microns) with an average of four segments. Five or more segments mean hypersegmentation, usually pointing to folic acid deficiency. We also see glossitis and a shiny, magenta-red tongue. This image is often indicative of depression, menopausal problems, and a tendency to heart attacks.

Hypersegmentation may also mean B-12 deficiencies associated with low HCL (hypochlorhydria), because if the parietal cells of the stomach are not producing HCL, they many times are not producing intrinsic factor. Hypersegmentation may also cause folic acid deficiencies late in pregnancy. The two deficiencies--of B-12 and folic acid--often appear together.

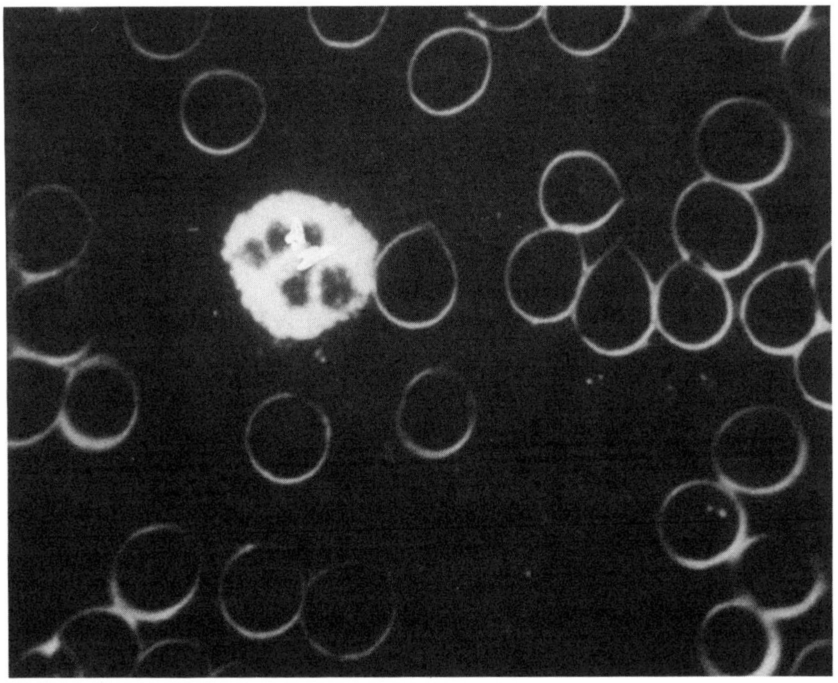

Neutrophil Hypersegmentation

Clumping of neutrophils on a darkfield image always indicates impaired immunity. Testing for the problem should include a mineral analysis for signs of malabsorption, plus a CBC and sed rate. If minerals aren't low, an SMA would be more appropriate, looking for elevations of liver enzymes. If clinical correlation merits it, an immune evaluation could be helpful.

DMG (dimethylglycine) apparently enhances oxygen utilization and neutralizes free radicals, extremely reactive substances in the body that cause chain reactions of cellular destruction. Agents that act against free radicals are called antioxidants. (More about these in Chapter Eight.) One of the most powerful antioxidants nature provides is called S.O.D., superoxide dismutase. It is produced in the body but requires sufficient manganese, zinc and copper to function properly. This is still another reason to do a mineral analysis. Another powerful antioxidant is proanthocyanidin, which is extracted from the grape seed. This substance is said to be 50 times more potent than vitamin E, one of the major antioxidants.

For the diet, we suggest calf liver once a week, along with lots of green, leafy vegetables, kidney and lima beans and other legumes, asparagus, whole grain cereals, and nuts.

Because the normal bacteria of the colon produce B-12, we would use the urine indican test; a very positive urine indican could mean insufficient B-12 production. Mineral analysis may show many low minerals, i.e., a pattern of malabsorption consistent with the hypochlorhydria we have mentioned.

Supplement	Mild	Moderate	Severe
Multi vitamin/mineral formula including:			
Folic Acid	**400 mcg/day**	**1,000 mcg**	**5,000 mcg**
Raw Stomach	**2**	**3**	**4**
B Complex	**1**	**2**	**3**
B-12	**250 mcg**	**500 mcg**	**1,000 mcg**
Liver	**2**	**3**	**4**
Betaine HCL/Pepsin (after meals)	**1**	**1-2**	**2**
Thymic Fractions	**1-2**	**2-3**	**3-4**
DMG	**1**	**2**	**2**
SOD	**1-2**	**2-3**	**3-4**

Eosinophils

This is another kind of white cell, also nucleated, usually having only 1-2 lobes, very bright, almost yellow, in darkfield examination. Its granules are much larger than the neutrophil's, and usually the ameboid movement is less obvious. These types of cells make up about 1 to 3% of the white blood cell count. Higher percentages are associated with allergies and parasites, and poor immunity in bacterial or viral infection. Eosinophil presence is also usually higher in lymphomas or Hodgkin's disease. Certain tumors such as eosinophilic granuloma also cause an increase in production of eosinophils.

Patients with food allergies sometimes show more eosinophils. But candida should always be ruled out, since such allergies often lessen or disappear totally after candida cases are cleared up.

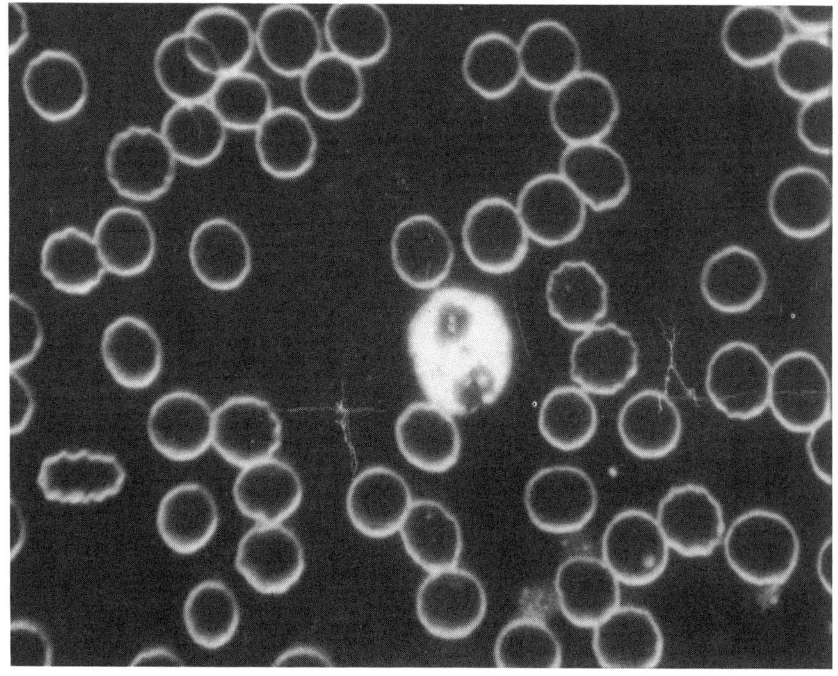

Eosinophil

The eosinophil suspect should be observed for dark circles under the eyes, white spots on the fingernails (a possible sign of zinc deficiency), eczema, periorbital edema, fluid retention in general and poor energy.

Supportive testing would include a urine indican; testing for candida or allergies; mineral analysis; and F.I.C.A. (Food Immune Complex Assay--not a test for Social Security) done after a scientific nutritional program plus enzymes, which works most of the time.

Note that my recommendations include large amounts of vitamin A, particularly for the severe cases. It is worth mentioning again that taking such large doses can be potentially toxic over the long term. Symptoms of vitamin A poisoning could show up. To avoid these serious problems, only use amounts of 50,000 and more for a month at a time.

Supplement	Mild	Moderate	Severe
Multi vitamin/mineral formula including:			
Vitamin A (water soluble)	**10-20,000 IU**	**25-50,000**	**50-100,000***
Vitamin C	**1-2 gr**	**2-3 gr**	**3-6 gr****
Vitamin B-6	**100 mg**	**200 mg**	**300 mg**
Pantothenic acid	**250 mg**	**500 mg**	**750 mg**
Adrenal	**2**	**3**	**4**
Zinc Picolinate	**15 mg**	**30 mg**	**45 mg**

***Remember the warning about Vitamin A.**
****(or to point of loose stools)**

Erythrocyte Aggregation

We know them simply as red blood cells. Formally, they are erythrocytes. Technically, they are bioconcave discs with a diameter of about 7 microns, a maximum thickness of 2 microns and about 1 micron thick in the center. Red blood cells are like sacks that can be endlessly reshaped without damage. This flexibility is due to the large quantity of membrane relative to the amount of material inside. Other cells would rupture easily with such treatment.

The concentration of red cells in the blood is normally 5,200,000 (plus or minus 300,000) in men, and 4,700,000 (plus or minus 300,000) in women.

When the red blood cells are drawn together as if by a magnet, we have an erythrocyte aggregation. Such an aggregation can be life-threatening, worse than rouleau, and even more detrimental to the downloading of oxygen. Saturated fat and abnormal protein cause sticky red cells. The problem also correlates with the sedimentation rate.

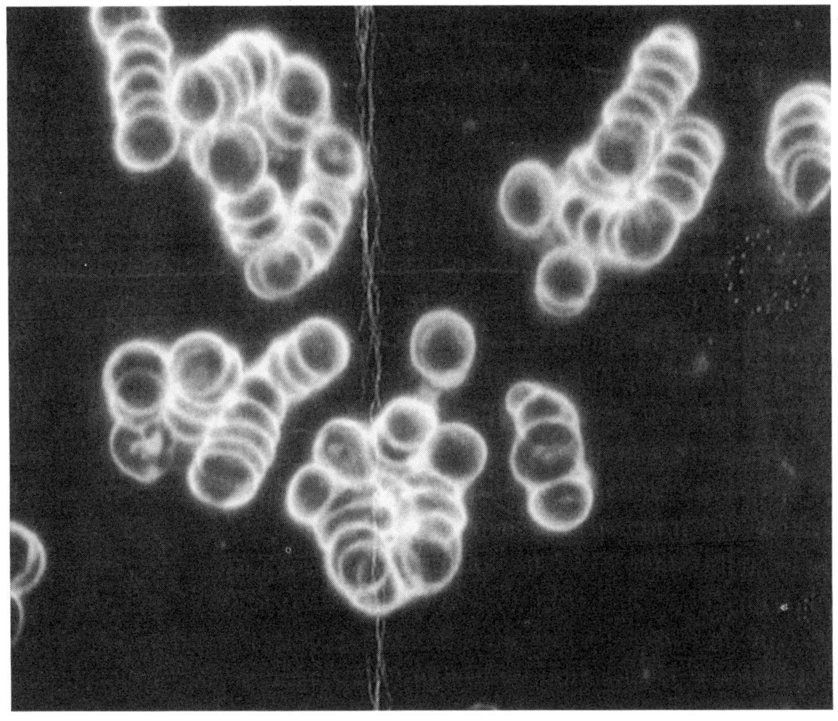

Erythrocyte Aggregation

At the Medical College of South Carolina, M. Knisely reviewed this subject at length. In more than 40 pages, he observed "agglutinated blood as seen in the bulbar conjunctiva of 600 human patients diagnosed as having 50 different pathological conditions and disease."

Heparin has been shown to reverse red cell aggregation. Again, that is why I suggested it to my friend's doctors, in the tragic story we told in Chapter One. Since niacin stimulates most cells to release heparin, we use this along with HCL, which is also very helpful.

Supplement	Mild	Moderate	Severe
Multi vitamin/mineral formula including:			
Betaine HCL/Pepsin	**1 after meals**	**2**	**2-3**
Niacin (non-flush)	**250 mg**	**500 mg**	**750 mg**

We also recommend a urine indican, which measures toxemia of the colon; and an SMA 24, along with liver function tests such as a GGTP.

Spicule Formation

Frequently, we see this condition along with sticky red cells and chronic, degenerative diseases. With spicules, we usually suspect a liver damaged by blood pressure medication, anti-histamines, non-steroidal anti-inflammatory agents, antibiotics and other drugs, alcohol or viruses.

Under the darkfield microscope, you see a picture akin to spokes around an empty space, like a pinwheel. Often, the spokes are irregular as in red cell aggregation. When we prick a patient's finger for blood to conduct a darkfield exam, we notice that if the blood is left on the fingertip for any time, red cell aggregation and spicule formation is the rule. The heavy paraproteins are acute phase reactants, so, if repetition of the test rules out technical problems, liver function should be evaluated.

Spicules probably consist of fibrin or alpha 2 macroglobulin, since they are the heavier proteins in the blood. Fibrinogen is of course involved in clotting. Recently, along with beta thromboglobulin, it was implicated in thrombocyte aggregation (clotting). So, spicule formation is still another problem we encounter in degenerative disease. Hydrochloric acid and heparin have been helpful, the latter derived from either lung or duodenal tissue. Needless to say, any causative drugs should be discontinued, after which, if spicules persist, or therapy fails, we recommend the following tests: SMA 24 with sed rate and GGTP, fibrinogen levels, urine indican and mineral analysis.

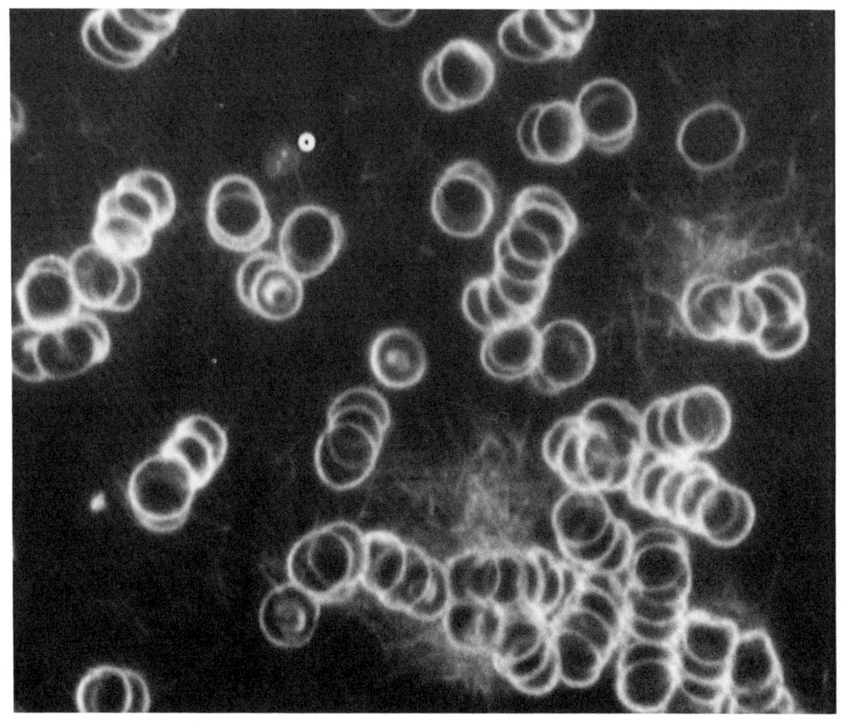

Spicules

Supplement	Mild	Moderate	Severe
Multi vitamin/mineral formula including:			
Betaine HCL/Pepsin	1 after meals	1-2	2
Liver	1 after meals	2	3
Choline/inositol/ methionine (see chylous material section)	2	4	6
Vitamin C	2 g	4 g	6 g
Duodenum	1	2	4
Lung	1	2	4
Olive leaf extract (if problem is virus-caused)	1	1-2	2-3

Poikilocytes

These are deformed red cells. If you have too many of them, you have poikilocytosis. Researchers believe that free radical damage causes membrane rigidity, that is secondary to oxidant-induced cross-linking of the membrane skeleton. Remember that 50% of the membrane is fat that is subject to peroxidation in the presence of oxygen. Antioxidants such as A, E, C, selenium, proanthocyanidins and glutathione (very rich in spleen) protect against this kind of assault.

Recent work by Dr. Jeffrey Bland, Ph.D., of Puget Sound University, and Horvitt, has shown that these cells have an increased tendency to hemolyze, since cell membranes contain considerable unsaturated and other fat. The idea occurred to Dr. Bland to give patients antioxidants to protect the cell wall from oxidative damage. He found that 600 units of Vitamin E did the job. Because of his research, and (supporting evidence cited in the anthology entitled *Hematology*, edited by William S. Beck (Boston, Massachusetts Institute of Technology, 1981, p. 201), we believe these deformed red cells occur because of antioxidant deficiency.

Fatigue usually accompanies poikilocytosis. One reason is that deformed red cells can't efficiently carry oxygen to the tissue cells. Such deformed cells are also seen in cases of post-splenectomy, since the spleen's function is to remove damaged cells. We find that many people with this condition eat considerable amounts of junk food.

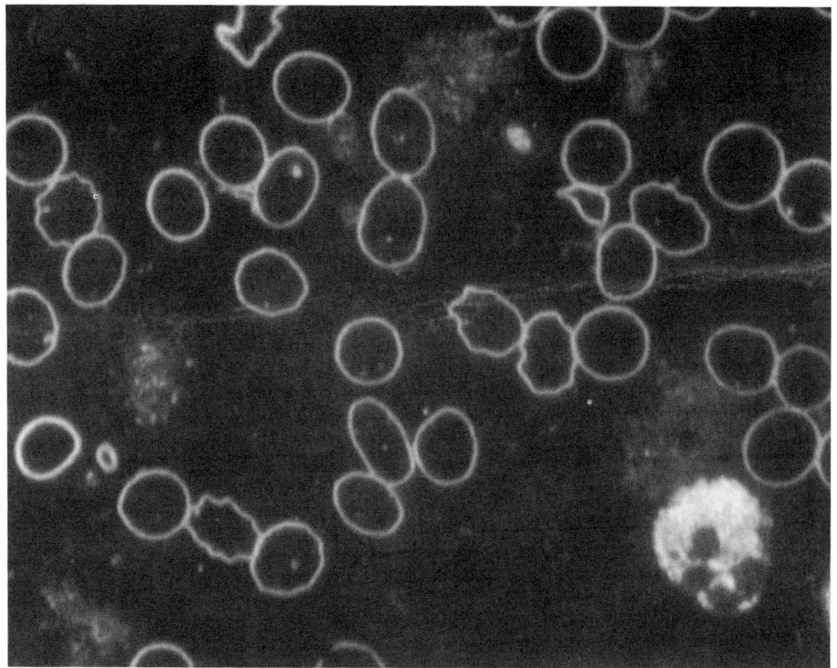

Poikilocytes

For instance, hamburgers, fries, fried food, and especially hydrogenated fat, such as chips. People who work in the sun, and patients who have undergone radiation and chemotherapy, often complain about fatigue. With regard to the sun, increased heat speeds up oxidative reactions in the skin, which can be slowed down by antioxidants. We recommend testing for serum Vitamin E if the test is inexpensive, and for zinc and selenium in a mineral (hair) analysis.

Supplement	Mild	Moderate	Severe
Multi vitamin/mineral formula including:			
Vitamin E (mixed tocopherols)	**1,000 IU**	**1,000 IU**	**1,000 IU**
Selenium	**200 mcg**	**400 mcg**	**600 mcg**
Vitamin C	**1 g**	**2 g**	**3 g**
Vitamin A	**15,000 IU**	**25,000 IU**	**50,000 IU***
Beta Carotene	**15,000 IU**	**25,000 IU**	**50,000 IU**
Spleen	**2**	**3**	**4**
DMG	**1**	**2**	**3**
Proanthocyanidins	**30 mg**	**60 mg**	**90-150 mg**

***Not for more than one month**

Anisocytosis

When you have abnormally shaped red cells, you have anisocytosis. This aberration is commonly associated with iron, folic acid and B-12 deficiencies. Anisocytosis is seen in autoimmune hemolytic anemias, liver disease, megaloblastic anemia of infancy, pernicious anemia (B-12 deficiency), and sickle cell disease (crescent-shaped red cells, a dangerous condition seen most of the time in blacks).

Supplements	Mild	Moderate	Severe
Multi vitamin/mineral formula including:			
Stomach extract	**1**	**2**	**3**
Betaine HCL/Pepsin (after meals)	**1**	**1**	**1**
Liver	**1**	**2**	**3**
Kelp	**2**	**3**	**4**

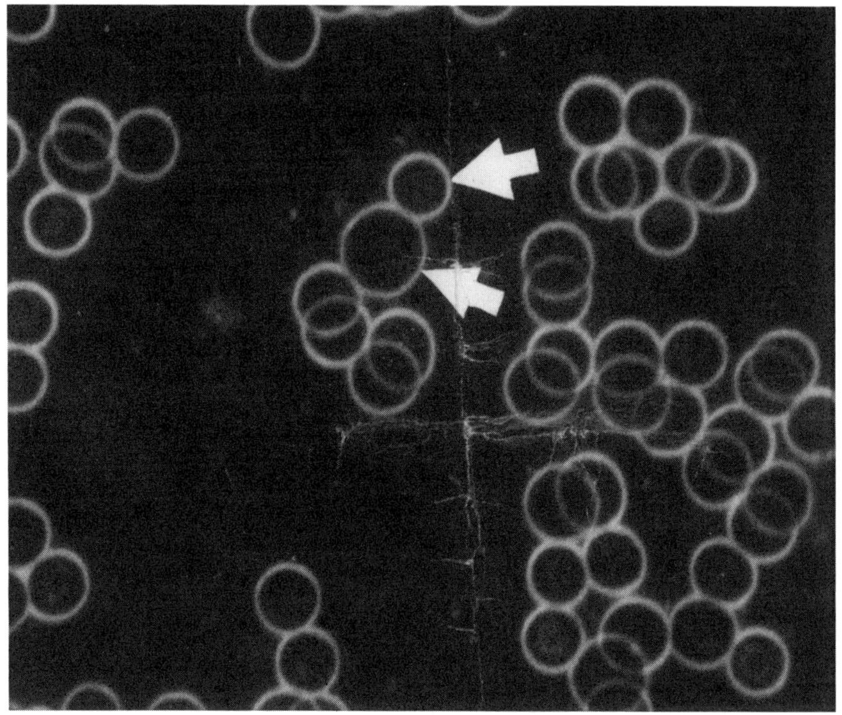

Anisocytosis

Stomach substance is used because it strengthens the patient's own stomach. The stronger the stomach the patient has, the more hydrochloric acid it produces, and HCL helps the absorption of iron. One source of iron is kelp. Testing would include a complete blood count, and a serum ferritin, the most sensitive test we have for iron.

Ovalocytes

These of course are oval, red cells, which usually have more total volume than normal red cells. We find them in folic acid and B-12 deficiency. Without folic acid or B-12, DNA synthesis is interrupted, causing megaloblastic hematopoiesis. Ovalocytes are also found with iron deficiency. According to W.R. Platt, M.D., in the *Color Atlas and Textbook of Hematology* (second edition, p. 232), "There are 15-25% ovalocytes in hypochromic microcytic anemias."

Junk food is one of the main causes of ovalocytes. We also see them in late pregnancy, depression, individuals with problems digesting fat, in alcoholics, in patients on birth control pills and other drugs, such as diphenylhydration (Dilantin) and trimethroprim (Septra).

Supportive testing would include a serum folic acid, and an MCV to see whether it is over 100. Supplements would depend on the number of ovalocytes seen in the dark field examination.

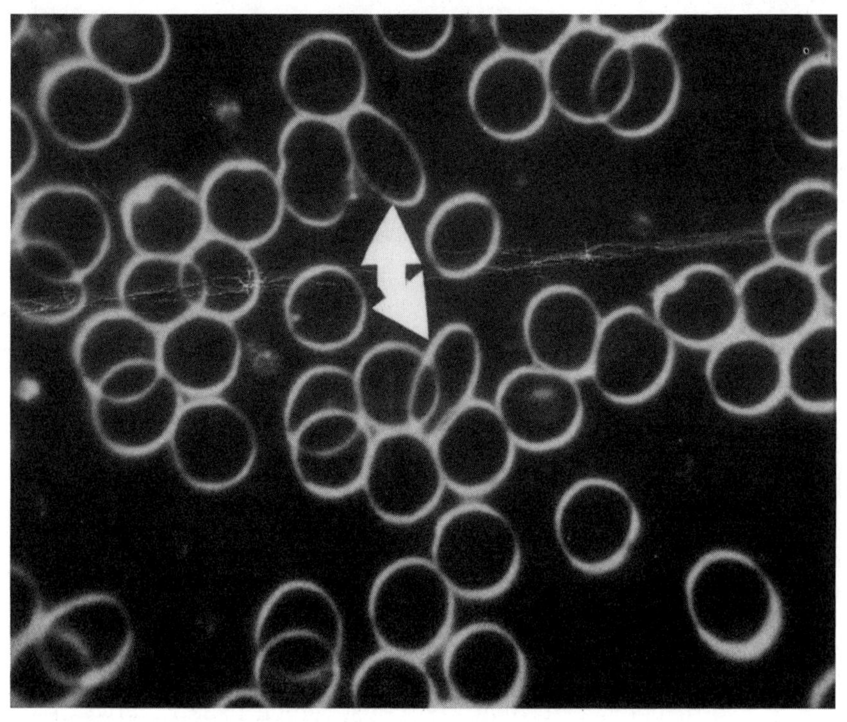

Ovalocytes

Supplements	Mild	Moderate	Severe
Multi vitamin/mineral formula including:			
Stomach	**2**	**3**	**4**
Liver	**3**	**4**	**6**
B-12 lozenge (1,000 mg)	**1**	**2**	**3**

Macrocytes

These are large red cells with a diameter greater than 9 microns, and an average size of 7.2 microns (W.R. Platt, M.D., in *Color Atlas and Textbook of Hematology*, second edition, p. 181). Macrocytes are found in B-12 and folic acid deficiency. Some of the conditions that may be associated with macrocytes are poor absorption, pernicious anemia, lack of hydrochloric acid and quick food transit. Macrocytes are also frequently seen in patients who have had stomach surgeries, tumors, non-functioning bowel loops, small bowel inflammation, parasitic bowel infection and inflammation of the pancreas.

Foods containing B-12, such as beef liver, are recommended. Supportive testing would include urinary methymalonic acid levels, serum B-12 levels, Schilling test and test for associated anemia.

Supplements	Mild	Moderate	Severe
Multi vitamin/mineral formula including:			
Stomach	**2**	**3**	**4**
Liver	**3**	**4**	**6**
B-12 lozenge (1000 mg)	**1**	**2**	**3**

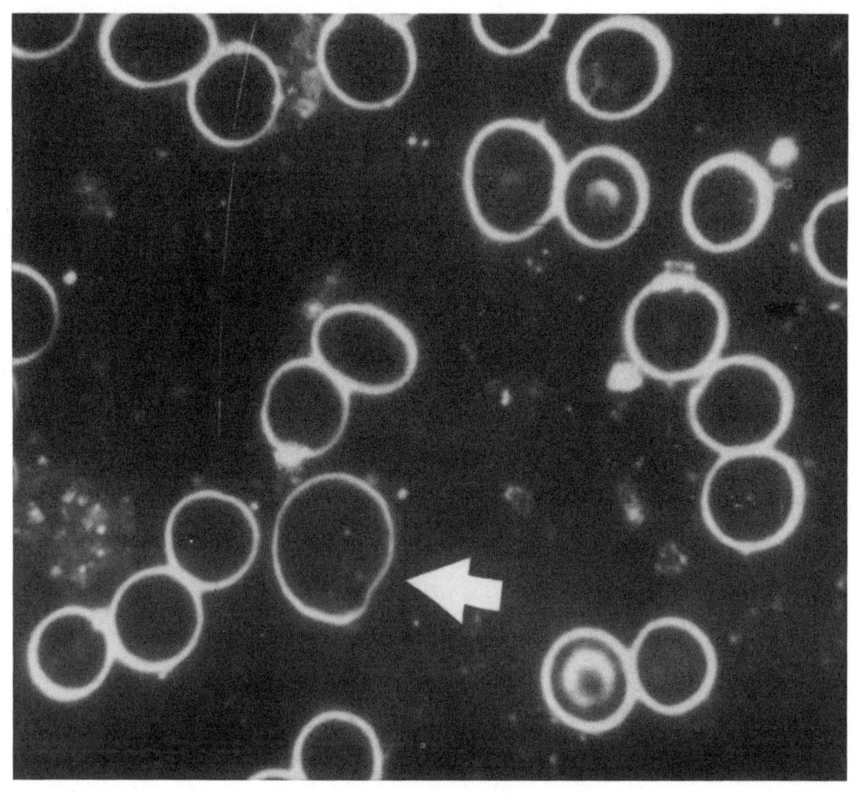

Macrocytes

Chapter Four
More Darkfield Squiggles

icrocytes are small, red cells, with a diameter of less than 6 microns, and frequently with an MCV of less than 80-82 cubic microns.

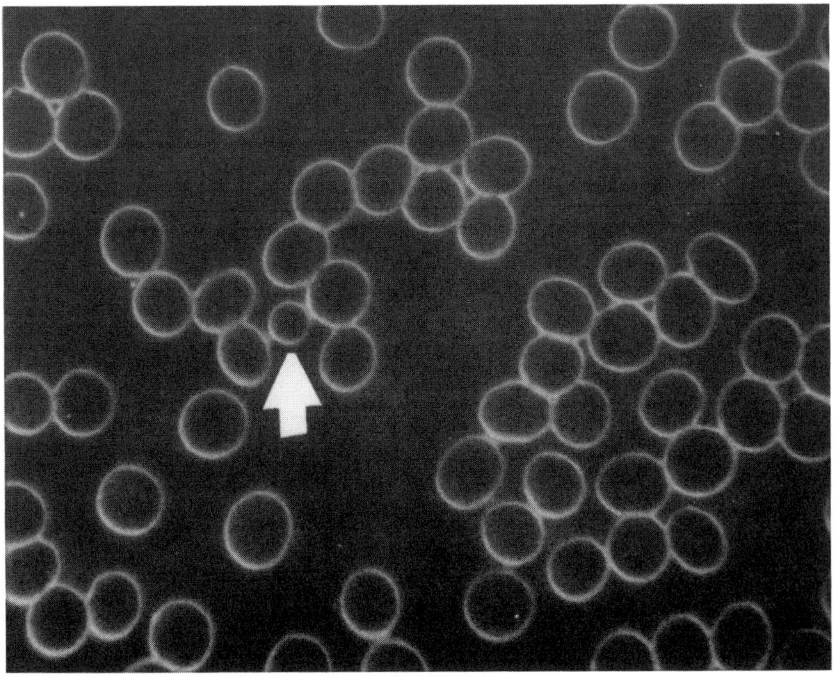

Microcytes

Microcytes often have less hemoglobin than normal cells and therefore are seen in iron deficiency anemia, spherocytic and Mediterranean hemolytic anemias. For supplementation, we suggest the usual multi vitamin and mineral foundation with extra iron, vitamin C and bone marrow. The dosage would be 2-4 tablets, depending on the number of microcytes seen.

Supplement	Mild	Moderate	Severe
Multi vitamin/mineral formula including:			
Liver	**1**	**2**	**3**
Iron	**1**	**2**	**3**
Vitamin C	**1 g**	**2 g**	**3 g**

Target Cells

These are red blood cells that look like "bull's eyes" because they have holes in them. Target cells can indicate iron deficiency or reduced hemoglobin synthesis. Less often, target cells indicate thalassemia, or hemoglobins (S,C,D,E) whose solubility is poor.

Pale skin, poor energy and malabsorption may accompany target cells. In women, target cells frequently appear during heavy menstrual bleeding and pregnancy. Target cells are seen in a third of hypothyroidism cases, anemias, hemorrhoids, colon cancers and when there is substantial loss of blood, as in ulcers (especially duodenal).

In addition to the usual diet, we suggest added iron, from kelp, brewer's yeast (if you are not sensitive to yeast), beef liver, black strap molasses and wheat germ.

Supplement	Mild	Moderate	Severe
Multi vitamin/mineral formula including:			
Liver	1	2	3
Iron	1	2	3
Stomach substance	1	2	3

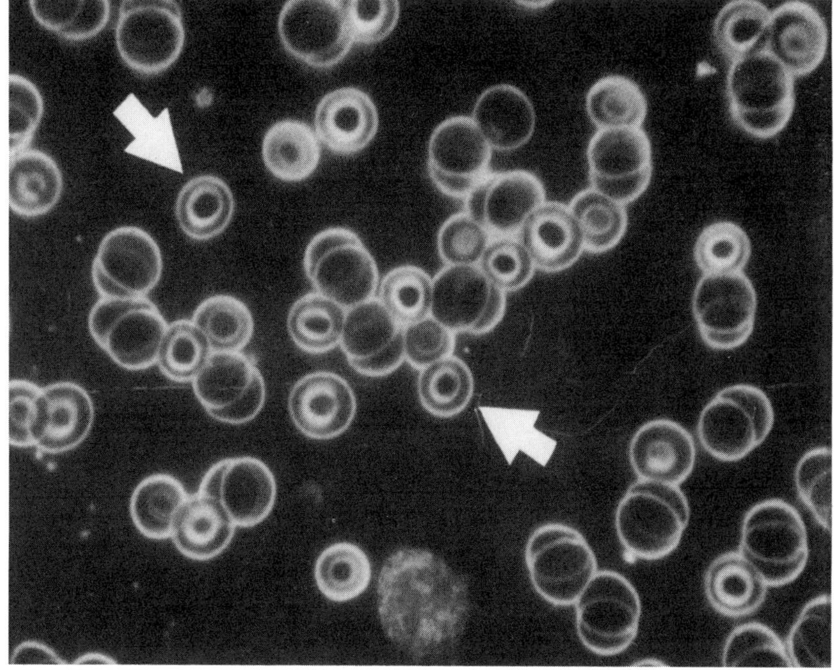

Target Cells

Supportive testing would include a CBC for hemoglobin, and a total red cell count, along with a serum ferritin. The stool should also be checked for occult blood.

Plaque

These structures often accompany heart disease and arteriosclerosis. They are different from protoplasts, which are discussed later. Plaque is a localized, irregular, hard or soft, abnormal formation, that is either stuck to the intima of an arterial vessel or free-floating in the blood. We can sometimes observe the latter type with darkfield microscopy.

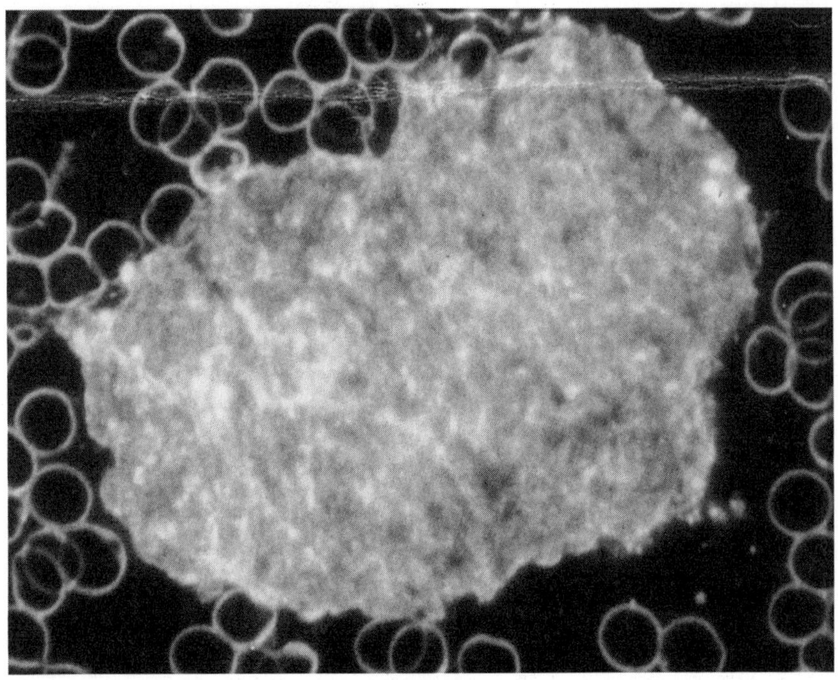

Plaque

Plaque composition can vary, but most of the time it contains a lipid core and fibrin deposits, along with thrombocyte aggregations (thrombosis), plus glycosaminoglycans (mucopolysaccharides), hemorrhage, calcification and collagen (having presumably broken off from an atheroma).

Conditions that may be associated with plaque include: cold hands and feet, poor circulation, reduced energy and stamina, pain in calves when walking, angina (chest pain), high blood pressure and diabetes with a history of heart attack or stroke.

We recommend the usual diet plus lots of fish.

Supplement	Mild	Moderate	Severe
Multi vitamin/mineral formula including:			
Vit. E 400 (mixed tocopherols)	**400 IU**	**800 IU**	**800 IU**
Garlic capsules	**1 after meals**	**2**	**2**
EPA/DHA	**2**	**3**	**4**
Carnitine	**1 g**	**1.5 g**	**2 g**
Vitamin C	**2 g**	**3 g**	**4 g**

When we see plaque in the blood, we recommend an SMA 24 test, with special emphasis on fats, especially adding the HDL. Cardiovascular testing, including echocardiography with Doppler and plethysmography may also be of value. Recently, a non-invasive, fast cat scan of the heart to indicate the amount of plaque formation in the coronary arteries has become available. If these tests prove impaired circulation, intravenous chelation therapy is often beneficial.

L and Rod Forms, Red Cell Microbes

We see all these things with the darkfield microscope. Virginia Livingston, M.D., believed they are forms of the pleomorphic "cryptocydes" microbe, which she classified under the family actina mycetales; they stain intermittently acid fast.

L-Forms must be distinguished from fat particles. They are larger, and occasionally appear yellow on the darkfield screen and much brighter than fat. They are luminescent and spherical, and they "dance" actively under scrutiny. L-Forms are described as embryonic bacteria that lack a rigid wall, but can grow and divide; on the other hand, the protoplast may increase in mass, but is unable to divide.

Low immunity with L-Forms is associated with all the chronic, degenerative diseases. The patient may be chronically ill with frequent colds, earaches or boils. He may lack energy. General nutritional deficiency and L-Forms seem to show up together, for which reason we recommend the usual diet.

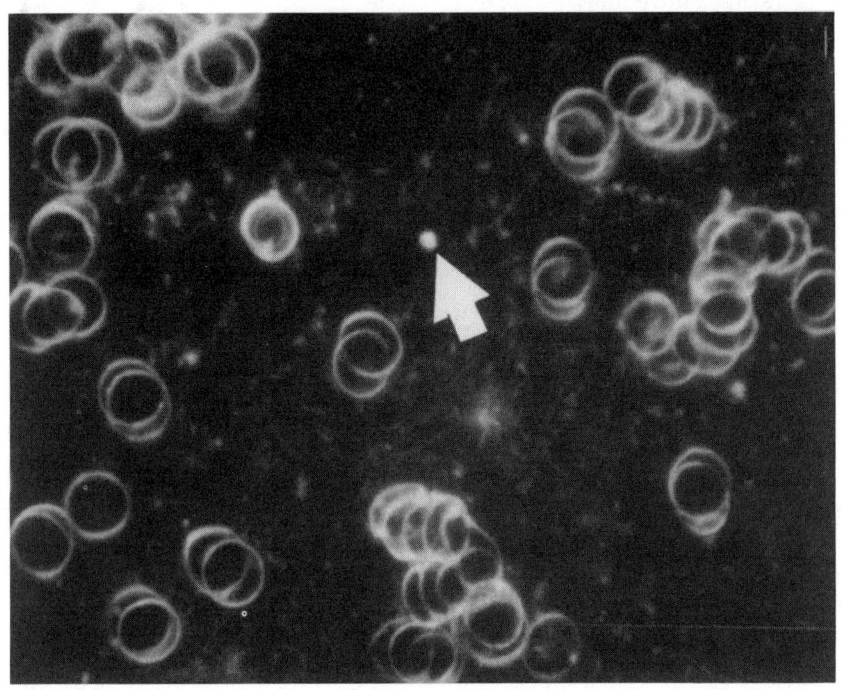

L Forms

Supplement	Mild	Moderate	Severe
Multi vitamin/mineral formula including:			
Vitamin C	**2 g**	**4 g**	**6 g**
Acidophilus	**1-2**	**2-3**	**3-5**
Thymus	**2**	**4**	**6**
Vitamin A (water soluble)	**25,000 IU**	**50,000***	**75,000***
B-6	**100 mg**	**200 mg**	**300 mg**

Pantothenic Acid	250 mg	500 mg	1,000 mg
Zinc Picolinate	15 mg	30 mg	45 mg
Propolis	1	2	3
Garlic capsules	2 after meals	3	4
Echinacea	100 mg	200 mg	300 mg

***Do not take these higher amounts for more than 1 month. Such prolonged use could be toxic.**

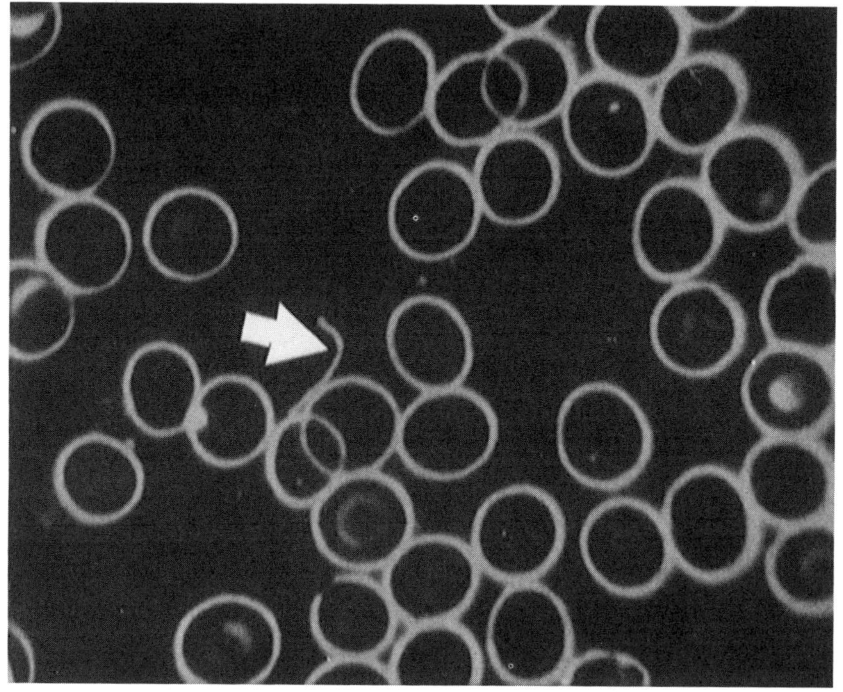

Rod Forms

If a dark field re-examination in 30-60 days shows L-Forms still present, we recommend an immune evaluation, which would include T and B cells, natural killer cells, and activated T cells. Also, immunoelectrophoresis may well be considered to assess immunoglobulin deficiencies. A mineral test should be conducted to evaluate zinc level and possible malabsorption at least, since many authorities think hydrochloric acid keeps infection from entering the bowel and proceeding to the blood. A urine indican and an SMA-24 would be helpful.

Rod Forms appear almost exclusively outside the red cells, and, as in any infection, the quantity is important. They are usually present when L-Forms arc plentiful. Urine cultures usually show a positive growth. Rods are large, cylindrical, motile, filamentous structures, usually smaller than 7 microns in length, but, rarely, they can be giants of 15 microns and more. They can look like dumbbells, sometimes with hollow cores, or like tubes. They are considered more serious than L-Forms, but, again, the two often occur together.

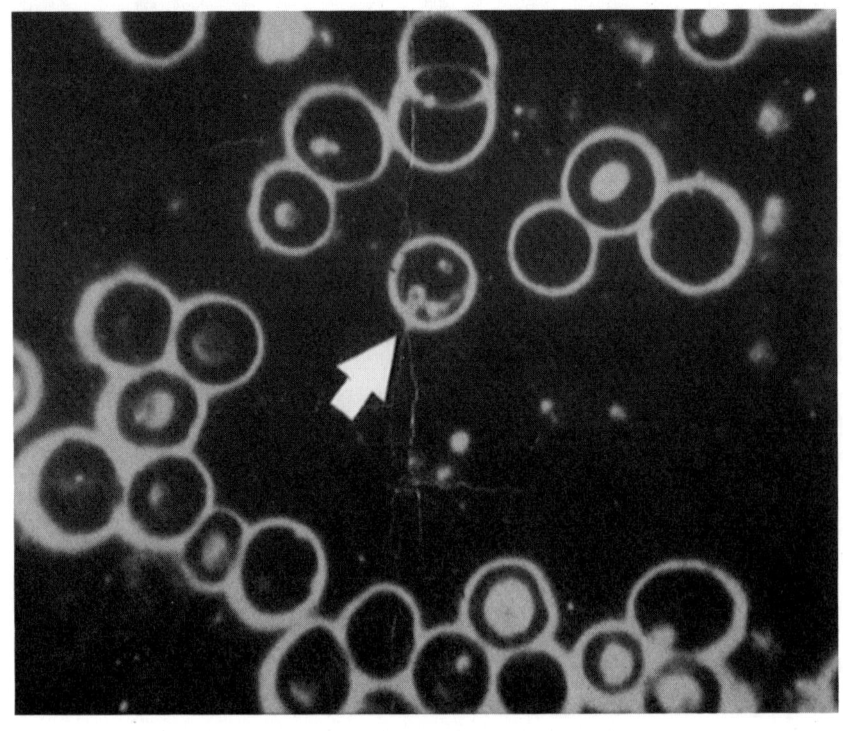

Red Cell Microbes

Testing would be the same as with L-Forms, in addition to possible treatment with vaccines, parenteral support, and anti-microbial agents such as colloidal silver and olive leaf extract.

Supplement	Mild	Moderate	Severe
Multi vitamin/mineral formula including:			
Zinc Picolinate	**15 mg**	**15 mg**	**15 mg**
Acidophilus	**1/2 tsp 2 x day**	**1 tsp 2 x day**	**1 tsp 2 x day**
Propolis	**2**	**3**	**4**
Thymus	**2**	**3**	**4**
Vitamin A*	**50,000 IU**	**75,000 IU**	**100,000 IU**
(emulsified or mycelized)			
Echinacea	**100 mg**	**200 mg**	**300 mg**
Silver (colloidal)	**1 tsp**	**2 tsp**	**3 tsp**
Olive leaf extract	**3**	**6**	**9**

***Do not take these higher amounts for more than 1 month. Such prolonged use could be toxic.**

Red Cell Microbes are usually embryonic bacteria, but are occasionally rods or cocci. Often, the only symptom will be a nagging fatigue, which is usually observed clinically in patients with other symptoms of poor immunity, such as yeast infections or skin fungal problems. In general, red cell microbes are thought to be more serious than L-Forms, but not as serious as rod forms. The patient usually responds well to immunological enhancement and stress reduction. We recommend the usual diet.

Supplement	Mild	Moderate	Severe
Multi vitamin/mineral formula including:			
Propolis	**2**	**3**	**4**
Acidophilus	**1 tsp daily**	**1 tsp 2 x day**	**1 tsp 3 x day**

Echinacea	**200 mg**	**300 mg**	**400 mg**
Pantothenic Acid	**250 mg**	**500 mg**	**750 mg**
B-6	**200 mg**	**400 mg**	**600 mg**
Vitamin A (mycelized)	**25,000 IU**	**50,000 IU***	**100,000 IU***
Spleen	**2**	**3**	**4**
Thymus	**1**	**2**	**3**
Silver (colloidal)	**1/2 tsp daily**	**1 tsp**	**2 tsp**
Olive leaf extract	**3**	**6**	**9**

***Do not take these higher amounts for more than 1 month. Such prolonged use could be toxic.**

Red Crystals

According to Dr. Livingston, these crystals are composed of actinomycin, which had a mild antibiotic effect in agar plates compared to pure actinomycin. Dr. Livingston wrote on them extensively in *Cancer: A New Breakthrough* (p. 152), and in *Compendium* (pp. 115-129). Occasionally they appear more orange than red. They can occur either in protoplasts or in plaque, or, more rarely, they can appear alone as large as 50 microns or even more in greatest diameter.

Red crystals are found frequently in drug users, cocaine sniffers and marijuana smokers. We have also seen them in cancer patients. Like junk food users, red crystal patients often have positive bowel toxemia tests (urine indicans). Reversing the toxicity with digestive enzymes, acidophilus or yogurt, and a good bowel cleanser should get rid of these toxic crystals.

Besides the urine indican, a mineral analysis for signs of malabsorption is helpful. Also recommended would be an SMA 24 with GGTP (the most sensitive liver test).

Supplement	Mild	Moderate	Severe
Multi vitamin/mineral formula including:			
Colon Cleanser	**1-3**	**2-3**	**3-4**

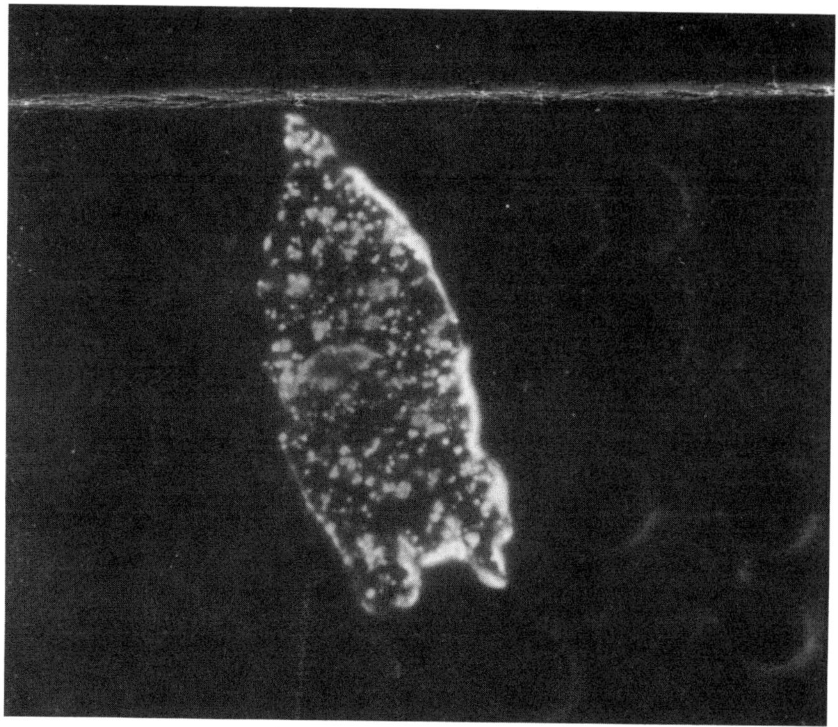

Red Crystals

Protoplasts

These are believed to be large forms of the pleomorphic "cryptocydes" microbe, probably a "parent." Dr. Livingston shows a protoplast with L-form inclusions or a release of mesosomes (similar to L-forms) secondary to shriveling of a protoplast. It is extremely difficult to distinguish these bodies from plaque. Morphological examination and clinical correlation are helpful. The plaques are very dense, while protoplasts are more translucent and frequently red. The color is supplied by toxic actinomycin. With protoplasts present, severe degenerative disease or toxemia should both be considered, as in a patient with damaged immunity.

Supplement	Mild	Moderate	Severe
Multi vitamin/mineral formula including:			
Thymus Fractions	2	3	4
Vitamin A (emulsified) or mycelized	25,000 IU	50,000 IU*	100,000 IU*
Colon Cleanser	2	3	4
Bromelain	1/before meals	2	2
Pancreatin	1/before meals	2	2
Vitamin C	2 g	3 g	4 g
Colloidal Silver	1 tsp	2 tsp	3 tsp
Olive leaf extract	3	6	9

*Do not take these higher amounts for more than 1 month. Such prolonged use could be toxic.

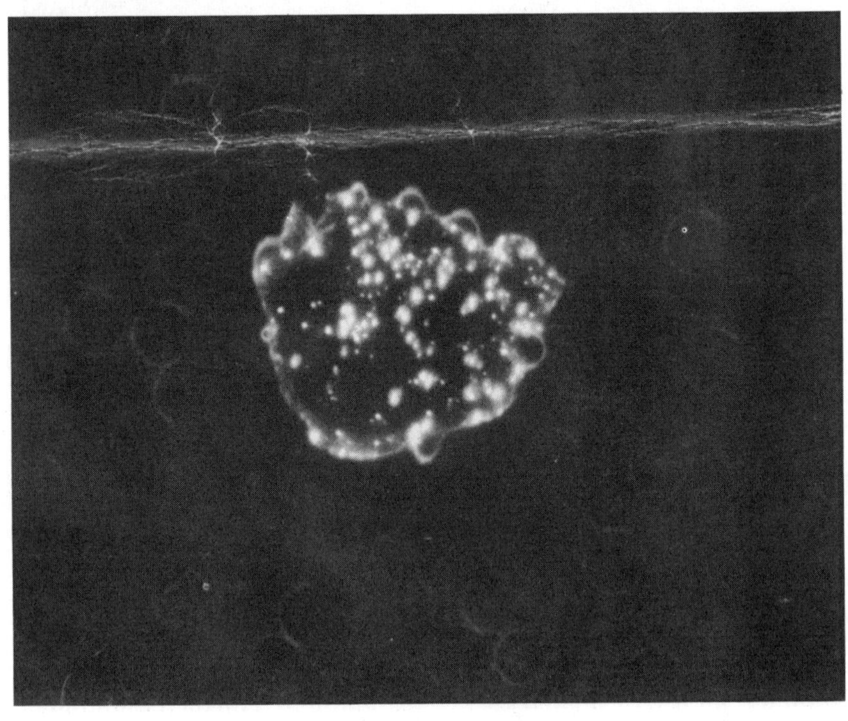

Protoplasts

Chapter Five
Why Patients Go Alternative

Why do patients go to holistic doctors? It's simple. Our prevailing medical system is not really delivering health care. It specializes in the *business of disease care treatment*, primarily with drugs, radiation and surgery, most of which are known to have serious side effects, risks and questionable validity. According to the Office of Technology of the U.S. Government, 80 percent of conventional medical therapies have no basis in science. Very slowly, the public is becoming aware of the hazards and failings of orthodox medicine, and is seeking alternative and preventive medical methods that include nutrition, herbs, homeopathy, acupuncture, Ayurveda, Chinese medicine, stress reduction, and chelation therapy.

When something isn't working, different options should be freely available. Bernard Jensen, one of the pioneers of nutrition, put it this way in a *Let's Live* magazine interview: "Wisdom is the ability to find an alternative. We find today that many of the drugs and methods in use are turning out to be detrimental to our bodies. We are living in side-effects, time bomb effects and genetic effects as a result of this. The age of alternative is coming in. It cannot be stopped because, as my mother used to say, if you give a man enough light he is bound to find his way."

I hope Jensen is right, that change is coming. It has to. The country can't really afford the present medical system. According to a 1991 *Los Angeles Times* editorial, employee health costs for big businesses "have skyrocketed from single digits to 25 percent and even up to 50 percent of profits in recent years." The term "health cost" bears scrutiny. We get a lot of cost and dubious health. Conventional treatment is expensive. What is all this doing to the economic viability of America, and the cost of producing goods and services? And look what's ahead--the baby boomers are coming of medical age.

Americans spent $847 billion on medical bills in 1992, says the U.S. Commerce Department. By 2000 the figure is expected to skyrocket to $1.3 trillion. And despite these ever rising numbers, progress against major disease killers is hard to find. Two out of five Americans are expected to develop cardiovascular disease during their lifetimes. Bypass surgery can exceed $40,000. More than 250,000 Americans undergo them each year--at a cost of about $18 billion--the number one health bill in this nation. Angioplasty, the so-called "balloon technique"--is elected by almost 400,000 new patients a year at about $10,000 per procedure. Yet, despite this staggering expense, up to a half of bypass grafts re-occlude after little more than five years, and a third to a half of arteries that are angioplastied wind up reblocked again after just four to six months. The original procedure then is performed again for still more money.

And despite the "war on cancer," that disease is expected to overtake heart disease as the No. 1 killer by the turn of the 21st century. The statisticians tell us that one out of every three men, women and children alive in this country today (a full third of all living Americans), doubtlessly will develop some type of cancer during his or her lifetime. Those odds are of course unwelcome and the projections fully expect them to shorten to two out of five (40%) by the year 2000.

What do all these catastrophic, depressing figures clearly say about the prevailing medical system? Well, what do you do if your team has a pitcher in the ballgame who is giving away hits and taking a beating? You yank him out of the game. You go to another of your pitchers, because it ain't working. The U.S. spends more for medical care than any other country; yet, we rank an abysmal 16th in life expectancy, and an even more embarrassing 23rd in infant mortality, despite the stupendous expense, increasing every year.

So, it's easy to understand why so many patients are presently flocking to the offices of doctors who offer true alternatives. Most of the time, those people already have seen orthodox physicians and most of the time those doctors have not been able to help. Their approved therapies are just not working. Question: Would patients see another doctor for more and different treatment, if they had already been cured, or adjusted, or controlled, etc.? Do you take a pitcher out of the game when he is pitching a no-hitter, or even a shutout? Of course not. You stay with him.

Even though the vast majority of chronic illnesses are preventable, the existing medical system emphasizes treatment and gives scant attention--often just lip service--to prevention. The result, as physician Charles B. Simone, M.D., tellingly explains in a February, 1996, article in *Energy Times Magazine*, is a "cost-explosive situation that will grow exponentially through the rest of this decade and into the next century. Our losing war against cancer illuminates this grave challenge."

Despite this massive spending on cancer research over the decades ($80 billion in 1992 alone), the number of new cases of every form of cancer has increased over the last 60 years, says Doctor Simone. All federal government research funding still pursues the myth of "finding a silver bullet . . . while the results of treatment continue to be unimpressive."

Simone adds: "About 90 to 95 percent of all chronic illnesses are preventable. Yet this continuing de-emphasis on causative factors, with a growing emphasis on treatment is the root contradiction in American life that must be addressed before health care costs can be contained."

Funding is but one proof of medical system bias. Another is the way case histories are regarded. The proof of the pudding is in the eating, and the truth of any treatment is in the effect on symptoms. "Lockstep medicine" contemptuously ignores case histories when they prove alternative therapy has worked. They would reject such accounts even if we were to present a gigabyte of such histories in 24 point type. But they relish case histories when we fail, which happens in many cases because conventional medicine routinely has sent those people home to die. Yes, we do fail, like every other doctor in history, but, with some exceptions, our failures are nowhere near as egregious as the wholesale slaughter and poisoning inflicted by conventional medical methods. Yet we have not demanded that sincere conventional physicians be locked up, and we expect the same courtesy. Yes, we fail, because there is much we still don't understand. The difference is that, when we fail we admit it; the "approved" doctors usually don't, no doubt because their failures are legion. I hope that one day soon those of us health professionals practicing preventive and truly alternative medicine, will no longer be tormented by America's present medical dictatorship. The fact is that freedom of medical choice does not exist in this country today. I can fondly remember when it did, however today--while other countries (such as little Costa Rica) enjoy much more medical freedom--we Americans suffer under alien, medical totalitarianism severe enough to make Dr. Mengele drool. When lost freedom returns to doctors' offices and hospitals in the United States--and it will--there will doubtless be a historic celebration, not to mention a substantially healthier, happier country.

On the following pages are the experiences of patients with a long list of problems so many people encounter. All of them first sought help from so-called "orthodox, conventional, approved" therapies. They all benefited from alternative methods after those therapies failed to provide significant help.

Karen A.

This patient is a real estate broker in sunny southern California. She had suffered for many years from serious headaches. She had PMS, but she didn't know it. She had an immune system difficulty, but she also didn't know that.

"I saw so many doctors. None of them could help me. Nothing worked.

“I would go in agony to see my gynecologist. Two weeks before my period, my breasts would feel inflamed, as if they were infected. I couldn't sleep at all on my stomach. At such times, life was a nightmare. The gynecologist was a ‘sweet guy,’ but shrugged, and said: ‘This is all just part of being a woman. I’m sorry, but there's nothing I can do.’

"Physicians are not an open minded group. They feel they have been educated, so they won't listen, especially when it comes to nutrition. They want to give you drugs. It's very annoying.

“A few months later, recommended by a friend, I visited Dr. Privitera for the headaches. He took a history, did a darkfield, looked at my blood on the monitor, and didn’t see any clumping. ‘You don't have a headache right now,’ he said. I was truly amazed. As he said, I didn't have one then.

“He asked me whether my breasts hurt. I thought he might be a pervert. I thought he wanted do a breast exam. I thought, 'No way.' What could headaches have to do with breasts? I was suspicious so I lied and said the breasts were no problem.

“He gave me a list of nutritional supplements to take. I figured I would take them one time, and if they didn’t work, I wouldn’t come back.

“After just six weeks, my breasts no longer hurt. The pain was completely gone. I was stunned, because I hadn't seen him for that reason. I thought it was out of his realm. I went for headaches.

“The headaches also were cleared up, especially after I got used to drinking a cup of flaxseed oil. I had been afraid to drink that much oil. But Dr. Privitera assured me that some oil is good and some is actually necessary to correct imbalances and deficiencies in the body.

"As a result of this experience, I have become somewhat of a crusader among my female friends. I am always asking them whether their breasts hurt. Most of these friends have the problem but not all of them can afford the testing, so I buy the bagfuls of vitamin and mineral supplements at Dr. Privitera's office for them. One of my girl friends was so relieved that one day she actually jumped up from her desk to hug me. She was grateful. Her breasts don't hurt anymore."

Harvey L.

Harvey, now retired, was a civilian employee for the military. He was 64, arthritic, and breathing hard whenever we played tennis. At one point he wore a back brace because of arthritic spurs of the spine. Harvey thought he might have to quit tennis.

"For years I had been seeing a physician at one of the very well known California HMOs. He prescribed the anti-inflammatories Naprosyn and Ansaid. I took them daily and they worked to some extent. I also took aspirin.

"After I met Jim Privitera on the tennis court a number of times, we became really quite friendly, and he suggested that my condition very possibly might be helped with a good program of supplementation with vitamins and minerals. Jim was enjoyable to play with but tough to beat with a tricky assortment of utterly ridiculous chips, chops and spins. I hoped maybe if I could feel better I could beat him.

"I visited his clinic. Jim took hair samples, drew blood, did darkfield microscopy, and found my blood in fairly good condition. Among the supplements he recommended were a calcium-magnesium complex, and a mucopolysaccharide complex from bovine bone cartilage extract. I was low in hydrochloric acid, which I understand from him that many older folks are, so we added some of that, as well.

"Within a few weeks, I definitely felt improvement, with less pain in the back. When I ran out of supplements, I just quit taking them for some time, and definitely felt 'third set' discomfort playing tennis. When I renewed my supply, I improved again.

"I was really doing much better on Jim's program. I quit the anti-inflammatories, and most of the aspirin. I discovered that the supplements just work better. I told this to my regular doctor, but he scoffs at the nutritional program and he sarcastically wishes me good luck."

We get very good results with many types of bone spurs. However, the program takes time to work. Remember always that these supplements are not drugs--they are *supplements;* they are additions to the diet--so we cannot expect immediate relief. Not only that, you are working on bone tissue--as opposed to a simple cold--so improvement obviously is going to take a while. Patients often report benefits within two to three months.

B. B.

Here is the sad story of what anorexia and bulimia did to a very beautiful, young girl.

"In the tenth grade at an all-girls school, I became uncomfortable with my body. I was heavy. More than 150 pounds. I really watched what I ate--one meal a day--but that wasn't fast enough. I literally became afraid of food and so I used to eat a meal and throw up. I decided to eat only a piece of sugarless gum and water, and exercise constantly. For instance, I played field hockey. Despite the bizarre diet, I wasn't tired. In the shower, I would hit myself, either with a field hockey stick, or, at home, with a plastic brush.

"My parents took me out of that school, and put me in a hospital for a month. I had gone from 170 pounds all the way down to 120. My parents were threatening to force feed me, with tubes. They wouldn't let me go to the bathroom or shower by myself. They feared I would throw up or hurt myself. I threw up anyway. At first, I needed at least 30 minutes to vomit. With time I was able to perfect the technique. You can make yourself throw up. I shoved my whole wrist in my throat. I could get everything out in four minutes flat.

"Eventually, doctors put me on anti-depressants. I knew I wasn't cured. I lied to them by saying I knew I needed food.

"I started at public school. I weighed my food, didn't allow any fat in the diet and drank only water. I lied about how many calories I ate. The doctors wanted me to eat 2,000 calories a day, but I ate only 1,500. After a while I would eat only 300.

"I never got hungry. I was 17, 5'7", and weighed only 79 pounds. I wore size one but I was still 'too fat.' in my mind. I wanted to lose more.

"The doctors thought I was completely cured, but I had no menstrual periods. My hair was falling out. I was suffering from extreme malnutrition. My skin lost pigmentation.

"I would fight my parents every night about taking drugs like Prozac. They would count pills. They were thinking of taking me to court; to declare me incompetent.

"Finally, a lady gynecologist told me that I was extremely selfish and that I shouldn't give my mom such grief. I asked my mother for help, told her that I hadn't realized how my problem was hurting other people. Because of the stress, my mother, a labor relations specialist, was also losing her hair. But in therapy, I admitted that my weight had been more important than my parents.

"By now, the doctors had tried all the prescription drugs on me, along with just about every anti-depressant they could think of. Dr. Privitera was the last hope. He was a 'vitamin doctor,' my mom told me.

"I was trying to get back into private school. I had to gain weight. Everything else had failed. I thought I may as well try this.

"Dr. Privitera pricked a finger, put a drop of blood on a slide, and we both looked at it on the TV monitor. He said my white cells were low. There was much clotting. I wasn't eating enough green foods. All kinds of stuff. I was low in calcium and iron, according to a hair analysis.

"He prescribed many supplements. He gave me a long list: thiamin; folic acid; zinc picolinate; fish oils; thyroid; lysine; PMS multiple; aqueous liver extract; selenium; lipo-3 factor; licorice for burning stomach; kelp; Super enzyme; calcium; muscle octane.

"I expected him to want my parents' money, as usual. I didn't care; it wasn't mine. Other doctors said they should put me in the hospital. They forced me to take drugs. They talked to my parents about me in my presence. Dr. Privitera didn't talk to my mother. He talked to me. He wouldn't force me to take pills.

"He didn't act like the typical doctor, who wants to get in and out. He was personal. He pushed some button in me. Long ago, a doctor said I was a beached whale. On the contrary, Dr. Privitera took my hand and told me, 'You're such a very beautiful girl. I don't understand why you need to keep losing weight.' Without Dr. Privitera, I know I could have died. I know I would have kept losing weight. My blood and organs would certainly have quit completely in a while. There was no drug that could have helped as fast as vitamins. All those doctors told me I should have died.

"I developed a desire to get better. My appearance improved. My color returned. I built muscle. The hair loss stopped."

Life has turned around for B.B. When we talked last she was 18, her weight a normal 135, and she was entering college as a freshman.

John H.

This patient is 78 and retired. He was a sailor on the U.S.S. Lexington at Pearl Harbor. He worked in the aerospace industry many years. He's 6'2" and always weighed 172.

"Fifteen or twenty years ago, I read that the government was planning to put Jim Privitera in the pen, for putting people on laetrile. I knew I wanted him to be my doctor.

"I had dropped 35 pounds in two months, was hacking and coughing. It was very painful. I was afraid one of the dentists had given me AIDS. There were horrible chest pains. When the tests came back negative, I wanted them to check me for TB. Again the results came back negative. No TB. Finally I had X-rays, and they said I had lung cancer, although I hadn't smoked in 50 years. The hospital said I couldn't deliver the X-rays myself to Dr. Privitera, however I insisted.

"At Dr. Jim's office, a urine test showed that I was pre-cancerous. I was deficient in all kinds of things. The hair test showed I had an excess of iron. It actually ran off the page. The last thing I needed was any more iron supplementation, but I did need just about everything else to restore my immune system.

"My prescription was an I.V. containing many interesting things: 40 grams of vitamin C; 400 c.c. lactated Ringer's; 3 c.c. B-6; 10 c.c. calcium; 10 c.c. dilute 1/500 HCL; 10 c.c. adrenal cortex; 5 c.c. magnesium; 2 c.c. B-complex; 1 c.c. chromium; 1 c.c. zinc; 1 c.c. copper; 1 c.c. manganese; 5 c.c. germanium; 6 c.c. selenium.

"Every week I would drive 240 miles from the desert to Dr. Jim's office. One week I do the I.V., the next week chelation. I also was getting Essiac, an herb tea that inhibits cancer, and colloidal silver, which knocked out the chest pain. Food stores have it, without prescription. Colloidal silver is clear, like water. Three squirts in the mouth let me eat, chew and swallow without trouble.

"I was pretty low when I started treatment. Like 2 to 3 on a 10 point scale. Now I'm up there around 7, I guess. My weight's coming back, up to 150 from 135. Now I'm always eating. This is the treatment I wanted. Jackie Onassis with all of her millions could still be alive. Instead, she went to chemotherapy. The doctors killed her. To hell with them."

Pam W.

For 35 years, Pam had been seeing orthodox physicians for severe respiratory and food allergies. Despite treatment, she continually felt "clogged up," was tired, and had dark circles under her eyes. At age 28, she realized she was allergic to milk. She was over 40 when she finally came to see me at the clinic. I did a darkfield analysis, along with hair and urine tests. Her hair calcium and magnesium were off the chart, meaning that they were not being absorbed. Osteoporosis was a danger. I gave her Cal-Mag citrate and Hydroxy-Cal, which "have helped a lot," iodine drops for thyroid and liver extract for low blood sugar. Her legs were "jittery," so I gave her KM, which is loaded with potassium. Her husband also takes it for his legs. She takes 2,000 mg. of C daily and now says she "almost never get colds." The clotting is almost totally gone from darkfield analysis. She is still tired, because of candida, but I give her colloidal silver for it. Nystatin worked for a while, but it's a drug. A broad spectrum antibiotic would kill everything, but the silver has no side effects, and there is no more foggy head.

"In 1990, my son Danny was six. He was tired. I thought he had flu. His stomach would turn over in the car. It got worse. His neck hurt. So did his head behind the ears and his groin. His lymph nodes were swollen.

"It was Sunday. We were on the way to church. I took Danny to a clinic for X-rays. They didn't have any idea what was wrong. They thought perhaps it was a virus. They told me to 'wait until it gets worse so we can find out.' It did. Danny's stomach distended. His face puffed up badly. The doctors thought it could be chronic fatigue syndrome.

"I took Danny to see Dr. Privitera, who did a darkfield analysis. The doctor prescribed a vitamin C I.V. every day.

"A week and a half passed. Danny's doctors didn't know what he had. They were just stumped. Danny got no better. At least he was still alive. Dr. Privitera was calm, but I could see that he was alarmed. 'You need to get him to the hospital right now,' he said. Of course, I took him right away. Later, his nurses told me Danny was the sickest looking child they'd ever seen.

"We arrived after 11 p.m., yet we had to pay for that whole day. Why worry? Because of the miracle of insurance and the federal government, it's 'free!' Tests said that Danny had leukemia. His bone marrow was dangerously low, so they operated. I tried to keep calm, but I shook for hours. The hospital said Danny must start on chemotherapy right away. But I saw my first husband take chemotherapy. It almost killed him. The doctors explained that because of improvements in the treatment of childhood leukemia over the previous 12 years, Danny would have a 60% chance. I said he must continue with the vitamins, and they said all right, even though they didn't let any one else do that. Danny entered the hospital on January 25th. By means of a catheter inserted in the neck, doctors gave him Vincristine, Methotrexate and Prednisone, a corticosteroid that weakens the adrenal glands and immune system. Meanwhile, Danny continued Dr. Privitera's I.V., and I believe the vitamin C kept his immune system strong. I also gave him vitamins when the nurses weren't looking. By February 14th, he was in remission. The doctors couldn't understand why his blood was so good, and why he hardly got sick at all. What the doctors didn't know was that the vitamins had been rebuilding Danny's weak immune system, while the chemotherapy was depressing it.

"Danny took chemo for three years, along with Dr. Privitera's I.V.s and lots of prayer. It looks like he is going to make it."

At last report, Danny had been off the chemo treatment for 16 months and was doing fine.

Sherry R.

More than 25 years ago, at age 19, Sherry was first diagnosed with discoid lupus erythematosus. She suffered scaly patches of the skin, scars throughout her scalp, and damage to her kidneys. She lost her hair; had to wear wigs.

"My health record says I'm a malingerer. Back east in 1971, a famous Cincinnati specialist told my husband I might live two or three years with care. At the U.S. Navy hospital in Long Beach, a doctor gave me blood and urine tests, then put me on Prednisone, 60 mg a day. For the first two weeks, I was awake, then I peaked out and crashed. My adrenal function was affected. I could have died. I actually thought I was going to die. A physician sent me to the Navy hospital in San Diego, where they figured out that

Prednisone was wrong. But it was hard to kick; I couldn't do so for 3 months. I didn't care if I lived or died.

"Earlier, back in North Carolina, the Navy doctors had said my problem was that the state was 'too wet.' In Long Beach it was 'too dry.' They said I was starting to get hysterical; that I would have to take Mylanta with the Prednisone, to avoid an ulcer.

"I was not hysterical. But I was rapidly coming to the conclusion that doctors are just drug salesmen. A doctor gave my father, 74, a new antibiotic for emphysema. It was very strong, and the surprise side effects were hallucinations. The doctor didn't warn him about it, because he didn't know himself. The doctor was surprised to hear it.

"The U.S. Navy doctor in Long Beach said, 'There's not a whole lot I can do for you,' and warned me about quackery. I called him a quack.

"My husband, Dean, sent me to Dr. Privitera's clinic. The technician who did the darkfield procedure looked at the monitor, saw clots, and asked if I had headaches. I hadn't said anything but I was having one right at that moment. I came home with two bags full of supplements. Within two weeks, I was alive. I was awake for the first time in ten years. And we had a sex life again.

"Lupus often causes divorce, because the mate doesn't understand. Lupus headaches are not the ones you hear about in Henny Youngman jokes. The disease can affect any organ. Two years later, Dean ran into the same Navy doctor and told him how well I was doing. There was no interest. Dr. Privitera restored my life. And whenever I see him he knows whether I've been backsliding. 'You're not taking your fish oils,' he yells. I feel better because he treated all of me--the whole person. To him I was a human being, not just a symptom. The attitude is so different in his clinic. Patients are joking. They are being treated the same way."

Elizabeth L.

In August, 1977, this lady was going through a nasty divorce and developed serious ovarian cancer, diagnosed by physical manipulation. The cancer was huge, and luckily she was very thin. Had she been fat, perhaps they wouldn't have detected it, because this was before MRI. She was 36.

"I went to three or four gynecologists. They all said get surgery immediately. I went to a wonderful surgeon who took as much as he could off both ovaries, but the cancer had metastasized and was spreading to the stomach lining and intestines. As a precaution, he sent me to an oncologist.

"I couldn't stand him. He was obnoxious, and full of himself. You had no right to ask questions. He prescribed a mild dosage of a chemotherapeutic drug called Alkeran. I took one pill a day, five days a month. He also told me to eat a balanced diet. But I didn't know what that was. My 'balanced diet' was a thick steak, candy bars, and black coffee. He didn't explain what a balanced diet is. Did he know? I took the pills one month. I questioned him. I said I didn't like taking poison. He said, 'You must do it. In 14 months we'll take a look see.' By 'look see' he meant exploratory surgery. I was incredulous.

"My uncle had gone to Dr. Privitera too late with pancreatic cancer. We lost him, but uncle was pleased with the program. In the hospital, an LVN whispered, 'Honey, there are other things you could do. Please don't tell anyone I'm saying this, but there's a doctor in Covina.' The nurse couldn't remember his name, but it was the same Dr. Privitera.

"I went to see him. I was still smoking. I knew nothing. I was such a mess that he didn't even want to look at my blood. Instead, he put me on I.V. vitamin therapy, and gave me a list of eating instructions: stop smoking and drinking; no coffee; cut down on meat. That was November, 1977.

"I took ninety pills a day. Then I took the tests. I was feeling better. I had gained weight. I had stopped eating meat altogether. The oncologist called and asked me to come in. There would be no charge. He said, 'You know, Mrs. L., what you're doing is wrong. The cancer is still there.'

"I went to Dr. Privitera, hysterical. He said, 'Your oncologist is an M.D. I'm an M.D. too.' He sat me down in his office, put an elephantine book in my lap, and said, 'Read about Alkeran.' The book said it would greatly increase my chances of getting leukemia in middle age. Dr. Privitera told me to do what I thought best.

"I thought this made sense. Later, I thought of the oncologist. The little son of a gun, how does he know it'll come back? So, I decided to use my own judgment. If I prayed long enough, I'd be shown what to do. I never did go back.

"In those days, 1978, Dr. PT was still being hounded as a 'quack.' The hospital and my family kept calling. Even a professor of medicine called. All said I should take the chemotherapy, but I resisted.

"After a year, Dr. Privitera cut the supplements back. Now, I eat vegetables, pasta, greens, and, once in a while, fish. No chicken. I'm almost a vegetarian. I'm afraid to get a mammogram. Dr. Privitera says I don't really need one right now. But I do get a pap smear and a regular physical exam from a family doctor, who tells me I'm healthy. I took a treadmill test, which said my heart is sound. In another test, they injected a dye, and then followed it on camera. My kidneys and urinary tract were perfect. So was a chest x-ray.

"All the things the doctor told us twenty years ago are now coming true. Fortunately, he has a good sense of humor. He's not bitter. I drank quarts of carrot juice. Now they talk about beta-carotene. Conventional doctors call my recovery a 'remission.' Until a few years ago, the hospital where I had my surgery called my sister every year, asking whether I was still alive. I am. I work as a bus driver. Look for me the next time you take the Sunset Boulevard route to downtown Los Angeles."

Beverly L.

A personnel clerk for a California school district, Beverly is 50 and has two grown children. In May, 1992, she had breast cancer surgery, and seven weeks of radiation. In July, 1993, she had a fish sandwich for lunch, and woke up at two in the morning, intensely nauseated. She was nauseous for three weeks. Nothing would stay in her system. Her HMO doctors called it "irritable bowel" syndrome, gave her some antibiotics, and recommended diets. But no medication would stay with her, no food. She lost at least ten pounds and couldn't go to work. She was sicker than ever before in her life. It was worse than the cancer. Her oncologist said it had nothing to do with the radiation, but it exhausted her.

"I went to see Dr. Privitera. He explained that radiation affects the entire body, quite obviously because all the blood circulates throughout it. He gave me a darkfield test, along with urine and hair analysis. These tests found a low level of antioxidants in my system. A cortisone shot with nutrients stopped my bowel spasms. I started to absorb again.

"I started out on vitamins and enzymes, but when the enzymes ran out, I didn't get any more. The spasms came back. At the clinic, Dr. Privitera was very adamant. 'Enzymes are the key,' he said. 'And you have to stop eating indiscriminately in restaurants any more. Be very aware of your eating. Avoid fatty foods and sugar. Eat fiber, but not too much, which for you could be just as bad.'

"Dr. Privitera saved my life. No orthodox doctor knew what to do. At the HMO, my primary doctor said, 'Give me his name and phone number. When I get sick, maybe I'll call him.'

"Dr. Privitera told me that his entire goal is for the patient to get well. I've never heard any other doctor say that. I don't think many doctors are open to other forms of healing. Here's an example. One of the HMO doctors said bacterial poisoning perhaps was my problem, but, 'if there's no proof of that, maybe it's totally psychological.' I'll never go back. Of course there was no poisoning. Recently, I saw another HMO doctor, and gave him my symptoms. I had barely finished, before he prescribed Donnagel, a prescription for diarrhea. He had a pre-set notion, like my oncologist, who wouldn't consider the possibility that radiation could have harmed me."

At last report, Beverly is still stabilized, is taking her supplements and doing well.

Cindi H.

This 36-year-old secondary school art teacher suffered for many years from very low blood sugar (hypoglycemia), and wasn't getting much help from approved medicine.

"I always was confused, exhausted, nauseous, afraid I would fall asleep at work. I had to force myself to stay awake. I came very close to falling asleep while driving the freeway. It was terrifying. My skin was dry and itchy. My hands and feet were on fire. I couldn't wear shoes, only sandals. I would fall asleep right after I ate white flour.

"I had gone to 'regular' doctors for six years, the first one at college. The doctor would tell me to come in, but I couldn't, because I was too sleepy to drive. I saw five or six doctors and three or four nurse practitioners. An internist at my HMO said it was 'all in your head.'

"Another doctor there said there was 'nothing more we can do.' They told me to eat little meals, but a lot of them. I had to carry a big bag of food. I couldn't eat out; couldn't go to a restaurant. I went to work, but had no energy.

"I suffered from depression, and took anti-depressants. The doctors said I would be on them for life. But, by this time, I had read something on low blood sugar. My husband pointed out that I would fall asleep right after eating white flour. He found a book called *The Yeast Connection: A Medical Breakthrough* [William G. Crook, New York, Vintage Books, 1986], which listed some 'unorthodox' doctors. Dr. Privitera was the one closest to my home.

"I told about him about my problem, and he immediately knew what was wrong.

"'It's a classic case.' he said.

"I asked, 'If it's a "classic case," how come no one knows about it?' I had lost hope. I had been to so many doctors.

“Dr. Privitera did a darkfield exam and found tiny clots causing chest pains. He said the solution was as simple as fish oils to oxygenate the blood. He did a hair analysis, explaining that all my problems were closely related. Candida clots blood, and makes the blood soupy instead of thin, which then cuts down on healing and enzyme absorption, so I couldn't tolerate sugar. I lacked oxygen. I couldn't tolerate white flour, couldn’t even tolerate artificial sweeteners.

“Because yeast was causing trouble, I took supplements to strengthen my liver and kill the yeast. Starting in March, 1994, I took 6 g of vitamin C a day, a B complex, and 30-40 other supplements.

"Within 15 minutes of first taking them, I was so much better, I could hardly believe it myself. Now, I'm off those anti-depressants altogether. The depression is gone. My whole attitude changed from negative to positive. Before, marriage was always difficult. We hurt each other. Now, I feel better, and my husband responds.

"My husband gets migraines, and used to have to lie down in a dark room. Dr. Privitera told him to take 3 fish oil capsules every hour, along with vitamin C. Now, he is able to stay in a room with the lights on, watch television and talk to me during an attack.

“I take lithium orotate now because lithium was low on my hair analysis. I can go several hours now without eating, and my hypoglycemia is manageable. I used to smell sweaty. No more. Now, I smell like herbs."

P.A.L.

Traditional medicine says this lady should have been dead many years ago, but she won't cooperate. When she was 23, P.A.L. had her fourth child. For five years, the doctors said she had precancerous lesions of the cervix. Finally, when she was 28, the doctor cauterized her cervix. Within months, her Pap Smear went to class IV cancer, with squamous carcinoma. The doctors told her that, without surgery, she might not live another six months.

"I asked what my survival chances were with surgery. I couldn't get a straight answer. Six months? A year? Five years? No one seemed to know. And why do I have this so young? Still no answers from the doctors. I went to the U.S.C. medical library, and spent the whole day searching for an answer. The more I read, the more I realized that the only sensible thing to do was nutrition.

"I went to the Hoxsey clinic in Mexico, where they use herbs, laetrile and high potassium. People from all around the world were there. At the time, I had medical insurance, which covered any prescription from a licensed practitioner. However, the insurance company refused to pay for my laetrile. I took them to court, but they won, claiming it was not a drug, but a vitamin, and they do not cover vitamins.

"Around this time--it was March of 1974--the manager of a health food store near my home recommended Dr. Privitera. I started with darkfield and hair analysis tests, lots of minerals and vitamins, and a coffee enema to detoxify my colon. Also, I stopped eating beef, pork and canned foods, but some fish and chicken was allowed. The cost to be treated by Hoxsey and Dr. Privitera was a 'drop in the bucket' compared to surgery and chemotherapy. Vitamins were a minimal cost next to possible lost time from surgery.

"By December, 1974, my Pap Smear was back to Class I. One doctor was very angry about that, and insisted that the lab check it again. It still came back Class I.

"I had been examined by four different doctors using four different labs, yet when I got better they all tried to tell me that the cancer was a mistaken diagnosis by their lab. I asked them, 'If I tell you what I did, will you share this with your other patients?' They said they wouldn't. 'Don't you even want to know what I did?' I would ask. They weren't interested. Many times since then I have shown various doctors my Pap Smears from 1974, and all they will say is, 'You are very lucky to be alive.'

"I stayed with the nutritional program for just a year, then quit.

"Several years ago, when I was 46, my gynecologist told me I had a cyst on an ovary. Later, he said it was too firm for a cyst, and maybe was a tumor. I returned to Dr. Privitera, and he gave me the usual shopping bag of supplements. But they sat on my shelf. I wasn't motivated to take them. Then, a year later, a different gynecologist said I had a Class II Pap, and that the cyst could indeed be a tumor. The gynecologist recommended a hysterectomy.

"I have no fear of death, but I do fear surgery. I told the gynecologist I would wait until my daughter got married in two months. Meanwhile, I took Coenzyme 10, folic acid, Biodyne and other vitamins--everything, in fact, that Dr. Privitera had recommended--for about eight weeks. He said that if the cyst/tumor got any bigger, I should go ahead with the surgery.

"I returned to the gynecologist, thinking that if the growth were the same size or smaller, I would postpone the surgery and continue with the nutrition. Would you believe it, the doctor said it was gone! Recently, another Pap Smear was 'within normal limits'

"Two years ago, I went to an eye specialist, who said I had macular degeneration of the eyes. Another eye surgeon concurred. The specialist said I could gradually go blind, but there was 'nothing we can do. Come back in a year, we'll do an annual exam, and see how the disease is progressing.' They said laser surgery wouldn't help, so, off to Doctor Privitera I went.

"He put me on a bovine extract for the eye. Later, I visited an eye specialist for a check-up, and he said I was doing better than a year ago. I asked him: 'Don't you want to know what I've been doing?' He was very blasé. He said, 'If it works for you, do it.' But he wouldn't tell his patients.

"For years, I also had a serious blood pressure problem. It was very low, consistently 84 over 42. Dr. Privitera said I was suffering from adrenal exhaustion, and gave me adrenalin shots. I also took biotin. My blood pressure came up to normal: 110 over 70. All along, other doctors had said they didn't know what was causing it, and didn't know what to do.

"I also suffered from osteoporosis, which other doctors insisted was just regular arthritis. Hair analysis showed I was discharging unbelievable amounts of calcium. Now, I take calcium/magnesium tabs and the condition is fairly well stabilized."

Her father also did well on the program. "My dad had surgery for cancer of the bladder. Later, he had two surgeries on his sinuses, and then he developed cancer of the sinus as well as possible skin cancer on his cheek. Doctors wanted him to have more surgery. Dr. Jim gave him the usual supplements. He also got Laetrile from Oklahoma. The cancer disappeared. He died at 81, but not from cancer. He fell and broke a hip, had surgery and died 3 months later. Again, the doctors had no explanation for the disappearance of the cancer."

P.A.L. works full-time at a credit union in customer service. The last time I talked with her, she had already put in a full day's work, mowed the front and back yards, washed her truck and gone grocery shopping. Not bad for someone who was supposed to be dead for twenty years.

Mary B.

When she was 18, a physician treated her for rheumatic fever. In her twenties, she developed swelling in her joints, and a doctor prescribed cortisone.

"It wasn't good for me. My condition deteriorated. The swelling got worse. It affected all my joints. At age 38, I went to a rheumatologist. He said I had rheumatoid arthritis. He didn't believe I had ever had rheumatic fever.

"He put me on 16 aspirins a day, and gold shots. They made me comfortable and reduced the swelling, but, after four years, they gave no more relief. The rheumatologist increased the dose, but still it did nothing, so he stopped them.

"One night, I had a complete collapse. I barely got home. After two hours, I couldn't move. I called the rheumatologist, who told me to take pain pills to survive the night. The next day, in his office, he put me on penicillimine. It took away my taste completely, and didn't help the swelling. By now, he was out of ideas, so I left. I was 42 years old, and desperate..

"I heard from some friends about Dr. Privitera, so I went to see him. He did a hair test and live cell analysis via darkfield. He said my immune system needed rebuilding, and sent me home with a bagful of supplements: copper, vitamins C and E, minerals, pancreatin, iodine, etc.

"Within a week, I was greatly improved. The swelling went down. Within three months, I was in remission. Today, ten years later, I still am. I take my supplements, but not as many.

"When I returned to see the rheumatologist, I mentioned the vitamins and minerals. He was totally against them. I never went back. The same man was rude to my aunt, who was dying of cancer. All he could do was try to camouflage symptoms, but this is more of a cure."

Cherilyn T.

"In May, 1992, after laboratory testing, I was diagnosed with diabetes. My blood sugar level was 247. At that time I felt exhausted most of the time no matter how much I slept. I felt depressed and mentally 'foggy.'

"I went to see Dr. Privitera and had around 46 chelation treatments during the next year. My blood sugar level was 87 when last checked. I've experienced greater circulation to my left foot which was previously numb much of the time. I've had very few yeast infections which were a real problem before. My energy level has increased dramatically and I feel much more alert."

Ed D.

"We went through the triumvirate of cut, burn and poison," says Ed D., a retired dentist. In 1975, his wife, Pat, found a lump on her leg above the knee. X-ray said it was not a lipoma (a benign, fatty tumor), but a malignant liposarcoma, but, says Ed, "the first son of a bitch didn't believe the X-ray. Because he was a greedy son of a bitch, he operated anyway, and found that the problem was a liposarcoma, just as the X-ray had said. He closed Pat up, explaining that he wasn't qualified to finish. Another surgeon had to do it. I'm still furious that Pat was subjected to unnecessary suffering. Had I known of the first surgeon's incompetence at the time, I would have sued. The biopsy said she was Stage III.

"Ten days after the surgery, she took chemotherapy. Her white cell count cratered to 400. She lost her hair. I watched helplessly as she puked her guts out on Christmas day. In January, she quit: 'If this is living, I'd rather be dead.'

"We decided to try apricot kernels, which are a good source of laetrile. I ground them up and kept them in the refrigerator. Pat took three teaspoons a day. She also took radiation. The only doctor who was honest with her was Dix Morgan, the radiologist. He insisted on regular chest X-rays--a liposarcoma typically invades the chest--but the only thing he found was lungs. Because she was doing so well, Morgan asked her privately whether she was taking laetrile.

"I took Pat to see Jim Privitera, who gave her Vitamin C shots, forbade junk food and prescribed handfuls of supplements three times a day for a year. Cancer victims' families in the neighborhood started calling. Pat was supposed to be dead. Why was she doing so well? I told them all about Dr. Jim. I even got a call from a physician in London, England, who said his wife also had a liposarcoma.

"Today, some twenty years later, Pat is more ornery than ever, which she denies. In her aerobics class, other ladies believe the gouge in her leg was the work of a shark. She still eats no junk food, but backslides somewhat. By the time I was diagnosed with poor circulation, I had learned my lesson about our medical system. I took chelation. My carotid sound tests went from abnormal to normal."

Hillary Clinton says medical costs today are out of control. We agree. *Why* are they out of control? Here's one reason. Each shot of Pat's chemo cost $175. Her surgeries were $22,000. The total cost of her licensed, approved, orthodox, consensus therapy was $30,000. Remember that this happened in 1975, when the dollar was still worth a few cents. The approved therapy didn't work. Our approach did work, and cost $800. In fact, as we have seen, that is why lockstep medicine hates it so much--precisely because it is so inexpensive.

C.H.

"Loma Linda is one of the finest hospitals in the world. I have no doubt about that. In March of 1991, I spent a week at the hospital. I got a series of EKGs, ecograms, angiograms, oxygen, saline, glucose, heparin, monitors, needles, and other tests. Fourteen doctors of the highest degree told me I couldn't live without triple bypass surgery. It was imperative. They all agreed triple bypass was the 'only' way they had to keep me alive. Surgery or death. The finest nurses were comforting me. That's really living. I was lying there with the wealthiest people in the country, each of us with his own private room, monitored constantly in case we needed anything.

"My choice was to walk out of Loma Linda and start a chelation program without surgery or drugs, with Dr. Jim Privitera. I believe that the quality of life includes not having to worry about damage to the immune system. I believe that God built a cage over the heart for a reason. It doesn't need to be messed up with a knife. The only thing that changes common sense reasoning is $$Politics$$ with a capital $ and the power that corrupts any system.

"One day in Loma Linda, while waiting for my turn on an E.K.G. machine, I noticed a man sitting in a wheel chair, waiting for his doctor to administer anti-rejection medication. He was wearing a mask and explained he had a transplant. The mask bespoke his decimated immune system. He had been a smoker most of his life and had come to Loma Linda a year before for a 'change of heart.'

"The message I would like to convey to the world would be to take a long, hard look at the A.M.A., the F.D.A., and a whole bunch of political three-letter words that would take away our rights to 'quality of life.'

"By the way, do you know what is the fastest thing on two wheels? A baboon on a bicycle going through Loma Linda!!

"Some patients don't have a choice. I have skipped the scalpel 5 times in my life. I thank God I was stubborn enough to make my own choice of doctors."

C.H. bypassed the bypass and is doing fine. He has been on a chelation program since 1991. He 's an avid cyclist and loves to bike 25 miles a day.

W.K.

Here's another bypass story. Before he became a patient of mine, W.K. had developed high blood pressure and chest pains. His cardiologist recommended an angiogram. The tests indicated he had significant arterial blockage. A surgeon said he needed bypass surgery. He might have gone for it except for the next thing the surgeon told him:

"He said to me he would receive $55,000 for the procedure, but would have to give a kickback of $20,000 to the referring cardiologist."

A disgusted W.K. decided to investigate alternatives. He learned about chelation therapy and recently started a series of chelation treatments.

Hilla Futterman

The following testimony, entitled, "It's Been 5 1/2 Years," was actually copyrighted by a patient of mine. We use it here in its entirety with her permission.

"Five and a half years ago, in late August, 1989, a team of doctors performed a very complex, eight hour surgery in order to remove an adenocarcinoma that had metastasized from my colon. The day after the surgery, the chief surgeon grouped with the other doctors at the foot of my bed in the intensive care unit and said, 'We got it all.' Being on a respirator, unable to talk, I signaled my feelings by raising my right hand and giving the hand OK sign. A month later, about to leave the hospital, I sat on my bed reading my discharge report. What jumped out at me was: 'Prognosis poor.' I was told later that the pathology report said that the healthy appearing tissue adjacent to the tumor was not 'clean'; cancer cells remained in my body. I refused radiation therapy and chemotherapy, having decided to take a therapy to strengthen my immune system so that it would destroy any abnormal cells and further growth of cancer.

"A number of weeks after being home from the hospital, I began Dr. James Privitera's therapeutic program which helped, immeasurably, to strengthen my immune system. The program consisted of vitamin and mineral supplements, other nutritional substances such as cod liver oil and liver extract, digestive enzymes and an 80 percent raw, natural foods diet guideline which included 2-4 cups a day of raw carrot, beet or apple juice, or any combination of them. I found I could not tolerate the prescribed digestive enzymes, so I ate a larger percentage of raw food. Besides the juices Dr. Privitera prescribed, I drank orange or grapefruit juice daily, and regularly took, once or twice a week, 1/2 to 3/4 of a cup of raw alfalfa leaf juice mixed with raw pineapple or apple juice. During a week, I also drank about a quart of raw pomegranate juice, each cup and a half blended with one or two raw eggs. Most of my food was organically grown. For a few months at the beginning of my therapy, I took an herb tea prescribed by Dr. Maoshing Ni, a Chinese herbalist, which included herbs the Chinese traditionally use to strengthen the immune system so it can inhibit abnormal cellular growth. The tea formula also included herbs to eliminate the heat I continued to feel for a few months after surgery. I also added three capsules of red clover blossoms a day to my supplement program.

"I stayed on my therapy for two years. Within the 5 1/2 years that have passed since my surgery, neither cat scan nor colonscopy, blood tests nor biopsy, could detect any cancer. Since you can't talk to me, reader, you can use the hand OK sign."

Part Two

Maximizing Health

Chapter Six
Eating Right

I have always felt that it is more important to eat right rather than count calories. In most cases, eating right takes care of weight problems and improves health. By eating right, I mean not only what you eat but *how* you eat as well.

In my opinion, the best general diet is one high in complex carbohydrates and low in fat. That means whole grains, vegetables and fruit should be emphasized. This provides the body with the best raw materials for energy and maintenance. This is also the kind of diet that will enable you to stabilize your weight at the level it is supposed to be. As much as possible, try to eat fresh, wholesome natural food. If you can purchase organic foods, that's even better. The fewer pesticides, herbicides and other unnatural chemicals in your food the better off you are.

But be practical. Be sensible. Be flexible. I always tell my patients to take it easy with their diets and with themselves. When you become obsessive you create stress and that will cancel out all your efforts to eat well. What is important is what you do over the long-term. Do the best you can without being a fanatic. Stop castigating yourself if you "pig out" now and then on some horrendously decadent and delicious dessert. Just have the general attitude of eating the healthiest food and enjoying life.

You hear a great deal about the health benefits of a vegetarian diet. Indeed, vegetarians are weightlifters and champion athletes.

They are not suffering from lack of vitality and strength. I have several elderly patients who have been lifelong vegetarians. They are vibrantly healthy and robust. A strong relationship has been found in studies conducted throughout the world between the amount of animal foods eaten and rates of cancer, heart disease and osteoporosis. Given this evidence, I simply tell my patients to go easy on the animal protein. If you have the need or craving, don't deny yourself. That would be unduly stressful. Besides, we all have different body types and genetic makeup. Many of us shouldn't be vegetarians. Just don't overdo it. Eat those types of meat that are lowest in fat content and highest in protein. That means veal, fish, chicken, turkey and lamb. As a rule, I suggest no more than 50 grams a day--about two ounces. Or restrict the animal protein to flavoring, garnish or as an accent rather than a main course.

In 1978, a report entitled "Diet and Killer Diseases" compiled by the U.S. Senate Select Committee on Nutrition and Human Needs concluded that the average American diet is responsible for the development of chronic degenerative diseases. Little has changed. The same highly-processed refined carbohydrates (such as white bread, pastry and pasta made with enriched flour) comprise an estimated 60 percent of our standard diet. These are the "empty calorie" foods--poor in nutrition and high in fat--that force your body to "borrow" nutrient reserves to digest the junk. "Dead food," I call it. Indeed, this is a major reason why our country is so sick and why we have a runaway national medical bill presently costing more than $900 billion and soaring. You may fill your stomach with this kind of trash but not your requirement for good nutrition or your potential for a long, healthy quality of life.

You should also eat more beans, whole grains, egg-free pasta, brown rice, potatoes and corn. Why do I say egg-free pasta? Because commercial egg powder is used in many pasta products--an ingredient that through processing has become in part oxidized cholesterol. We know from animal studies that oxidized cholesterol contributes to clotting and arterial plaques.

In general, I have nothing against eggs. I eat them all the time. My advice is to eat them as close to raw as possible. Soft boiled is the best form. Over easy and over medium are OK. Hard boiled and scrambled are the worst. Hard boiled kills the enzymes. Scrambled involves high heat and oxygen that combine to create oxidized cholesterol.

Emphasize the vegetables and fruits recognized for their anti-cancer properties. Highly-pigmented foods--green, yellow, orange, and red--are known to have particularly protective qualities. The major protective groups of vegetables are categorized as follows:

1. Protease inhibitors (protease is an enzyme involved in the cancer process)--soybeans, chickpeas, lentils, limas, and red, black and white beans.

2. Cruciferous vegetables--broccoli, brussels sprouts, cabbage, and cauliflower. These foods are particularly high in natural compounds that enhance the body's ability to neutralize toxins.

3. Beta-carotenes--carrots, yams, sweet potatoes, tomatoes, green leafy vegetables, squash, pumpkin, apricots, spinach, asparagus, deep green lettuce and cantaloupe.

Fiber Keeps You Moving

A diet high in complex carbohydrates ensures getting plenty of beneficial fiber. Fiber is the portion of plant foods that human digestive enzymes cannot break down and provides the roughage important for healthy, frequent, and regular bowel movements.

The typical Western diet, high in meat, dairy, processed food, and refined carbohydrates, leads to slow bowel passage and constipation, the absorption of toxins, and the risk of serious intestinal disorders.

Fiber is another way to help prevent blood clots. After many years as a physician in Africa, Denis Burkitt, M.D., determined that the natural high-fiber diets eaten by native cultures was a major reason why they experienced few varicose veins, hemorrhoids, and blood clots. This typically causes straining to evacuate wastes. As a result of the downward pressure exerted, veins in the legs can become damaged. Blood may pool in these veins instead of returning upward to the heart. This noxious situation creates opportunities for potentially dangerous clots as well as the development of inflamed, painful veins known as thrombophlebitis.

In *Eat Right, Live Longer* (New York, Harmony Books, 1995), Neal Barnard, M.D., refers to new evidence suggesting meat-based diets encourage the growth of intestinal bacteria that produce compounds that accelerate clotting. "Meat also contains a type of fat, called stearic acid, that encourages clotting," Dr. Barnard adds.

Individuals suffering from hemorrhoids often report improvement of their condition merely by eating more of fiber foods.

The fiber foods provide the bulk that makes you feel satisfied. When you eat simple, refined carbohydrates with little or no fiber you tend to eat more calories in order to fill up. Fiber foods require more chewing which gives your body enough time to register the fact that you're no longer in need of food.

Furthermore, fiber may absorb dietary fat and carry it out of the body. Scientific studies have shown that high fiber diets can help prevent obesity.

Over the years, a number of researchers have suggested that a fiber-rich diet lowers the risk of heart attack. A major study conducted by the Harvard School of Public Health and published in 1996 confirmed this connection. The Harvard researchers tracked the health of more than 40,000 men for six years and found that fatal and nonfatal heart attacks were 41 percent less common among individuals who ate more than 28 grams of fiber daily, compared to those who ate less than 13 grams.

What do 28 grams of fiber mean in terms of food? A third of a cup of wheat bran yields 8.5 grams of fiber. A half-cup of cooked kidney beans yields 7.3 grams. A half-cup of peas 3.6. One apple with the skin is 3.5 and a banana 2.4 grams of fiber.

These same Harvard researchers reported that the connection between saturated fat intake and coronary heart disease "is almost entirely explained by lower fiber intake among the men who consumed more fat."

More On Fat

Fats are combinations of saturated and unsaturated fatty acids. The term saturation refers to the number of hydrogen atoms a fatty acid carries. Fatty acids have different degrees of saturation and length, factors which determine whether a fat is solid or is liquid at room temperature. Saturated fats tend to be solid and relate primarily to animal sources such as butter and the fat in dairy and meat. What matters most, researchers say, is that you reduce the amount of saturated fat in your diet.

Much research has been conducted on the connection between dietary fats and blood cholesterol. Olive oil, a so-called monounsaturated fat, and polyunsaturated vegetable oils such as corn, soybean and safflower all lower the artery-clogging low-density lipoproteins (the so-called LDL "bad cholesterol"). Which oil does a better job is moot, depending on the particular study you read. Many widely-publicized studies point to the consumption of olive oil by Mediterranean peoples as a major reason why they have a lower incidence of heart disease than Americans. Researchers also point out that people in Mediterranean areas eat more vegetables and fruit than Americans, foods that contain many natural substances beneficial for health.

Of course, these benefits assume that one is consuming such oils the way nature provides them, via whole olives, etc., which provide antioxidants along with the oils. Remember that those oils, while derived from vegetables, are all fat--vegetable fat. They do lower bad cholesterol, but, because they are fat, they increase the risk of cancer, because processing them to remove the oil from the vegetables removes the vital antioxidants. Indeed, animal studies show that the polyunsaturated fats are potent promoters of breast cancer. A steady increase in breast, prostatic, colon and pancreatic cancer among Americans has paralleled a sharp increase in the use of polyunsaturated vegetable oils since the 1960s. So, the way to enjoy the heart benefits of the oils without the cancer risk is obvious: simply replace the antioxidants the processing of those vegetables removes (vitamins A, C, E, etc.), in the manner and dosages we have discussed elsewhere in this book. Take the antioxidants along with the oils.

Statistics on breast cancer are shocking evidence as to the harm of a typically high-fat Western diet. Studies show that women in the U.S., Canada, Australia, and Northern Europe have five to six times mores breast cancer than women from Asia and Africa, where low-fat diets prevail. Some national differences are even greater. For instance, in Kenya the breast cancer incidence is 1.08 cases per 100,000 women--twenty-fold less than in the U.S. There are no exceptions to the findings that in countries with low fat intake the cancer incidence is low, and where dietary fat is high cancer is also high.

In China, where fat intake ranges from about 6 to 24 percent of calories, researcher T. Colin Campbell found a strong correlation to breast cancer. Those women with the higher intake--even though it was comparatively low by Western standards (we eat 30 or 40 percent of our calories as fat)--had the highest rates.

Migration studies show that women who move from areas with a low incidence of breast cancer (such as Japan) to countries where a higher fat diet prevails will have an increased rate of cancer. The daughters of these women have disease rates little different from women in their adopted country.

High-fat diets produce virulent, metabolic carcinogens (cancer-causing compounds). Natural "killer" cells are part of the body's immune system that fights infection and malignant growths. The activity of these cells increases on low-fat diets. Conversely, high-fat diets inhibit the immune system.

By all means, try to cut down your intake of total dietary fat to no more than 20 percent of your total calories and ideally down to 10 percent. Stay away from dairy, which is high in saturated fats that are believed to be causative agents for heart disease and to a lesser extent, for cancer.

Do you eat out a lot? Eat a lot of fast foods? Fast food is fat city in addition to loads of sugar, salt, refined carbohydrates, and chemical additives. Fast food meals contain on average more than 50 percent fat. Habituation will put you into the nutritional poorhouse.

Nuts and seeds are OK in small amounts. While they have a high fat content they are valuable for their essential fatty acids and vitamin E, both of which serve as cancer-fighting antioxidants.

It Isn't Just What You Eat, It's How You Eat, Too

"To eat is human; to digest, divine."--C.T. Copeland

Years ago as a young physician, I became friends with the late Emory Thurston, one of the great pioneers of nutrition. Over lunch one day, he told me, "Jim, you have to eat slowly and chew your food more. That way you'll outlive all those doctors who don't believe in nutrition." Thurston was full of practical advice and obviously practiced what he preached. He was a vital and hardy man who lived to a ripe age of 95.

Today, in an age where eating on the run has become a way of life, the primordial act of chewing is sorely neglected. Too busy to chew our food as we should, we often just gulp it down., with consequences that would appear truly beneficial only to the manufacturers of indigestion aids.

Chewing is essential to health, a lesson dramatized by a health enthusiast and weightlifter you probably never heard of. His name was Horace Fletcher and he was probably the greatest crusader for chewing the world has ever known. Before the turn of the century, he was a 40-ish college professor extremely overweight, beset with poor health, chronic indigestion and limited energy. During a trip to Europe to restore his vitality he came across a statement made by former English prime minister William Gladstone that bites of food should be chewed 32 times, or once for each tooth.

That made sense to Fletcher, so he tried it. And he tried other recommendations related to how you eat, such as never eating when you are tired, disturbed or angry, and never eating until you are hungry, and keeping away unpleasant thoughts at mealtime.

Applying these principles, Fletcher regained his health within a half-year, totally conquering fatigue and illness. With his newfound vigor he began entering long-distance bicycle races and even outperformed college athletes in feats of strength and endurance. He also wrote and lectured widely on his eating style, which became known as Fletcherism. Among his followers were leading physicians, politicians and the Rockefeller family.

On chewing, Fletcher went beyond P.M. Gladstone's suggestion and recommended 50 chews per mouthful. He told people to keep count while they chewed, to chew their food to a pulp until it practically swallows itself, and face downward so the food can easily slip through the "food gate" at the back of the mouth.

Some of his ideas now may seem extreme, but he did make people think more about chewing. Indeed, chewing is the very first step in digestion. Properly done, it breaks food down into smaller pieces that are more easily digestible and at the same time mixes the food with saliva. Your saliva contains enzymes which begin the digestive process, particularly for carbohydrates and starches, and lubricate the food for a smooth voyage down into the stomach.

As the chewing starts, the stomach begins to produce its own lubricating and breakdown juices that further enhance the digestive process.

The mechanical act of chewing is essential to digest vegetables. Most vegetables, especially raw ones, have fairly tough cellulose encasements around the nutrients in their cells and unless you mechanically break that down you don't really get the active nutrient release. Furthermore, there is a tendency nowadays to cook less, so that the food is crunchy, such as in stir fry. So unless you chew these foods properly, much of what you eat will just be wasted.

Chewing is not quite as important for protein foods. Ever notice the way a dog gulps down meat? Give him a piece of bread and he will chew it. The reason is that the acid in the stomach will take care of the protein even if it is not chewed down to a pulp. That doesn't mean you won't choke if you swallow too big a piece of meat.

Most people won't resist swallowing or talking for the 50 chews recommended by Fletcher, so for the sake of practicality and efficiency maybe we should aim for 20-25 chews per mouthful.

The Eating Environment

Rarely, it seems, do people sit down just to eat. They usually sit down to eat and talk, or to eat and read, or eat and watch TV.

"People talk too much and chew too little," said Susan Schiffman, Ph.D., head of a weight-loss clinic at Duke University in a 1990 article in *Muscle and Fitness* magazine. "Talking between chewing would be a better habit. It would slow you down."

Slowing down in fact may be a valid strategy for losing weight. Schiffman has learned from her patients that wolfing down food with hardly a break between bites results in excessive amounts of food in the stomach. By contrast, slow, careful chewing seems to put less food in the stomach. More time is spent chewing and less on swallowing, giving the person more of an opportunity to get in touch with feelings of fullness.

Additionally, the more you chew the more you taste. Chewing forces air--and odor--back into the nose through your throat. "That's the way we get most of our odor and taste from the food we eat," says Dr. Schiffman. "We don't smell it through the nostrils. We get it retronasally. When you put it into your mouth you may think it is taste, but it is really odor that is going up the back of the throat and being picked up by the nose."

It is perhaps for this benefit that devout Epicureans would argue that the meal table is a place for conducting the business of eating rather than conducting business while eating. "Conversation is the enemy of good food," was the way the late, great movie director and gourmet Alfred Hitchcock put it.

The late Arthur L. Kaslow, M.D., a Solvang, California, physician specializing in nutritional medicine, found a strong connection among patients between improper eating and indigestion, gas, constipation and diarrhea. He developed a special stool examination that determined, among other things, if a person was chewing his or her food well.

Dr. Kaslow said he often found incompletely digested food particles and evidence of improper chewing. When he asked his patients about chewing, they usually said they didn't pay much attention.

"These people usually have a lot of gas, a lot of bowel problems, a lot of difficulties, and they may even be in what we call secondary malnutrition," Kaslow said. "They may be taking good food into their mouths but don't get good nourishment out of it. I tell them that I can take care of your digestion, I can give you digestive enzymes, I can take care of the gas-forming bacteria, but nobody else but you can eat for you. That's your job."

Keep Cool To Keep Your Digestive "Fire" Hot

Emotions also affect digestion. In a 1987 study at Temple University's School of Dentistry, researchers reported that deep relaxation appears to be the single most important factor contributing to optimum oral digestion and subsequent absorption of complex carbohydrates, the most important food for high energy.

And when deep relaxation was combined with thorough chewing, the process of digestion was enhanced even more, according to the study. Stress, in the form of mathematical exercises performed during eating, was found to affect negatively the saliva and enzyme production necessary for breaking down foodstuffs in the mouth. Participants in the study attained deep relaxation through meditation.

These findings are in keeping with the oldest dietary recommendations in the world--India's Ayurvedic health tradition, some 5,000 years old. The ancient Indians believed that one should eat in a relaxed and quiet setting and focus on the food in order to get the maximum benefits.

In Ayurveda, there is a unique concept called *agni*, or "digestive fire," the bodily mechanisms and enzymes involved in digestion. "A primary sign of good health is that your *agni* is burning bright," writes Deepak Chopra, M.D., in his best-selling book on Ayurveda, *Perfect Health* (Buenos Aires, J. Vergara, 1991). "That means you are digesting your food efficiently, distributing all the necessary nutrients to every cell, and burning off waste products without leaving deposits of toxins. Nature has set up everyone's body in such a way that *agni* follows a cycle throughout the day; unless *agni's* daily rhythm is correctly set, digestion will suffer. One of the most valuable things to know is how to reset a flickering *agni* and coax it back into its natural groove."

To do that, Ayurveda says we need to recognize the digestive rhythms which make us slightly hungry in the morning, very hungry at noon, and moderately hungry in the early evening. Between those times, *agni* shuts down the appetite so that it can get on with the process of digestion. When the stomach is empty again, *agni* rekindles the appetite.

Ayurveda thus recommends having our largest meal at lunch, when digestion is strongest. Dinner should be a modest meal that can be digested before bedtime.

Nutritionists who say that a good breakfast is the key to a good day would be challenged by Ayurveda, which says if you are hungry in the morning, eat a good breakfast; if you are not hungry, don't eat.

Thus, one of the main rules of eating is not to eat until you are hungry. Your previous meal should be digested before you eat again.

From the wisdom of the timeless Ayurveda tradition, here are additional tips for maximizing digestion you might like to try:

- Always sit down to eat. Keep talk to a minimum when eating. Don't discuss business or stressful topics. By not paying attention to what you are eating, you are very likely to overeat. When you have finished, sit for a moment or two. That enables your body to settle into its digestive rhythm.

• Eat to the point of satisfaction rather than fullness. Ideally, you should get up from the table with about a quarter of your stomach empty. This doesn't mean you have to give up tasty desserts. Just don't top up with them. During a meal, put your attention on your stomach for a moment. If you're feeling satisfied, it's time to stop. Listen to your body.

"Your digestive tract will work more efficiently on smaller portions, and your body will find it much easier to control its weight automatically," says Chopra. "Don't be afraid that you will walk away from the table hungry. Being satisfied is not the same as being stuffed. If you leave a little empty room in your stomach, you will feel light, buoyant, energetic, and much fresher an hour after you eat. That is how a properly eaten meal feels, leading naturally to a properly digested one."

• Try to eat at regular times.

• Favor freshly prepared foods and avoid leftovers and reheated foods. Try to avoid cold drinks, particularly ice cold drinks, with meals. The reason: They extinguish *agni*. It's a major shock to your digestive system if you flood it with ice cold fluid during a meal. Ayurveda recommends sipping only a small amount of warm or hot water with a meal. Iced drinks cause a constriction of the villi in the intestines. These are the countless projections on the intestinal walls where food absorption takes place. Constriction interferes with the uptake of nourishment. Doctors say that gastric or indigestion problems often clear up as a result of abstaining from ice drinks during meals.

A Word On Weight-Loss Diets

A humorist once said that people will go to great lengths to avoid going to great widths. That's certainly true here in America, where dieting and weight loss long ago overtook baseball as the national pastime. Weight loss is an $18 billion-a-year business driven in large part by the misguided efforts of dieters to reach skinny heaven. This is a world of myth, fantasy, misinformation, ignorance, frustration and failure.

People will try anything. Drugs, diets, regurgitation of swallowed food, surgery and expensive ready-made meals. Maybe you have tried some of these things yourself.

Ninety-eight percent of weight reduction programs don't offer lasting results. Zeal for a new diet, for instance, may last a week, perhaps even a month. Before long, however, enthusiasm fades in the face of denial and effort. Old habits return, lost pounds reappear, and you proceed to the next fad that comes along, *ad infinitum*.

A diet advocating any type of suppression of hunger is doomed from the start. Hunger and appetite are natural expressions of health in every living creature. Food is the fuel of energy, cell growth and repair, and the countless number of biochemical processes going on within our bodies. To put on the brakes by "controlling" or "managing" appetite is to invite failure by denying the body its natural expression.

It makes sense to work with the natural laws of hunger and appetite. That's what I tell my patients.

Remember nobody says you have to be thin. Maybe it's not in your genes. Just be concerned about eating healthy.

Exercise

You know the importance of exercise. But I'll repeat it for the record. A wise man once said that "those who think they have no time for bodily exercise will sooner or later have to find time for illness."

Research shows that the beginning of obesity comes with a sudden decrease in activity level. If you want a pretty startling comparison, look at what happens with livestock. Ranchers, when they want to fatten up their animals for market, pen them up to restrict movement while feeding them the same or even lesser amounts of food.

There's no getting around it. You must exercise every day, even if it's just for a little bit. You know what your body needs to feel good. Try to get in at least 30 minutes daily at a moderate to high intensity, meaning raising your heart rate up to about 60-70 percent of maximum. Brisk walking is great. So is swimming. Cycling. Whatever turns you on. Just do it. Exercise does not, as some shirkers insist, add to your hunger. Studies show, in fact, just the reverse: that sustained vigorous exercise decreases appetite for many hours after it. Furthermore, it releases tensions and anxieties, which of course are common triggers for overeating, and last, but not least, it burns calories. The more you exercise, the more you burn and the more pounds you lose.

Below are a few simple suggestions that work for many people. In all cases, start out slowly and gently. You can use this program as a springboard to aerobics classes, walking, hiking or bicycle groups, or even gym membership.

1. A brisk walk--not window shopping, but striding out. Gradually build up intensity. Under no circumstances, should an obese person try running. It is too hard on the joints.

2. Exercise bicycles or treadmill. If you use a bicycle, make sure the seat is broad enough to accommodate you. Many seats are inadequate for seriously overweight individuals.

3. Weight training is highly efficient for weight loss. Don't let that term scare you. I'm not talking heavy stuff but light exercises for the main muscles of the body--the legs, chest, upper back, shoulders and midsection.

You will be amazed at the results. A tiny bit each day begins to reverse the effects of muscle disuse. Your muscles begin to grow slightly larger. When they do, they burn far more calories.

All you need to get started is a barbell, a few light weight plates, and a flat bench, something like a patio bench. Or you can join a gym and do it. If you decide to go this route, get advice and an easy program from a trainer.

Use common sense. Start the exercise program very delicately. Never push your body. Never overdo it. Begin at any level that is comfortable for you--even if it is one repetition.

With exercise it is important to do something that you enjoy. If you enjoy what you are doing, you'll stay with it. And if you can stay with it, you will succeed.

Chapter Seven
How to Increase Your Energy

Chronic fatigue drags more people to doctors than anything else. It's certainly the most common complaint I hear from patients. While fatigue is a general symptom associated with many infectious illnesses and disease processes, often a holistic physician can restore lagging energy levels by looking at a patient's lifestyle.

Diet is a good place to start.

The famous Spanish writer Cervantes once said, "the belly carries the legs, and not the legs the belly." The observation is as true now as it was in the seventeenth century. If you observe the contents of supermarket shopping carts or the things people put in their mouths at greasy spoons you have a good idea why fatigue is so rampant.

Our planet Earth serves up its tasty, life-sustaining food in the form of carbohydrates, fats and proteins. Their components--glucose, fatty acids, amino acids, vitamins and minerals--are the chemical substances used by the body, along with oxygen and water, to produce energy.

Carbohydrates are the most fundamental foodstuff for energy. The digestive system dismantles them into glucose (blood sugar), which is carried to the brain for mental energy or stored in the liver and muscles as glycogen for use elsewhere in the body.

There are two types of carbohydrates: complex and simple. In general, complex carbs can be said to break down slowly, putting a steady flow of glucose into the bloodstream. They include unrefined whole grain foods (whole wheat, oatmeal, barley, brown rice, buckwheat, etc.), fruits, vegetables, nuts, seeds and beans.

Research has revealed major differences among complex carbs as to how rapidly they are broken down into glucose. Some, such as the potato, are processed quickly and in fact cause a quicker rise in glucose levels than even table sugar. The rate at which foods are turned into glucose is called the glycemic index.

Boiled carrots produce a blood-sugar response that is 92 percent of glucose. Fructose, the primary sugar of fruit, has a low 20 rating. That means it is very slowly absorbed and converted. That's what you want. Choose your complex carbohydrates among the lower glycemic index foods for a steady injection of safe energy.

Here are some other examples of glycemic index ratings:

Potato chips 51	**Brown rice 66**
Sweet potatoes 48	**White rice 72**
Millet 71	**White spaghetti 50**
Raisins 64	**Banana 62**
Apples 39	**Corn flakes 80**
All-Bran 51	**Peas 51**
Lima beans 36	**Kidney beans 29**
Soybeans 15	**Ice cream 36**

Whole milk 34

(Source: A.S. Trusswell, Glycemic Index of Foods, *European Journal of Nutrition*, Supplement two, 1992)

Simple carbohydrate foods for the most part are absorbed quickly and cause a rapid rise of glucose. Pigging out on sweets will do that. The body reacts hormonally by driving the glucose level back down, usually even lower than it was before.

Low blood sugar typically brings on such things as fatigue and irritability, and many other symptoms. Constant ups and downs of glucose can wreak havoc with your energy. On a regular basis it can lead to debilitating hypoglycemia (low blood sugar) and even diabetes. Experts estimate that 9 to 17 percent of the adult U.S. population suffers from hypoglycemic conditions.

Simple, refined carbohydrates include table sugar, candy, honey, white bread, and sugary cakes and cookies.

Be alert to hidden sugar in foods such as donuts (which offer 6 teaspoons per glazed donut), desserts (7 per slice of chocolate cake with icing), soft drinks (8 per 12-ounce can!), and shakes (14!!). The best way to avoid energy crashes, is to avoid these foods.

Another negative side of simple carbs is that unlike complex carbs they are devoid of fiber, the "roughage" of unprocessed plant food that creates healthy, frequent, and regular bowel movements.

Fat is a high energy food with twice as much stored energy as carbohydrates and protein. Eating more fat can increase endurance but it will also increase your cholesterol level, clog your arteries, increase the risk of cancer and deplete potassium and magnesium, key minerals related to energy. Moreover, fat is difficult to digest. Sitting down and eating a meal high in fat is a sure way to drain your battery. Afterwards, you generally have one desire--a nice, long sleep.

Fat has gotten a bad rap basically because we eat so much of it. The body requires fat, just not as much as we eat. Protein is indispensable to muscle growth and repair, but is a poor source of energy. Certain amino acids, called the branched chain aminos, contribute 15-20 percent of total energy utilization during intense exercise and in endurance activity when glycogen becomes depleted. These aminos are converted to glucose in the liver and then released into the blood to be used by muscles as needed.

Rx For After-Meal Blahs

You don't have to be Einstein to figure this simple formula: Energy = food quality and quantity. What it means is this:

- Eat the freshest, most wholesome and least processed food available.

• Don't overeat. Eat until you are satisfied and stop. Heavy meals, particularly high in fat, condemn your body to hours of hard, energy-sapping digestive labor. This prolonged digestion diverts blood away from the muscles and brain to the gastrointestinal tract. Food should energize you. If you have the brain blahs or frequently feel like sleeping after a meal, consider how much you are eating. As Ben Franklin said: "A full belly makes a dull brain."

Brain Food

Speaking of the brain, it is worthwhile to observe how much food affects mental energy. Even thousands of years ago, Indian sages wrote about how food perturbed or relaxed the mind. Today, nutritional science is unraveling the biochemical nuts and bolts of this relationship.

Your brain is not some independent instrument operating on a different scale of notes than the rest of your body. The brain, the nervous system it controls, and in turn the muscles the nervous system controls, indeed the whole ball of wax that is you is an interrelated mind-body totality requiring good nutrition to function well.

As I mentioned a moment ago, this totality that is you must constantly be nourished by oxygen, glucose, fats, amino acids, vitamins and minerals. Muscles are fueled by glucose, which is the simple sugar broken down from carbohydrates. Yet the brain is the largest consumer of glucose in your body.

In today's polluted and chemicalized world, you must eat both offensively and defensively to maintain optimum physical and mental energy. Offensively means emphasizing those foods that will provide you with nutrients to keep your mind clear, focused and energized. Defensively means learning which foods or chemical additives boggle your brain--then staying away from them.

Optimum energy requires that you use your head to feed it, that you concentrate on what you eat if you want better concentration. If you don't you'll find yourself in the languid lane of life occupied by vast numbers of Americans whose poor eating habits cause chronic mood swings, mental ups and downs, and lack of concentration.

Hypoglycemia

This common condition--very often associated with chronic fatigue--occurs when your blood sugar level drops and sets off a variety of biochemical reactions. Eating large amounts of sugar and other refined carbohydrates (enriched-flour baked goods, processed grains, and alcohol) has a lot to do with making it worse.

In the treatment of hypoglycemia, many people cut out sugar and refined carbohydrates yet experience only partial relief. They may even feel worse--a withdrawal symptom from the sugar--or perhaps feel refreshingly "up" for days or parts of days. But the improvement doesn't last.

The reason is that such people need wholesome snacks of protein or complex carbohydrates every couple of hours to prevent blood sugar dips, as well as B complex vitamin supplements to fortify their nervous systems.

Persistent fatigue that develops from low blood sugar generally takes up to three months to be relieved once a corrective program is started.

Food And Environmental Allergies

Food you eat every day, and indeed love to eat often, may possibly be draining your energy. Both foods, and the chemical additives they contain, commonly trigger different combinations of allergic symptoms in sensitive individuals. In my clinic, many of the problems I treat, including fatigue, are related to food allergies.

Kareem Abdul-Jabbar, basketball's greatest scorer, suffered from debilitating migraines and loss of energy whenever he ate wheat, eggplant, tomatoes, milk or shellfish.

People in constant reaction are more tired. They have less stamina. When offending foods or substances are removed, energy is greatly improved.

Any food or additive has the potential to cause problems. Wheat, milk, corn, soy, cane sugar, chocolate, yeast and citrus fruit are major offenders. Sensitivities usually involve all foods containing these products. You may never eat an ear of corn but may react to corn syrup, corn oil, or corn starch widely used in the food industry. A sensitivity to grapes can upset you seriously when you drink wine.

Frequency is also important. Something eaten once a week may be fine, but on a daily basis may cause trouble.

Watch out also for chemicals in the workplace or home. Exposure to them is another overlooked cause of fatigue and stress. When you go to work and after a short period of time you find that your stress level shoots up rapidly, then you should become very aware of what you are smelling and touching. The first sign of an environmental allergy such as this is difficulty in breathing. That is often followed by irritability, headache, fatigue, or difficulty in concentration.

Nutritional Deficiencies

Survey after survey shows vast numbers of Americans grossly deficient in essential nutrients such as iron, zinc, magnesium, and vitamins A, B-1, B-2, B-6 and C. Even athletes who eat more than most people show regular deficits. Any deficiency is capable of impairing energy. Such deficits occur for many reasons, among them:

• Americans are overfed, but undernourished. It's not hard to see why. Today's food--from the grower to your gullet--loses nutritional value every step of the way. The loss of nutrients starts right at the source--on agricultural soil that is mineral-deficient from intense farming methods and long-term use of chemical fertilizers and pesticides. The practice of harvesting of crops before they are mature, so they get to the market ripe, further depletes vitamin content.

• Two-thirds of the food we eat is commercially processed and processing almost always occurs at the expense of good nutrition. Wheat, for instance, converted into white flour, loses more than 50 percent of its health-giving vitamins and almost 90 percent of its minerals.

• Sugar and highly-processed refined carbohydrates comprise as much as 60 percent of the American dietary intake. These extremely low-density nutrients not only deprive the body of essential nutrients, but crowd out other nutritious foods, creating marginal malnutrition.`

• The bombardment of food with chemicals for shelf life and eye appeal contributes to more nutritional destruction.

• Fast food, an American staple, is notoriously deficient in key nutrients, such as vitamin A, several of the B vitamins, iron, and copper.

• Alcohol, smoking and drugs (prescription or otherwise) devastate the vitamin B complex group, vitamins A and C, along with zinc, magnesium and calcium.

• Stress is the way we react--mentally, emotionally and physically--to the demands of life. Anytime you have stress you are going to have physical symptoms--and fatigue is one of the most common. The more stress you experience in life the more nutrients you burn up that are essential for protecting your brain and body.

By the way, stress increases adrenaline. This, in turn, makes platelets stick together, hampering the supply of oxygen to red cells. The consequence: fading energy.

Overcoming Deficiencies

Deficiencies are overcome by eating the best and least processed food you can buy. That's absolutely fundamental to any healthy lifestyle. On a strong foundation of good food, you can further enhance your nutritional intake with high-quality supplements. You start with a good multi vitamin and mineral. For fine-tuning and addressing individual nutritional needs, I strongly recommend consulting with a nutritionally-oriented health professional.

Some specific supplements for relieving fatigue include the following:

• Magnesium is a major partner in more than 300 enzymatic reactions in the body, including the generation of cellular energy and muscle relaxation. A mild deficiency can cause fatigue. All stress and trauma, whether physical or emotional, causes a loss of the body's stores of magnesium. Stress includes overwork, travel, too much exercise, and surgery.

According to Dr. Mildred Seelig, Ph.D., of Emory University, and one of the world's leading experts on magnesium, the negative effects of stress on the body may be compounded if you don't have enough magnesium to begin with. Surveys indicate that 75 percent or more of Americans are deficient.

Vegetables, nuts and whole grains are rich in magnesium, but most of us don't eat enough. The national preference for processed foods ensures a risky low magnesium intake.

The refining of whole grains eliminates most of the magnesium content. The processing of whole wheat to white flour causes a magnesium loss of 82 percent.

High fat diets also have a negative effect on magnesium. The fat forms soaps in the gut that washes out whatever magnesium is contained in the food.

Anyone who drinks alcoholic beverages is undoubtedly deficient in magnesium. Even a small amount drains magnesium. As for alcoholics, they are beyond mere deficiency, says Dr. Seelig. Colas and other soft-drinks that are rich in phosphates inactivate magnesium.

• Potassium stimulates nerve impulses for muscle contractions and assists in the conversion of glucose to glycogen. Mental stress, excessive sweating, alcohol, coffee, and a high intake of salt and sugar deplete potassium. The most proven combination for energy is magnesium-potassium aspartate, which reduces fatigue, increases stamina and delays the onset of metabolic exhaustion.[1]

• Zinc activates thyroid[2] and thyroid regulates metabolism, in the same way the accelerator of a car determines speed. Recently, selenium was shown to stimulate thyroid.

• Specific amino acids strengthen muscles. Branch chain amino acids, and, most recently, glutamine, are the latest on the list. Branch chain amino acids have been shown to increase vital muscle effectiveness in A.L.S. patients; body builders use them with good results.[3] Recent animal studies have shown that glutamine may be even more important in the stimulation of muscle protein synthesis than branch chain amino acids.[4]

• Carnitine strengthens the heart and regulates the delivery of triglycerides. It also causes a significant increase in the utilization of lactic acid as an energy source. Lactic acid normally is considered to be a waste product of muscle contraction that causes muscle fatigue and cramping.[5] Like carnitine, biotin reduces lactic acid formation.

• Phosphatidyl choline has been shown to reduce fatigue by as much as 35% in long distance runners. It is also a neurotransmitter and increases alertness.[6]

• Bee pollen, used mostly by European athletes, has also been shown to increase stamina. Some English reports claim as much as 40-50% increase in measured performance.[7]

• Ginseng is believed to build mental and physical vitality over time. Dr. K. Takogi, of the University of Tokyo, stated that "with the use of ginseng there is a significant anti-fatigue reaction in animals." Russian athletes were known to have made good use of this herb for years. Studies found that it increased endurance, reflexes, stamina, motivation, coordination and concentration. Ginseng is regarded as an adaptogen, a substance that systemically helps normalize bodily functions. It contains active compounds known as glycosides, which are chemicals bound to sugar. These glycosides are capable of stimulating protective, restorative responses to stress. Ginseng has been used around the world for centuries as a natural "upper."

- Octacosonal, a component of wheat germ oil, has been shown to improve reaction time, endurance and neuromuscular control.[8] Among other contributions to the body, it boosts muscle glycogen storage and extends the capacity for work or serious exercise.

- The 13 vitamins in the B complex family represent, as a unit, perhaps the single most important factor for the health of the nervous system. They are also essential to the conversion of food into energy. When a person exercises strenuously, the body quickly burns up its vitamin B resources. A shortage affects both performance and recovery. Among the B Vitamins most important to energy are:

Thiamine (B-1) is a major energizer of the heart muscle.

Niacin (B-3) keeps blood vessels dilated and promotes oxygen transport through the body. It also combines with chromium to facilitate glucose transfer into cells.

Pantothenic acid (B-5) contributes directly to cellular energy production. Controlled experiments with both humans and animals demonstrate improved endurance with supplementation.

- A deficiency of vitamin C is related to scurvy, where the body's immune system and structure literally collapses. One of the first signs of scurvy is chronic fatigue.

Vitamin C helps muscles use fatty acids as an energy source, thereby helping to economize on glycogen and enhancing endurance. Moreover, the vitamin is believed to slow down lactic acid buildup, which is associated with fatigue.

More than 20 years ago, the late Dr. Frederick Klenner, M.D., a North Carolina physician who pioneered the therapeutic use of vitamin C, tested the vitamin's effect on the fatiguability of a top professional football team, the Philadelphia Eagles.

"One week we gave them placebos and the next week vitamin C," Klenner reported. "We found that on vitamin C the players' fatigue was less in the final quarter.

"Anyone who takes vitamin C will notice that their endurance will increase," he added. "It's the No. 1 anti-fatigue vitamin."

• Iron is necessary for oxygen transportation throughout the body and storage of oxygen to fuel muscular contractions. Iron is easily lost through sweat, urine, feces and menstrual flow. A cup of coffee or black tea with meals or just afterward can block as much as 80 percent absorption of the iron in your food.

• Coenzyme Q10 is a fundamental biochemical found in all living organisms necessary for cellular respiration and energy production. People tend to become deficient as they age. Poor diet accelerates deficiency.

• Antioxidants are potent substances found in our bodies and in food. They deter harmful oxidative processes inside our body that can cause cellular destruction and disease. Coenzyme Q10 is one such antioxidant. So are vitamins C and E, and beta carotene. In recent years, medical science has found that an enormous variety of chemical compounds in plants known as phytochemicals, proanthocyanidins and flavonols is particularly effective. These substances are now available in supplement form. Included among their benefits is the ability to enhance the activity of vitamin C and increase the aerobic capacity of athletes.

Energy Help From the Olive Tree

Since early 1995 I have become familiar with a powerful phytochemical derived from the leaf of the olive tree. In supplement form, as olive leaf extract, it has shown a remarkable energizing and immune-boosting property. I have had excellent results with it in my practice. For more details on this exciting, new supplement, see Chapter Nine.

Rest

Do you get enough rest to compensate for the stress in your hectic life? Rest balances activity, a concept well understood even in ancient times. In the yin and yang principle of Chinese medicine, rest is yin and activity is yang.

The late Vince Lombardi, coach of football's Green Bay Packers, put great store on rest. He once fined all-star fullback Jim Taylor $25 for sitting on the edge of his bed in his socks and shorts at 11:01 p.m. Lombardi wanted his players in bed--horizontally--at 11 sharp.

Get enough sleep so that when you awake the next morning you feel rested. A fatigued person is much more prone to stress than someone who is well rested.

Caffeine

Coffee is the world's most popular drink, stimulant and drug--all in one. Yes, drug. It contains caffeine and other similar compounds that stimulate the nervous system. The average cup of drip brew contains 80-120 mg of caffeine. Instant contains 66-100 mg. Caffeine is also found in lesser concentrations in black tea (42-100 mg) and cola drinks (31-64 mg).

It's estimated that Americans swig over 400 million cups of coffee a day, many for pick-me-up purposes. Caffeine triggers the release of chemical substances from the adrenal glands that can cause the liver to release stored sugar into the blood, the heart to pump harder and the brain to think clearer. But the rise in blood sugar in turn stimulates the pancreas to pump insulin into the blood stream. This drives the blood sugar level down again, often below the normal level. When this occurs, you typically experience fatigue.

Arnold Fox, M.D., in a 1982 *Let's Live* magazine article entitled "Caffeine--Unexpected Cause of Fatigue!" wrote that "it may take as long as several hours before your body chemistry is returned to normal. Meanwhile, if you've had any more coffee, tea, cola, cocoa, or any caffeine-containing substances, the cycle begins anew. What you are doing is throwing a monkey wrench in your body's machinery."

Just as in all things, there are individual differences in regard to caffeine sensitivity. The average person, according to Fox, will have clearly discernible signs of caffeine stimulation after drinking as little as 250 mg, but the body already becomes affected with less. Fatigue is just one of the problems caffeine causes. It has also been implicated in nervousness, anxiety, depression, and sleeplessness.

According to research in Scandinavia, it may also create an undesirable effect on clotting by causing a rise in platelet activity. A mere 100 mg of caffeine is all that it takes to generate a four-fold increase in the presence of a certain platelet protein.

---

1. Kroenke, K., Wood, D.R., Mangelsdorff, A.D., et al., "Chronic Fatigue in Primary Care," *Journal of the American Medical Association*, 1988, 260:929 -34.
2. "Zinc Activates Thyroid," *American Journal of Clinical Nutrition*, August, 1980, 33:1767-1770.
3. "Pilot Trial of BCAA in Amytrophic Lateral Sclerosis," *Lancet*, May 7, 1988, pp. 1015-16.
4. MacLennan, P.A., Brown, R.A., Rennie, M.J., "A Positive Relationship Between Protein Synthetic Rate and Intracellular Glutamine Concentration in Perfused Rat Skeletal Muscle," *FEBS Letter*, 1987, 215:187-91
5. Thomsen, Dr. J., chief of cardiology, Middleton Memorial Veterans Hospital, Madison, Wisconsin, *Medical Tribune*, May 2, 1977.
6. Wurtman, R.J., et al., "Decreased Plasma Choline Concentrations in Marathon Runners," *New England Journal of Medicine*, October 2, 1986.
7. F. Roy Keght, "Athletes Use Pollen for Greater Performance."
8. Cureton, T.K., "The Physiological Effects of Wheat Germ Oil on Hormones in Exercise," Springfield, Thomas, 1972.

Chapter Eight
A Primer on Supplements

Despite all the evidence--more every year--authoritarian medicine continues to insist that "we get all the vitamins we need from our food." True enough, supplements were not needed in the Garden of Eden. The food was perfect, except for a problem with the apple. In the previous chapters, I have discussed some of the more important reasons why I believe supplementation is necessary. Let me cover a little more ground here.

Today, it still is possible to eat a "balanced diet," but for most that lofty goal is as unattainable as winning the lotto. One reason is that few of us can claim we have ideal eating habits. We now eat out more than in, and what we eat is often betwixt and between. Again, nutritional surveys without end show Americans to be deficient in nutrients that are critical for health.

Another reason is that studies show vegetables no longer contain as many vitamins and minerals as they once did. Artificially fertilized soil is not as good as soil naturally fertilized by animal excrement and decayed vegetation (compost).

Over the decades, the soil has been depleted, giving more than it gets. Artificial fertilizers kill the soil's microorganisms, yielding "dead soil." Crops grown on dead soil have a higher carbohydrate content, which is more vulnerable to greedy, unwanted insects. Transportation, storage and canning also deplete vitamins and minerals. Pasteurization of milk--a necessity when Louis Pasteur gave it his name, but now outmoded--destroys valuable enzymes, as well as other food factors, such as lecithin. Cooking itself destroys food values. That is why meat that is not overcooked and steamed vegetables are healthier for you.

The logical answer is to eat only organically grown food (grown on naturally fertilized soil, regularly checked for proper mineral levels). If we could do that, authoritarian medicine would be right. We could "get everything we need from three balanced meals." The trouble is that such food is not always available. When it is, it is often expensive, because chemical fertilizers have made it "unusual." Sometimes, it is only available in a "health food store." Please understand that we are by no means arguing against "better living through chemistry." Without the discoveries of chemistry, we would not enjoy many of the luxuries that have become necessities we now take for granted. We simply advance the modest assertion that, like everything else, it should be used judiciously.

In recent years, major cereal producers like General Mills and Kellogg have started selling whole foods containing few or no preservatives. Of course these companies are merely responding to the changing buying habits of enough people who have quit "junk" cereals and turned to natural, whole, non-preserved products. Needless to say, the Food and Drug Administration is still beating the drums for junk and fighting the supplement industry.

Since eating as we should is often difficult, we need to take supplements, starting with vitamins and minerals. Supplements give authoritarian medicine fits. The authoritarians could easily eliminate the need for them, by judiciously restoring the health of the soil, so we could "get everything we need from three balanced meals." Instead, as we shall see, they prefer to impose forcibly a monopoly in restraint of trade, in violation of federal law.

Vitamins

What are they? Vitamins are accessory, organic food factors existing in all foods in minute amounts, and necessary for the body to work normally. We know something is a vitamin if its absence causes malnutrition and specific deficiency diseases, including scurvy (Vitamin C deficiency), pernicious anemia (Vitamin B-12 deficiency), and rickets (Vitamin D deficiency), etc.

The authoritarians, because of either ignorance or malevolence (or money), say there is no difference between synthetic and natural vitamins, because chemistry is chemistry, and the body can't tell the difference. They are wrong. The two types of vitamins are structurally different. Examined under a polarized microscope, natural vitamins bend light to the right and are, therefore, "dextra-rotary." Synthetic vitamins bend light to the left and right and are, therefore, dextra and "levo-rotary." Proof of this is right on the Vitamin E label, for instance. D Alpha Tocopherol is natural. D-L Alpha Tocopherol is synthetic. Synthetic vitamins are less effective. They are made from synthetic elements like coal tar. Natural vitamins are derived from food elements that occur naturally, so your body assimilates them more easily. Synthetic vitamins make coal tar companies happy. Natural vitamins make farmers happy. Coal belongs in a furnace. Food belongs in a stomach.

Minerals

There are 96 times more minerals in the body than vitamins. Minerals are familiar elements like Iron (chemical symbol Fe), Copper (Cu), Magnesium (Mg), Zinc (Zn), and less familiar substances such as vanadium, rubidium and molybdenum. Like vitamins, they are necessary for life itself and combine with other basic components of food to form enzymes. Minerals act as catalysts in biological reactions and help enzymes do their work. Minerals are ingested through food and water. The American diet is deficient in many minerals, because of mineral-poor agricultural soil, the result of intensive farming and long-term use of chemical fertilizers and pesticides.

Antioxidants

It seems like only yesterday that we first heard the term "antioxidants." Now, everybody is talking about their ability to counteract the damaging effects of "free radicals," which are highly unstable molecular fragments unleashed within the body by strenuous exercise, chemicals, polluted air, stress, and other factors. "Free radicals" are involved in blood clots, damage to cellular components and DNA, as well as muscle pains, cramps and fatigue. Research has shown that "free radicals" cause or contribute to major diseases such as cancer, atherosclerosis, arthritis, dementia, etc.[1-10]

Technically speaking, free radicals are hydroxyl radicals, superoxide radicals and oxygen molecules with one electron. The normal, healthy oxygen molecule has two electrons (hence O_2). Lacking one, it tries to become complete again by stealing one from a healthy cell, thereby weakening and aging the body.

Antioxidants prevent that damage. By now, you are familiar with many of them. They include Vitamin E (especially the Beta, Gamma and Epsilon fractions); Vitamin C, selenium and beta carotene. Other antioxidants are superoxide dismutase, glutathione, coenzyme Q10, etc. In the last few years, many new and powerful nutritional antioxidants have appeared, among them the so-called proanthocyanidins and phytochemicals--compounds made from grape seed extracts and other plant material.

As we have seen, platelet aggregation causes more than 90% of heart attacks.[11] Antioxidants (C, E, beta carotenes and selenium) reduce platelet aggregation significantly, as shown in recent studies.[12]

Amino Acids

Aminos are the building blocks of protein. There are 24 of them, which form a countless variety of proteins. They all contain combinations of nitrogen, oxygen, carbon and hydrogen. Amino acids are either essential or nonessential.

Essential aminos must be derived from food. There are eight of them. L-isoleucine, L-leucine, L-lysine, L-methionine, L-phenylalanine, L-tryptophan, L-threonine, and L-valine. Two others, L-arginine and L-histidine, are essential for children.

Nonessential aminos are manufactured internally in the quantities the body requires. Their names are L-alanine, L-asparagine, L-aspartic acid, L-citruline, L-cysteine, L-cystine, L-glutamine, L-glutamic acid, glycine, L-ornithine, L-proline, L-serine, taurine, and L-tyrosine.

In recent years there has been an explosion of interest in amino acids. Research and clinical applications have increased in a major way. Today, aminos are being used to help people sleep and feel better, and overcome anxiety, depression and substance abuse. They are being utilized as components of new anti-aging compounds. Hospital emergency rooms are using them in the treatment of medication overdose and liver detoxification.

It has become clear that amino acid supplementation offers a new weapon in the fight against chronic illness.

The amino acid melatonin became the nutritional “discovery” of 1995 and attained superstar status with books, magazine cover articles, and television reports praising its anti-aging and sleep-producing properties.

Some important advances in the use of amino acids include:

Research demonstrating how tyrosine can help substance abusers quit their habits and counteract stress, chronic fatigue, and attention deficit disorders.

Tests for amino acid blood levels are being increasingly seen as important indicators of physical and mental illnesses. For instance, a new test that measures blood levels of homocysteine holds promise as a leading risk indicator for heart disease.

GABA, short for gamma-aminobutyric acid, is an amino acid that acts as an inhibitory neurotransmitter in the body. GABA helps keep the brain calm and orderly by inhibiting the excitation level of the brain cells in the cortex that are on the receiving end of incoming anxiety messages. If stress, anxiety and fear are prolonged, GABA stores are depleted, opening the way for a flood of alarm messages and mental imbalance. In supplement form, it helps calm anxiety disorders.

Scientific research has proven that body builders and athletes have been right all along about the use of branched chain amino acids--leucine, isoleucine and valine--to promote muscle development and improve performance. Not only do branched chain aminos aid athletes, but they also help speed wound healing after surgery.

Overshadowing the many positive developments in amino acid research and usage, is the continuing ban on tryptophan--an important amino acid--by the U.S. Food and Drug Administration. This is a towering example of criminal use of government power and interference in the free enterprise process. We shall talk more about this later.

Glandulars

These supplements go back to antiquity. For many years, liver has been used for pernicious anemia without interference from authoritarian medicine. Likewise, desiccated thyroid has been used for hypo(low)thyroid conditions.[13] It is interesting to note that the first thing a carnivore eats after a kill are the organs. Research has proven the effectiveness of animal gland products. Studies have shown that injected and radioactively tagged specific organ tissues are transported by phagocytes to the same organ in the target animal.[14] The good news is that oral glandulars work too.

Bone meal is a natural source of calcium, magnesium and phosphorous. Animals have it and enjoy strong bones; man must learn from nature or suffer the consequences of ignoring her.

Hydroxyapatite, the main element in bone meal, has recently been shown to inhibit cortical bone thinning, i.e., osteoporosis! In short, bone strengthens bone.[15] Heart substance contains ample concentrations of carnitine, which increases the heart's energy production.[16]

Ohio State University has been using nerve proteins on animals for a disease that resembles multiple sclerosis. Early results show such promise in 30 patients that the study has been extended to 120 patients who will swallow nerve proteins daily.[17] Non-toxic bovine myelin was recently shown to reduce the number of significant attacks in M.S.[18]

Adrenals contain many hormones needed for stress and energy, cortisone and adrenalin to name a couple. Pancreas contains enzymes needed for indigestion. Thymus contains thymosin, a hormone for immunity, and duodenum has been used for colitis, to strengthen the bowel.[19]

---

1 Demopoulos, H.B., Pietronigro, D.D., Flamm, E.S., Seligman, M.L., "The Possible Role of Free Radical Reactions in Carcinogenesis," *Journal of Environmental Pathology and Toxicology*, 1980, 3:273-303.

2. Harman, D., "The Aging Process," Proceedings of the National Academy of Science, U.S.A., 1981, 78:7124-28.

3. Dormandy, T.L., "An Approach to Free Radicals," *Lancet*, 1983, ii 1010-14.

4. Demopoulos, H.B., Pietronigro, D.D., Seligman, M.L., "The Development of Secondary Pathology With Free Radical Reactions as a Threshold Mechanism," *Journal of the American College of Toxicology*, 1983, 2(3): 173-84.

5. Demopoulos, H.B., "Molecular Oxygen in Health and Disease." Read before the American Academy of Medical Preventics Tenth Annual Spring Conference, Los Angeles, May 21, 1983. (Available on three audio cassettes from Instatape, P.O. Box 1729, Monrovia, CA 91016.)

6. Ames, B.N., "Dietary Carcinogens and Anticarcinogens," *Science*, 1983, 221:1256-64.

7. Dormandy, T.L., "Free-Radical Resection in Biological Systems," *Annals of the Royal College of Surgery*, England, 1980, 62:188-94.

8. Dormandy, T.L., "Free-Radical Oxidation and Antioxidants," *Lancet*, 1978, 8:647-50.

9. Levine, S.A., Reinhardt, I.H., "Biochemical Pathology Initiated by Free Radicals, Oxidant Chemicals and Therapeutic Drugs in the Etiology of Chemical Hypersensitivity Disease," *Journal of Orthomolecular Psychiatry*, 1983, 12(3): 166-83.

10. Del Maestro, R.F., "An Approach to Free Radicals in Medicine and Biology," *Acta. Physiol. Scand.*, 1980, 492 (suppl.):158-68.

11. William N. Kelley, M.D., et al., *Text Book of Internal Medicine*, 1989, vol. 1, p. 37

12. Salomen, J., et al., "Effects of Antioxidant Supplements on Platelet Function: A Randomized, Pair-matched, Placebo-controlled, Double-blind Trial in Men With Low Antioxidant Status," *American Journal of Clinical Nutrition*, 1991, 53(5): 1222-1229.

13. Bland, S., "Glandular Based Food Supplements, Helping to Separate Fact From Fiction," Monograph, Bellevue Redmond Mac Lab, Inc., 1980, pp. 29-32.
14. Kment, A., *Untersuchungen der meerschweinchenschilddrusen-aktivat mit radioisotopen* (J 131) *nach siccacell-preparaten, Bericht v.d. 5 Tagg. d.Forschungskreises, f.ZT*, 33-40, 1958.
15. Epstein, Owen, MRCP, Kato, Yahuhiro, M.D., Robert, Dick, FRCR and Sherlock, Sheila, FRCP., "Vitamin D, hydroxyapatite, and Calcium Gluconate in Treatment of Cortical Bone Thinning in Postmenopausal Women With Primary Biliary Cirrhosis, *American Journal of Clinical Nutrition*, 36, September, 1982, pp. 426-430.
16 Thomsen, Dr. J., chief of cardiology of Middleton Memorial Veterans Hospital, Madison, Wis. *Medical Tribune*, May 2, 1977.
17 Whitacre, Carol, Ohio State University, Briefing of Council for the Advancement of Science Writing, 1991.
18 Weiner, H.L., et al., "Double Blind pilot trial of oral toleration with myelin antigens in multiple sclerosis, *Science*, 1993;259:1321-4.
19 Haskell, Benjamin, M.D., Friedman, M.H.F., Ph.D., "One Year's Treatment of Non-Specific Ulcerative Colitis with Intestinal Extract," Department of Surgery & Department of Physiology, Jefferson Medical College and Hospital, Philadelphia, December, 1948.

Chapter Nine
Olive Leaf Extract

Science has long stalked the chemical world within plants to uncover their amazing, healing secrets. Lately, these investigations have repeatedly yielded discovery after discovery of natural compounds with promising health and medical potential.

Some of these compounds stimulate the production of anti-cancer enzymes in the body. Others bind and neutralize certain carcinogenic chemicals. Others have antioxidant effects, protecting the body from oxidation damage caused by harmful molecular fragments known as free radicals that contribute to aging and illness. Some are known to specifically protect cardiac and vascular health.

These natural compounds are found abundantly in roots, stems, leaves, fruits and vegetables. They go by a variety of scientific names like polyphenols, flavonoids, flavonols, pycnogenols, glucosinolates, isoprenoids, carotenoids, tocotrienols, and proanthocyanidins. To keep things simple and pronounceable, we will just call them phytochemicals or phytonutrients. Phyto stems from the Greek word for plant.

The volume of current research is intense. Some experts say these compounds may offer the best protection we know of against the diseases that plague us today. There's much yet to learn about the tissue-specific way they work. However, with time, these phytonutrients, in the form of supplements or medical preparations, may play a major role in anti-aging medicine and how we prevent and treat disease.

Among the many phytochemicals that have interested me, as a clinician, is oleuropein (pronounced oh-lee-or-oh-pin), a substance found in the olive leaf. I am not the only health practitioner who has found that a natural supplement of olive leaf extract contains substantial medicinal benefits. For instance, olive leaf extract boosts the energy among patients and aids in the treatment of herpes and other viral conditions, flu and colds, fungal infections, chronic fatigue and allergies. I have also been surprised by unexpected results generated by this supplement.

The Olive and Us

One particular member of the plant kingdom that has been exceptionally generous to mankind is the olive tree. Indeed, its special gifts to humans have been documented for thousands of years and it is a dove carrying an olive branch that in our day and age stands for the global symbol of peace.

The olive tree belongs to a plant family that includes the ash, jasmine and lilac. The cultivated olive is harvested from a tree known scientifically as Olea europa, native to the eastern Mediterranean region. Today, these trees are widely grown throughout the whole Mediterranean area (98 percent of the world's olive oil comes from there) and in other regions with a similar climate.

According to Greek mythology, the olive tree was the creation of the goddess Athena, who first planted one out among the rocky grounds of the Acropolis and endowed it with powers to illuminate the darkness, soothe wounds and provide nourishment.

Whoever the responsible party is for the olive tree, it has certainly lived up to its divine origins. The olive tree has given us:

- A hard and variegated wood that is esteemed by cabinet makers. Tourists returning from the Holy Land usually carry souvenirs made of olive wood.

• Olives for eating.

• Olives for olive oil. During the Roman Empire, olive cultivation, curing and oil production advanced to a fine art—an art that has survived largely intact for 2,000 years. So, too, have Roman recipes for the use of olives and olive oil in food. For cooking purposes, olive oil is recommended over other vegetable oils because it has been found to be less susceptible to heat-caused oxidation that changes the chemical structure of the oil into a potentially-harmful form.

• Olive oil for illumination. This was the lighting oil used in Mediterranean houses well into the 19th century.

• Olive oil for lubrication. It oiled the machines of the industrial revolution just as it had served the Romans in earlier times as axle grease.

• Olive oil for healing. Hippocrates, the father of medicine, prescribed olive oil for curing ulcers, cholera and muscular pains some 2,500 years ago. Over the ages, numerous folk medicine applications for olive oil have been described.

In more recent medical times, the health benefits of olive oil have attracted considerable attention. Many studies indicate that the consumption of olive oil by Mediterranean peoples is an important reason why they have less heart disease than Americans. There is also some scientific evidence that olive oil intake may reduce the risk of breast cancer for women.

Studies have also shown that olive oil is beneficial for blood pressure and blood glucose levels.

• The olive leaf for healing.

Throughout history, the utilization of the fruit and its oil have overshadowed the rest of the tree. But recent medical research indicates that the olive leaf, celebrated in the Bible and then relatively forgotten, may be a rising healing star.

The Olive Leaf in History and Medicine

It is hard to avoid the conclusion that there is something very special about the olive leaf. For one thing, it is the first botanical mentioned in the Bible.

"And the dove came in to him in the evening, and lo, in her mouth was an olive leaf plucked off. So Noah knew that the waters were abated from off the earth." (Genesis 8:11)

After the Great Flood we didn't hear too much about the olive leaf for a long time. Obviously this was a hard act to follow.

In a much later biblical time (Ezekiel 47:12), God speaks of a tree: "The fruit thereof shall be for meat, and the leaf thereof for medicine." Was it the olive tree?

Then, in Revelation, at the very end of the New Testament, there is an angelic vision of a "tree of life" whose leaves "were for the healing of the nations." Today, as modern medicine increasingly embraces phytochemicals it is interesting to speculate about the biblical "tree of life." Again, was it perhaps the olive tree?

The ancient Egyptians may have been the first to put the olive leaf to practical use. They regarded it as a symbol of heavenly power, and in keeping with that belief, they extracted its oil and used it to mummify their kings.

Later cultures found the leaf was better utilized for the living than the dead. Over the ages, there is documentation that it was a popular folk remedy for combating fevers.

The first formal medical mention of the olive leaf—an account describing its ability to cure severe cases of fever and malaria—was made almost 150 years ago. An 1854 report in the *Pharmaceutical Journal* by one Daniel Hanbury provided the following simple healing recipe: Boil a handful of leaves in a quart of water down to half its original volume. Then administer the liquid in the amount of a full wine glass every 3 or 4 hours until the fever is cured. The author said he discovered this effective tincture in 1843 and had used it successfully. This method became well known in England for treating sick Britons returning from His or Her Majesty's tropical colonies. The author believed that a bitter substance in the leaves was the key healing ingredient.

He was right.

Decades later, scientists isolated a bitter substance from the leaf and named it oleuropein. It was found to be one ingredient in a compound produced by the olive tree that makes it particularly robust and resistant against insect and bacterial damage. From a technical angle, oleuropein is an iridoid, a structural class of chemical compounds found in plants. It is present in olive oil, throughout the olive tree, and is, in fact, the bitter material that is eliminated from the olives when they are cured.

In 1962, an Italian researcher reported that oleuropein lowered blood pressure in animals. This triggered a flurry of scientific interest in the olive leaf.

Other European researchers confirmed this interesting finding. In addition, they found it could also increase blood flow in the coronary arteries, relieve arrhythmias, and prevent intestinal muscle spasms.

Around this time, a Dutch researcher determined the active ingredient in oleuropein to be a substance he called elenolic acid. It was found to have a powerful anti-bacterial effect.

By the late 1960s, research by scientists at Upjohn, a major American pharmaceutical company, showed that elenolic acid also inhibited the growth of viruses. In fact, it stopped every virus that it was tested against. A number of laboratory experiments with calcium elenolate, a salt of elenolic acid, demonstrated a strong effect against bacteria, parasitic protozoans and many viruses associated with common colds.

The compound worked effectively at low concentrations without any harmful influence on host cell mechanisms, the American researchers concluded. That meant they believed it to be extremely safe and non-toxic, even at high doses.

Following test tube experiments, the pharmaceutical company launched animal tests. Experiments showed the compound was indeed extremely well tolerated. There was a hitch, however. In the body of an animal, the substance rapidly attached to protein in blood serum, which made calcium elenolate useless. This binding action essentially took it "out of action," rendering it ineffective. Because of this obstacle, research into the compound as a potential virus- and bacteria-killing pharmaceutical drug was dropped.

Research into olive leaf extract continues, primarily in Europe. Among the most recent findings are these:

• In a series of experiments, oleuropein was found to inactivate bacteria by apparently dissolving the outer lining of the microbes.

• At the University of Milan's Institute of Pharmacological Sciences, researchers found that oleuropein inhibited harmful oxidation of low-density lipoproteins, the so-called "bad cholesterol" involved in heart and arterial disease. This revelation, if confirmed by further research, suggests that oleuropein may contain antioxidant properties similar to other phytochemical compounds.

Medical researcher Morton Walker, D.P.M., writing about olive leaf extract in the July 1996 issue of the *Townsend Letter for Doctors and Patients*, comments that the intake of flavonoids "is correlated with a lower incidence of cardiovascular disease, indicating that the daily intake of olive oil and/or olive leaf extract containing phenols will likely bring on a similar result."

At the present time, the cardiovascular research community is excited about such actions. Studies have show that some phytochemicals can reduce the harmful oxidation of cholesterol as well as slow down the accelerated clumping of blood platelets that can lead to dangerous clots.

• At Spain's University of Granada, pharmacologists determined that olive leaf extract causes relaxation of arterial walls in laboratory animals. Such results suggest a possible benefit for hypertension, an effect first mentioned by researchers more than 30 years ago.

• In Tunis, researchers found that aqueous extract of olive leaves reduced hypertension, blood sugar, and the level of uric acid in rodents. This finding again indicates potential in the treatment of hypertension, as well as diabetes and heart disease. An elevated uric acid level is a risk factor for heart problems.

Remember the biochemical snag mentioned earlier—that elenolic acid binds with proteins in the body to nullify any therapeutic use? That problem has now been overcome and the door opened for the development of effective olive leaf extract supplements.

Such products are now available, containing oleuropein and synergistic olive leaf extracts, including flavonoids. So . . .

The medicinal firepower is there.

The safety is there.

The added benefit of other phytochemicals is there.

In short, we now have an exciting new herbal with quite a promising future.

Olive Leaf Firepower

For the record, the researchers at Upjohn found calcium elenolate effective in test tube experiments against the following viruses: herpes, vaccinia, pseudorabies, Newcastle, Coxsacloe A 21, encepthlomyocarditis, polio 1, 2, and 3, vesicular stomititus, sindbis, reovirus, Moloney Murine leukemia, Rauscher Murine leukemia, Moloney sarcoma, and many influenza and parainfluenza types.

They found it effective against these bacteria and parasitic protozoans: lactobacillus plantarum W50, l. brevis 50, pediococcus cerevisiae 39, leuconostoc mesenteroides 42, staphylococcus aureus, bacillus subtilis, enterobacteraerogenes NRRL B-199, E. cloacae NRRL B-414; also E. coli, salmonella tyhimurium, pseudomonas fluorescens, P. solanacearum, P. lachrymans, erwinia carotovora; along with E. tracheiphila, xanthomonas vesicatoria, corynesbacterium Michiganese, plasmodium falciparum, virax and malariae.

The researchers credit a number of unique properties possessed by the olive leaf compound for such broad killing power:

- **An ability to interfere with critical amino acid production essential for viruses.**
- **Olive leaf extract is able to contain viral infection and/or spread by inactivating viruses or by preventing virus shedding, budding or assembly at the cell membrane.**
- **The ability to penetrate infected cells directly and stop viral replication.**
- **In the case of retroviruses, it is able to neutralize the production of reverse transcriptase and protease. A retrovirus, such as HIV, needs these enzymes to alter the RNA of a healthy cell.**
- **It can stimulate phagocytosis, an immune system response in which cells ingest harmful microorganisms and foreign matter.**

The research suggests that this may be a "true anti-viral" compound because it appears to block selectively an entire virus-specific system in the infected host. It thus appears to offer healing effects not addressed by pharmaceutical antibiotics.

The Clinical Perspective

Clinically, olive leaf extract has been used for a relatively short time. Health professionals began using it early in 1995 when it first became available. Although we do not have long-term perspectives as yet, initial results are very positive. We see a very promising and unique herbal with multiple applications. It shows considerable therapeutic action against many common conditions. In short, it appears to be living up to its unique background and expectations.

From research and clinical experience to date, we can say that supplemental olive leaf extract may be beneficial in the treatment for conditions caused by, or associated with, a virus, retrovirus, bacterium, or protozoan. Among such conditions are influenza, the common cold, meningitis, Epstein-Barr Virus (EBV), encephalitis, herpes I and II, human herpes virus 6 and 7, shingles, HIV/ARC/AIDS, chronic fatigue syndrome, hepatitis B, pneumonia, tuberculosis, gonorrhea, malaria, dengue, bacteremia, severe diarrhea, blood poisoning, and dental, ear, urinary tract and surgical infections.

In our clinic, we use olive leaf extract for a variety of infectious and chronic conditions. We also believe that many people who lead stressful lives or who may be particularly susceptible to colds and viruses may benefit from long-term use of olive leaf extract as a preventive agent.

As I mentioned earlier, I am surprised and delighted all the time by unexpected benefits reported by patients. This indicates that we are perhaps just scratching the surface in our understanding of phytochemical benefits. Patients have told me about improved psoriasis, normalization of arrhythmias (heart beat irregularities), and less pain from hemorrhoids, toothaches and chronically achy joints.

I myself cured a chronic toenail fungal infection after starting on the supplement. It had not responded to the many other nutrients that I take.

One female patient with bad allergies reported significant improvement and a level of energy she hadn't felt for years.

One elderly male with severe arrhythmia told me his condition had vastly improved in about eight days just from taking olive leaf extract alone. A woman with mild arrhythmia said her condition improved substantially while she took the supplement and then slowly became irregular again after she ran out of it.

We know from the oleuropein research done in the 1960s that the substance improves blood flood to the heart and acts to normalize arrhythmias. Presently, we are learning much about the cardiovascular benefits of the phytochemical compounds found in grape seeds, onions, kale, green beans, broccoli, and other vegetables. It will be interesting indeed to see what benefits the particular phytochemicals in olive leaf extract produce for heart and circulatory health.

Phil Selinsky, a naturopathic doctor at the Institute for Holistic Studies in Santa Barbara, and biochemist Arnold Takemoto, who has been developing patient nutritional programs on behalf of physicians in Arizona for 15 years, have found olive leaf extract to be an effective addition to their array of natural healing tools.

After using the supplement in dozens of cases for over a year, Selinsky is impressed with the benefits and looks forward to continued use and greater understanding about its most effective applications.

There is no doubt that olive leaf extract has real healing power. In a moment I will go into much greater detail on how it has helped patients.

It is important to remember, however, that, like any other nutritional supplement, it should not be considered a cure-all or panacea. In holistic practices such as mine, individual supplements are part of a comprehensive program that includes better diet, exercise, and stress control methods. That's how we maximum health and minimize symptoms.

In such a program, a patient may start with supplements X, Y and Z, get involved in an exercise program, and experience perhaps 50 percent relief for a given condition. That's a lot of relief but then we keep trying to improve the situation. We now add another supplement, let's say the olive leaf extract, and we get another degree of improvement, often quite large. In this manner, we continually tailor the program of an individual patient for the best results. And in this scheme of things, olive leaf extract is making a very positive contribution. It complements all the good things patients are doing.

There is always the possibility that one ingredient, one supplement, can fill a large gap or particular need in the body and by itself lead to major improvement. We see that happen all the time. But usually it is all the elements in a nutritional program working together—like a team of horses pulling a wagon—that gets the job done most effectively.

Biochemist Arnold Takemoto puts it this way: "Olive leaf extract is not a single magic-bullet. There are very few such things, especially in non-pharmaceutical medicine. In many cases it takes a whole lot more than just one ingredient to get over a particular condition. Yet I find it a very valuable addition against chronic fatigue syndrome and many other viral conditions, especially those that are more tenacious. It fills a hole that we haven't been able to fill before."

In the *Townsend Letter* article, Takemoto told Morton Walker that he has "yet to discover another herbal substance that accomplishes antimicrobially what this substance achieves."

Takemoto went on to say that Lisa Weinrib, M.D., one of the physicians he works with, treats many cases of fibromyalgia and chronic fatigue syndrome. "Dr. Weinrib has noticed that patients with these problems exhibit much improvement from use of the extract. It's the missing link that functions as an antiviral and antiretroviral agent by slowing down the organism's reproductive cycle. A slowdown . . . allows the patient's immune system to go on the attack."

Takemoto says olive leaf extract has helped patients eliminate stubborn viral infections they have had for years. One patient, who had suffered from shingles (herpes zoster) for nine years, experienced complete relief within two days of starting olive leaf extract and other supplements.

"In my approach," Takemoto says, "I target key antibody responses for specific viruses, stimulate the immune system, and with olive leaf extract attempt to inhibit the reproduction of the virus. It takes everything to get over some of these real chronic conditions."

More Energy

One of the most frequent comments we hear from patients after they start taking olive leaf extract is that they feel more energetic and have a greater sense of well-being. Many want to continue the supplement even after the treatment program has cleared up or reduced specific problems.

Some patients are energized to the point that they inquire whether there is an "upper" in the product. There is not. It simply generates a natural "upper" effect. Healthy people who take it say they also feel this infusion of energy.

One of my patients is an 18-year-old professional ice-skater who says that one or two olive leaf extract tablets a day helps her sustain the high energy level she needs for practice and performance.

In my clinic, as in many others, fatigue is the No. 1 complaint. I am not referring to serious chronic fatigue situations but just routine tiredness, likely caused by a combination of consuming a dead food diet and not exercising. The average person, of course, is not going to change eating habits and is not going to go on a regular exercise program. In such cases, the olive leaf extract looks like a good source of pep for the pepless.

Chronic Fatigue

In my experience, olive leaf extract also has helped in many chronic fatigue cases, even the most serious. One female patient described to me what she called a "really quite unbelievable" recovery within one month of taking the supplement:

"For the last few years I have not been feeling like myself. I've had little energy and enthusiasm for anything. This is not my usual nature. I attributed it to weight, unemployment and just being down. My head was always somewhat achy and I couldn't figure out why. The only way I could describe it would be as a constant low-degree headache which never left.

"I started taking olive leaf extract and noticed an immediate elevation of my spirits. What I liked about the product was that it was effective but gentle and didn't make me hyper or unable to sleep. Quite the contrary, I slept better.

"After a few days I began to notice more energy and a stronger sense of well-being. The cobwebs in my brain started to diminish. I also noticed a bad shoulder and a bad knee started to get better. The pain associated with these joints remarkably improved.

"The only side-effects I had were a couple of headaches in the beginning which disappeared with some aspirin.

"I started to feel much, much better. It was amazing to see the fatigue disappear and my general health improve. I couldn't believe I felt so well.

"I stopped taking the product after 30 days and experienced no withdrawal or anything. I simply felt better and that has stayed the same for the last 60 days without the product."

Another female patient with Epstein-Barr Virus reported that the supplement "has helped me very much in overcoming the tiredness I feel. It has given me energy."

For some very sick individuals, including people with chronic fatigue syndrome or particularly heavy loads of virus or bacteria in their bodies, olive leaf extract may possibly generate detoxification symptoms—known as the "die-off effect"—that may be unpleasant.

Such people may actually feel worse for a short time before feeling better. As an example, many chronic fatigue patients suffer from an associated depression. Patients of mine who toughed it out through the "die-off" period emerged highly energized and no longer depressed.

The "die-off effect," or Herxheimer Reaction as it is medically called, refers to symptoms generated by a detoxification process. If you are sick and use this product, you should be aware of the possibility. For this reason it may be advisable to consult first with a holistic health practitioner before using it.

If you have ever used Nystatin to fight yeast infections, you are probably familiar with this situation. Nystatin kills yeast. As the body becomes full of dead yeast, you may experience a variety of detoxification symptoms. Symptoms may intensify to the point where you need to stop or reduce the dosage of the medication in order to give your body a chance to eliminate the toxic waste. Of course you would need to experiment with this.

Olive leaf extract is potent stuff. It can generate an internal cleansing action that may similarly cause significant detoxification symptoms. There are ways of minimizing such a reaction and eliminating the discomfort.

The "Die-Off Effect" and How to Deal With It

"Die-off" symptoms can begin almost immediately after starting the supplement. It can hit different people in different ways. Reactions include extreme fatigue, diarrhea, headaches, muscle/joint achiness or flu-like symptoms. Severity differs also from person to person, depending on the extent of infection.

Keep in mind that such symptoms are positive signs. Nevertheless, they can be unpleasant. Some people may not want to continue because of the discomfort. Others handle it better. Others experience no such effect.

Here's what to do in case of substantial detoxification symptoms:

- Reduce the number of tablets, or even stop them altogether, if only for a while.
- You may need a day or two, or even a week, to allow your body to process the "die-off."
- When you feel better, you can resume the supplement at a low dose and increase slowly.
- Holistic practitioners can usually provide a supportive detoxification program for individuals who experience a strong "die-off" response. In my clinic, this program includes taking vitamin C to bowel tolerance. Such a regimen is best done under professional guidance.

Other than the "die-off" detoxification effect among some individuals, olive leaf extract appears to create no side effects.

Past research with calcium elenolate, the derivative of oleuropein, included safety studies with laboratory animals. They were dosed orally and also via injection. The only symptom observed was a mild irritation of the mucous membrane among some animals at the injection site. Since olive leaf extract is taken orally, this observation is basically irrelevant.

The research indicated that even doses many times higher than recommended are unlikely to produce toxic or other adverse side effects.

During 1993 testing of the liquid form of the product against the herpes virus, there were no observed or reported side effects.

Potential Against Serious Infectious Diseases

Deaths from infectious diseases, formerly on the decline, have recently taken an alarming upward turn in this country. According to worried federal researchers, such deaths rose by 58 percent from 1980 to 1992, pushing this category of illness up behind heart disease and cancer in the No. 3 spot of killer diseases.

While the AIDS epidemic accounts for most of the rise, experts say there has been an unusual increase in mysterious respiratory infections among the elderly and blood infections among people of all ages. When you eliminate the AIDS factor, the death rate during the same period for all other infectious diseases rose by 22 percent.

The World Health Organization (WHO), back in 1978, looked to the future and issued a report which contended that by the year 2000, sources other than Western, technological medicine would be needed in order for all people to have adequate health care. The organization subsequently adopted the report that recommended the use of traditional forms of healing and medicine, such as the use of herbs, to meet the demands of an exploding global population.

As we approach the year 2000, the wisdom—and the urgency—of this advice is obvious in the light of the serious side-effects and shortcomings of pharmaceutical drugs.

With the emergence, for instance, of antibiotic-resistant bacterial strains, natural products such as olive leaf extract take on greater importance. Even if new antibiotics are developed, new infectious bacteria would emerge that are resistant to new drugs. In the case of herbal medicinals, their complex chemistry may often render them potentially more effective against a wide variety of microorganisms for which pharmaceutical drugs prove to be ineffective.

AIDS

It will indeed be interesting to see if olive leaf extract can benefit AIDS cases. We know that it inhibits the production of reverse transcriptase and protease, enzymes necessary for certain viruses, such as HIV, to damage healthy cells.

Informal, preliminary reports are promising. Mark Konlee, editor of *Positive Health News*, a newsletter on alternative treatments that circulates widely in the AIDS community, has reported exciting, initial results attained by individuals using olive leaf extract, either in the tablet supplement form or directly as a tea brewed from leaves, along with other ingredients.

Those other ingredients, according to Konlee, have been found to be highly beneficial over the years. They include:

- Naltrexone, an immune-stabilizing drug used in the treatment of heroin and alcohol addiction. Clinical trials conducted by Bernard Bihari, M.D., a New York City physician specializing in HIV/AIDS, demonstrated that this preparation stops the progression of the disease and the decline of the immune system in a majority of patients who take it regularly. Naltrexone stimulates key hormones regulating the immune system and the communication between the brain and immune function. No side effects have been reported.
- DNCB (dinitrochlorobenzene), which is a chemical used in photography labs that is applied in small doses on the skin. This compound acts as an anti-viral agent by stimulating killer cell activity. An estimated 7,000 patients with AIDS have used this substance for some 10 years.

• A blend of olive oil/whole lemon juice. This "grassroots" recipe appears to be uniquely helpful in reversing neuropathy, swollen lymph nodes and the wasting syndrome associated with HIV.

For more specifics on this approach, interested individuals may contact "Keep Hope Alive," P.O. Box 27041, West Allis, WI 53227, or by phone at 414-548-4344.

Konlee reports that the combination, with added olive leaf extract, "has produced stunning results," including viral loads dropping dramatically within a month. Among the cases he describes are these:

1. A patient had been using Naltrexone since October, 1995, along with weekly topical applications of DNCB. He had not used the olive oil/juice blend. In August of that year he had had a CD8 count of 700. CD8 refers to killer T cells, which, along with so-called Natural Killer cells, are major immune destroyers of virus-infected cells. They reduce viral loads and inhibit damage to the body's defenses.

In January of 1996, his CD8 count had risen to 1380. In March of 1996 he added olive leaf extract at the standard dose of one capsule four times daily. He initially experienced a mild headache, a probable "die-off effect." Within days, he reported a significant increase in energy along with the disappearance of swollen lymph nodes. He said he felt 20 years younger. On March 21, his CD8 count had soared to 1920! His physician said never before in his career had he seen such improvement in an AIDS patient.

2. One patient reported that after he finished a bottle of olive leaf extract, one of three Kaposi Sarcoma lesions on his chest vanished. He experienced headaches and flu-like symptoms for about two weeks, again a probable "die-off effect."

Continuing with a second bottle, he said that the second lesion was completely gone and the last one was "fading fast."

His HIV viral load, as measured by PCR technology, had dropped from 160,000 to 30,000 in about two months time. Soon afterward, he reported that his PCR results for HIV were now down to 692!

3. An HIV patient reported his genital herpes vanished within four days of starting on the olive leaf extract.

4. Another patient with Kaposi's Sarcoma and retinitis began adding five capsules daily along with Naltrexone and DNCB. He reported that the sarcoma lesions stopped growing after he started the olive leaf extract. This prompted him to stop two drugs he had been taking—Ganciclovir and Biaxin—because of severe intestinal side effects. A few days after he discontinued the drugs, his digestion returned to normal. He soon reported improved vision. His lesions were becoming lighter in color.

5. One patient took the olive leaf extract by itself for about 3 1/2 months. His HIV viral load dropped nearly in half as a result, along with significant improvements in his white blood cell counts. After he added Naltrexone and the lemon/olive oil drink, his improvement accelerated.

Herpes

I have recommended olive leaf extract to many patients with herpes. The results have been encouraging.

One man in his early 40s suffered from repeated lesions plus fatigue. In a week after starting the supplement, his lesions disappeared and his energy level increased. He told me that olive leaf extract was the only preparation that had ever cleared up the herpes. "Even the most minute blisters are gone," he said.

A female patient had an unusually stubborn herpetic cold sore in the mouth for four months. She also suffered from cancer, thus there may have been some significant immune exhaustion involved. After one week with the olive leaf, the sore disappeared.

These and other, similar clinical successes are consistent with a private 1993 herpes study in humans. In that investigation, a weaker and ethanol (alcohol-based) form of olive leaf extract was used by six individuals with herpes. All reported symptomatic relief. Three said their lesions disappeared within 48 hours.

The remaining three, who experienced no improvement, then received a stronger dose. One said that three days later, most of the lesions were gone. The other two also reported doing better. All six subjects said the olive leaf extract produced better results than Acyclovir, which they had previously used.

Flu and Colds

Results to date indicate that olive leaf extract may be a good weapon against the common cold and flu. Consider the following letter written to me in August of 1995 by a female patient suffering from persistent flu symptoms:

"I became ill with the flu in February and had several immune boosters, extra vitamins and three antibiotics. My fever was 102-103 every afternoon and this continued even after the antibiotics. I developed paralyzing chest and abdominal pain, being confined to the couch for weeks--hardly able to walk. My weight dropped to 84 pounds. Medical tests revealed nothing specifically wrong.

"I started taking olive leaf extract on July 18. Within a few days my temperature started dropping and it is slowly and steadily going down, so that some days I haven't needed to take Tylenol to reduce it. The pain is subsiding gradually and my appetite and strength are returning."

When she took her next, routine medical examination, the woman's temperature had been normal for a week. She hadn't needed pain-killers for two weeks.

I received a striking testimony from an elementary school teacher with a history of asthma and vulnerability to colds and flu. She felt that olive leaf extract fortified her system against the constant exposure to germs circulating throughout her classroom.

"I used to get sick all the time," she told me. "One school year I got strep throat eight times. If you sneezed at me, the chances are I would get sick. Not any more. When many kids in my class were coughing, sneezing, and blowing their noses before Christmas, I caught a slight cold and that's it."

Bacterial Infections

The ability of olive leaf extract to destroy bacteria was demonstrated dramatically in the case of a 64-year-old physician who had been bedridden for several years following a serious stroke. He also suffered recurrent bladder infections which caused considerable pain, smelly urine and fever.

All efforts to alleviate his condition had been generally unsuccessful. Even a $1,000 antibiotic specially made for him had not worked. He had constant discomfort. His urine was cloudy "and looked like soup." Often, it was bloody.

After the doctor took the olive leaf extract one month, the infections completely vanished. After six months, the condition has not recurred.

The doctor also suffered from frequent allergies and colds and had to take medication to keep these under control. The incidence and severity were significantly minimized with the supplement, with the happy a result that he requires considerably less medicine.

Naturopath Phil Selinsky reports success against bacterial infections in a number of cases. These include sinus and bladder infections and oral infections associated with tooth or gum disease.

"Some patients have told me that olive leaf extract took down their dental-related infections within hours," according to Selinsky. "They were quite impressed by the response."

The general recommendation for olive leaf extract is four tablets daily. For these kinds of infections, Selinsky recommends patients begin with two tablets followed by another every four hours.

"That usually gets you on top of the situation," he says. For more serious infections, tablets can be taken at shorter intervals.

One night a patient of mine developed swelling and intense pain from an abscess and decided to take several tablets at one time. It reduced the pain. In the morning, when the pain returned, he took a "handful" of tablets--about eight or nine, he guesses. An hour-and-a-half later, the pain and swelling were gone. The pain did not return but a dental examination determined that the involved tooth had to go.

Diabetes

Researchers have found that the natural olive leaf compounds can decrease the level of blood sugar. I have had several cases in my clinic confirming this finding.

One involved a 15-year-old girl with juvenile diabetes. The teenager had been regularly taking 350 units of insulin daily for control. After one month on olive leaf extract, she was able to maintain similar control with just 220 units.

In another case, the blood sugar level of a diabetic, elderly priest dropped from 450 to 160 after three months. In yet another instance, the blood sugar of a middle aged man stabilized at 140, down from 250, after one month. He reported a great increase in energy during this time.

These results are truly exciting. I look forward to more opportunities to gauge the benefits of olive leaf for diabetics. Will it generate improved blood circulation and antioxidant effects to help against the destructive vascular complications of diabetes that contribute to stroke, heart disease and peripheral circulatory problems? Time will tell.

Rheumatoid Arthritis

A number of patients have experienced significant easing of joint pain. We don't know yet precisely how this is happening.

A male patient, who had been diagnosed with rheumatoid arthritis five years before, had this to say: "After taking all the medicines I could stand with no real results, I was informed about some nutritional supplements. One of them was an olive leaf extract.

"After taking it for three weeks, I noticed more flexibility in my fingers, elbows and neck. There was marked relief of muscle tension surrounding joints. Overall I am enjoying olive leaf extract with my daily routine."

Multiple Symptoms

One of our clinical observations is that olive leaf extract appears to work on many different levels in the body. As a result we often hear reports from patients that a variety of symptoms begin improving.

One woman with chronic fatigue, frequent colds, asthma, and vaginal yeast infections said that all her symptoms had virtually cleared up within five weeks. The woman, a teacher, was able to take on new projects she wouldn't even begin to think were possible before.

A male patient wrote a detailed letter about his experience:

"I became ill in December, 1993 and was diagnosed with a stomach and prostate infection. I was treated with high doses of antibiotics, but never fully recovered.

"I was troubled with multiple symptoms, some of which were back and neck pain, fatigue, flu-like symptoms, swollen glands, sinus and digestive problems.

"I was subsequently diagnosed with fibromyalgia (chronic fatigue syndrome) and the physicians recommended Prozac-type antidepressants and anti-inflammatory drugs. But I refused them.

"I began taking olive leaf extract along with my regular vitamin and mineral supplements in August of 1995 at the rate of one tablet every six hours. I increased the dosage after five days and began feeling better.

"I tried different dosages for a number of days until I found the optimum amount for me. Today I take three tablets four times a day. My overall health has greatly improved and so has my energy and disposition.

"One very interesting thing has occurred. My finger nails were infected, by whatever infection I had, leaving them wrinkled-looking. Now they are slowly returning to their normal shape."

A female patient, after taking olive leaf extract for a month, gave me this happy report: "It has improved my allergy-like psoriasis, and symptoms of a kidney infection. I have been having back aches for almost a year and frequent urination. These have improved a lot also."

Fungus and Yeast Infections

Earlier I mentioned my own positive experience with olive leaf extract. I started taking the supplement and it completely cleared up a stubborn toenail fungus infection. A number of other patients have told me similar stories.

A woman with an infection of the large toenail said that within 60 days her condition was about three-quarters healed. For five years, she had tried many types of medication and natural agents without success.

More than 10 million Americans are said to have disfiguring fungal nail infections, a widely ignored medical problem. It is frequently found among patients with AIDS, cancer and diabetes, athletes, elderly individuals, people who spend considerable time standing or who wear the same shoes day after day, or who wear artificial fingernails. Drugs taken for cancer and AIDS lower resistance and are believed to make people more susceptible to infection.

For the first time in 35 years, a new drug has been approved for the condition. It is called Sporanox and is reported to be more effective than previous anti-fungal preparations. But none of these preparations comes cheap. Patricia Anstett, of the Knight-Ridder Newspapers, reports that two 100-milligram pills of Sproranox are taken daily for about three months at a cost of $900. Older drugs, taken for 12 months or more, cost double or more that amount over the longer duration. Even with the new drug, the condition may return if the medication is stopped.

Olive leaf extract may offer a natural—and, for sure, less expensive—method of self-treatment.

One patient said a fungal infection of the tongue he had had for 30 years responded virtually overnight to the olive leaf. "I had tried all kinds of diets, treatments and regimes, but to no avail," he told me. "Within three weeks on olive leaf extract the fungus disappeared!"

More than a dozen patients with candidiasis have reported significant improvements. They say they have fewer infections, allergic reactions, less dullness and more energy. One woman said she was finally able to clean out her dust-ridden garage. Before olive leaf extract that would have been impossible for her.

One 36-year-old woman, who had suffered repeated vaginal yeast infections for several years, told me this account of her experience with olive leaf extract:

"I have seen several doctors using conventional medicine. They prescribed every medication available to combat yeast, all to no avail.

"After less than three weeks of taking the olive leaf supplement, all symptoms cleared up and have not returned. As a sufferer of herpes simplex II, I would experience outbreaks several times a year. Now, I have had no more flare-ups."

Skin Conditions

A chronic scalp infection that had stubbornly resisted all treatment for more than 10 years responded directly to olive leaf extract within 60 days. The patient wrote me this detailed letter:

"The condition would flare up causing very painful eruptions and lesions in my scalp, which, over time, have killed quite a few hair follicles. Modern medical doctors and dermatologists have been unable to eradicate the condition. I had resigned myself to the fact that there was no cure.

"I am satisfied that I am getting some significant results from using the olive leaf extract. My scalp remains a little tender, but the eruptions have all but ceased. I am continuing to use the product about twice a day, and the skin color is much healthier than it has been in recent time.

"No matter what drug therapy my doctors have prescribed in the past, none has provided me with the level of relief I am currently experiencing. I would gladly recommend this product to others suffering chronic skin ailments."

A female patient reported better energy and the disappearance of a rash in 30 days. The rash occurred in winter, or during times of extreme cold.

Tropical Illnesses

Olive leaf extract may offer considerable potential in the treatment of tropical infections such as malaria and dengue. Malaria is caused by parasitic protozoans injected into the body by infected mosquitoes. Protozoans, in case you are interested, are one-celled organisms, the simplest creatures in the animal kingdom.

As far back as 1827, reports appeared in medical literature indicating the benefits of olive leaf extract in the treatment of malaria. In 1906, one report stated that olive leaves were, in fact, superior to quinine for malarial infections. Quinine was preferred, however, because it was easier to administer. In studies performed by the Upjohn company, calcium elenolate, the substance within oleuropein, was found to be effective against the malaria protozoa.

Now in tablet form, there may be renewed interest in olive leaf extract as an anti-malarial agent. Preliminary reports from Latin America are promising.

A full-fledged case of malaria at a clinic in Mexico was totally cured with a dosage schedule of two olive leaf extract supplements every six hours. A clinic report said that the 34-year-old female patient made a steady recovery and, after six months, "she was without any of the malaria symptoms, not even anemia or shivers. Her breath is good. Her state of mind is excellent and she does not show any signs of chronic or contagious disease."

Malaria has been reported recently in Texas and continues to be a leading cause of illness and deaths worldwide, particularly because of the development of drug-resistant strains. "It is a continuing concern in the United States because of increased international migration, travel, and commerce," according to the publication *Morbidity and Mortality Weekly Reports*.

Another serious tropical disease giving concern to public health officials is dengue fever. This ailment is also mosquito-borne, in this case caused by a virus, and occurs mainly in tropical Asia and the Caribbean. It can cause vomiting, high fever, loss of appetite, and abdominal pain, and is deadly in 50 percent of cases. Some 50 million people are affected each year and about half a million require hospitalization, according to the UN's World Health Organization. Researchers are trying to find a vaccine but no breakthroughs have occurred yet.

In 1995, large outbreaks of dengue were reported by health authorities in 12 Latin American and Caribbean countries.

Dosage

Olive leaf extract is currently available in the form of 500 mg. tablets. The routine dosage is one tablet every six hours or four throughout the day. Take the supplement between meals for best results.

In the case of bad colds or flu, you can use two tablets every six hours. For acute infections, some individuals have taken more—three and even four every six hours—and reported rapid relief.

If you encounter a "die-off" effect, cut back on the number of tablets you are taking or temporarily discontinue them. See the section on the "die-off effect."

For healthy folks seeking more energy or the preventive benefits of olive leaf extract, we suggest one or two tablets a day. The younger and cleaner the body, the more responsive it is to supplements such as this. When a person becomes older and more toxic, more of the supplement is required to do the job.

References

Cruess WV, and Alsberg CL, The bitter glucoside of the olive. *J. Amer. Chem. Soc.* 1934; 56:2115-7.

Samuelsson G, The blood pressure lowering factor in leaves of Olea Europaea. *Farmacevtisk Revy,* 1951; 15: 229-39.

Panizzi L et al, The constitution of oleuropein, a bitter glucoside of the olive with hypotensive action. *Gazz. Chim. Ital; 1960;* 90:1449-85.

Petkov V and Manolov P, Pharmacological analysis of the iridoid oleuropein. *Drug Res., 1972;* 22(9): 1476-86.

Veer WLC et al, A compound isolated from olea europaea. *Recueil, 1957;* 76: 839-40.

Juven B et al, Studies on the mechanism of the antimicrobial action of oleuropein. *J. Appl. Bact., 1972;* 35:559-67.

Renis HE, In vitro antiviral activity of calcium elenolate. *Antimicrob. Agents Chemother., 1970;* 167-72.

Elliott GA et al, Preliminary studies with calcium elenolate, an antiviral agent. *Antimicrob. Agents Chemother., 1970:* 173-76.

Soret MG, Antiviral activity of calcium elenolate on parainfluenza infection of hamsters. *Antimicrob. Agents Chemother., 1970:* 160-66.

Heinze JE et al, Specificity of the antiviral agent calcium elenolate. *Antimicrob. Agents Chemother., 1975: 8(4), 421-25.*

Hirschman SZ, Inactivation of DNA polymerases of Murine Leukaemia viruses by calcium elenolate. *Nature New Biology, 1972;* 238:277-79.

Kubo I et al, A multichemical defense mechanism of bitter olive olea europaea (Oleaceae)--Is oleuropein a phytoalexin precursor? *J. Chem. Ecol* 1985; 11(2): 251-63.

Gariboldi P et al, Secoiridoids from olea europaea, *Phytochem., 1986;* 25(4) 865-69.

Zarzuelo A et al, Vasodilator effect of olive leaf, *Planta Med., 1991; 57 (5), 417-9.*

Department of Pharmacology and Toxicology, Society of Pharmaceutical Industries of Tunis, Hypotension, hypoglycemia and hypouricemia recorded after repeated administration of aqueous leaf extract of Olea europaea, *Belgian Pharmacology Journal,* March-April 1994; 49 (2), 101-8.

Visioli F and Galli C, Oleuropein protects low density lipoprotein from oxidation, *Life Sciences,* 1994; 55 (24), 1965-71.

Chapter Ten
Allergies and Nutrition

Allergic diseases develop in people who are unusually sensitive to substances that are otherwise harmless. The most common of these disorders are asthma, eczema, hay fever and hives. Asthmatics seem to have an increased tendency to clot. Any organ in the body may become the site of an allergy. That's why symptoms are so varied. They can include restlessness, fatigue, headache, irritability or stomach problems, unexplained chronic illness, nausea, diarrhea, rashes, sinus congestion, aches and pains, confusion, even temporary insanity. Your boss may not be crazy, just allergic to you!

Substances capable of causing allergy are called allergens, or antigens. When an allergen gets inside the body, it causes an irritation in the susceptible tissues; for instance, the nose starts running like the beer spigot at a clambake. There is itching and stuffiness. The bronchial tubes are afflicted with coughing and asthmatic wheeze. The skin may erupt in edema, eczema or hives. Allergic patients may be sensitive to more than one allergen, i.e., to pollens, molds, dust, feathers, animal danders, foods, chemicals and drugs. In California, most of the vegetation pollinates in the spring, when asthmatics and other victims lightly turn to thoughts of sneezing. Doomsday can come at any time of year, depending on the mating habits of the flora in your area.

Some patients can't tolerate chemicals, fumes, vapors, even odors, including tobacco smoke, perfumed hair sprays, strong cooking odors, gas fumes from stoves and heaters, turpentine, paint, chlorine, waxes, insect spray, detergent and cleansing powders, vapor from plastic bags, synthetic fibers (nylon, naugahyde, etc.) and car exhaust fumes.

There are three ways I believe allergy can be effectively treated. First, and most important, I believe, is a nutritional tune-up. Doctors have long used nutrition for allergic problems. For instance, Vitamin C is a natural antihistamine; studies and clinical practice show it to be effective both for nasal allergies and asthma. Sufferers are usually deficient in zinc, which stimulates immunity, magnesium, which inhibits clotting, as well as molybdenum, Vitamin B-6, and fish oils (Omega 3 fatty acids-EPA). Many of these supplements counteract inflammation of the recently discovered prostaglandin system. We also use bioflavinoids, hydrochloric acid, selenium, Vitamin B-12 and licorice.

I always try to convince allergy patients of the importance of optimizing their nutritional intake. In 70 to 80 percent of cases, this can eliminate the need for allergy testing. Through improved nutrition and supplementation, immune function is so enhanced that allergens are effectively neutralized and detoxified by the body. The system is fortified. The individual is less reactive.

The second step in treating allergy is to separate the allergen from the patient. This can be done when the incriminating allergen is relatively limited in supply, such as feathers or corn. The allergen may be a cleaning product, in which case Bon Ami may be substituted. If paint or a chemical in a cleaning solvent is the culprit, these should not be used near the patient. Drugs should be taken sparingly, only when your doctor insists. Flavored soda pop, candy and icings, all instruments of Satan, should be avoided. When the allergen is airborne seasonal pollen, mold spores, dust, a husband or a wife, and cannot be eliminated without living in an igloo or costly court action, we use the third method, in which we desensitize by injection, usually administered weekly.

Unfortunately, in allergy there is no miracle cure, because there are too many variables. Allergy is not just one thing, like hernia. However, desensitization has provided dramatic relief to many of our patients. In our clinical experience, about 85% of them improve after two years of antigen injections. There are few absolutes, and the degree of improvement, as well as the time needed to show it, varies considerably. We just don't know why, but some people are unable to manufacture the necessary, protective antibodies. Too much stress can also aggravate allergy problems and prevent good response to treatment.

If you are on medication, you should be aware that some drugs, such as antihistamines, may act like sedatives and make you sleepy, in which case you shouldn't work around dangerous machinery like automobiles. Recently, a couple of non-sedating antihistamines, Seldane and Hismanal, were released, followed by a third antihistamine, Claritin, with even fewer side effects.

Answers to Frequently Asked Questions About Allergies

• Are allergies inherited?

The tendency to develop allergies is inherited, yes, but the offspring's allergy may be entirely different. For example, a parent may have asthma but the child may have eczema.

• Does moving To a different climate help?

Sometimes, moving to a warmer, drier area helps, but most of the time the allergies return. Patients suffering from asthma, emphysema or chronic bronchitis, should seek an area free of smog or industrial air pollution, if such conditions aggravate lung symptoms.

• Do colds trigger asthma?

Yes. Potential asthmatics may only have symptoms when triggered by colds. Sooner or later, however, asthma will strike between colds; so, these patients should consider seeing an allergist.

• Do you desensitize against foods?

As a rule, no. One need only avoid the suspected foods for a short time. In most cases, the foods can later be tolerated when reintroduced into the diet. However, the patient may have to avoid certain foods--i.e., nuts, eggs and fish--for life, unless enzyme supplements improve digestion by reducing those foods to basic constituents, that is, simple amino acids, sugars and fats.

• Can food cause allergies?

We find such allergies mostly in youngsters, but many adults are sensitive to certain foods. Major offenders include beans, beef, beets, carrots, cheese, chocolate, coffee, corn, eggs, fish, milk, nuts, oats, oranges, peas, pork, potato (white), sea food, tomato, wheat and yeast. Almost anything we ingest can be an allergen to someone. If you suspect foods, your allergist will be grateful if you keep a diary of everything you eat for a couple of weeks, along with the day, time and duration of symptoms. If important foods are implicated and omitted from the diet, you must replace them with non-offending substitutes to avoid weight loss and malnutrition.

• Could refusal to respire overcome house dust?

Yes, but it is ineffective, and could adversely affect life span. Dust is impossible to get rid of, because dust thou art, and unto dust shalt thou return, but the home should be made as dust-free as possible. Cover heat vents (registers) with cheese cloth or filters and change them when necessary. Clean closets thoroughly, and give old clothes away, along with outgrown toys. Get rid of boxes and papers not in use. Strip beds and vacuum mattresses and box springs thoroughly; then cover them with non-allergenic zippered covers. Don't use feather pillows. Don't use chenille-type candlewick bed spreads; they're too linty. Use dacron blankets and comforters. There are many allergy-free products available for the home. If your husband complains, tell him to call us. We'll back you up. Who knows? Your home could wind up in *House Beautiful*, and you won't be coughing and wheezing when they come to take the pictures.

• Can drugs be taken during allergy treatment?

Please do not take antihistamines the night before or the day of testing. During desensitization, however, patients may use medication for relief, such as antihistamines and asthma tablets.

• May we keep pets or must I get rid of my allergic husband?

Keep your husband, but your other pets may have to go. You can try to desensitize your husband to animal danders, which isn’t always that easy. Cat dander, in particular, is a problem.

• Could nasal allergy or hay fever trigger asthma?

A victim of one allergy can develop another. Allergic rhinitis very often leads to asthma, so it is important to treat the allergy before the asthma develops.

• How can one tell an allergy from a cold?

A cold usually lasts a few days. If symptoms persist, you could have an allergy. Sometimes, colds and allergies happen together, and both must be treated. If a disgusting, green or yellow mucous pours from your nose and chest, causing general revulsion and ostracism, you could have a cold.

• How often should nose drops be used?

With restraint, no more than twice daily, for only a few days, and in only one nostril. Nose drops can give temporary relief, but constant use causes the membranes to "rebound," often with swelling worse than the original complaint.

Part Three

Organized Quackery

Chapter Eleven
The Empire Strikes Back

Having now seen the cornucopia of benefits offered by darkfield technology, the reader will no doubt be mystified to learn that for many years, the medical establishment has orchestrated a reign of terror against it, including quack propaganda concocted by tax-exempt front groups, commando raids on clinics and labs by FDA and the Internal Revenue Service, the outrageously misnamed California Board of Medical Quality Assurance, hereinafter known as CABOMQUA, threats, downright lies, and criminal activity that would land anyone else in prison. The purpose of the terror is to persuade Dr. Privitera and other physicians around the country not to use live cell analysis, darkfield technology, or chelation, and not to use the supplements we have previously discussed.

On June 14, 1985, Victor J. Rosen, M.D., of the Brotman Medical Center, in Culver City, California, wrote to Adrian Mayer, M.D., of CABOMQUA (pronounced KABUMKWA), citing a long list of scholarly articles, letters, a manuscript and reprint, from the most prestigious medical journals in the world, among them the *New England Journal of Medicine*, which Mayer had sent him for review as part of CABOMQUA's investigation of Dr. Privitera. The material discussed the role of clotting in asthma, heart disease and other problems, despite which Rosen concluded that his mind remained unchanged on the subject of "live cell analysis in the diagnosis of nutritional deficiencies." Rosen later died of cancer, another sacrifice on the altar of the consensus medicine he worshipped.

Five days later, Dr. Mayer wrote another letter, this one to Arnold R. Abrams, M.D., of the Department of Pathology at St. John's Hospital in Santa Monica, California. Mayer asked: "Is there any validity in Dr. Privitera's methodology? I understand that something like this was done in the 30's or 40's." Despite his recognition that "something like this" has been done for forty or fifty years, Mayer asks Abrams to characterize Dr. P.'s use of darkfield technology as either gross negligence, incompetence or negligence, or some combination thereof. In other words, Mayer offers Abrams the choice of only three versions of guilty. The CABOMQUA "investigation" started with a conclusion, and now was asking these outside doctors to underwrite it. Mayer also tells Abrams this: "When you render an opinion on a physician for the Board of Medical Quality Assurance, you have immunity from liability . . . ." In other words, you may say anything you like without fear of being sued. And: "The Board's policy is to pay $50 an hour for the preparation, evaluation and writing of your opinion. . . ." Does this prove Abrams was in it for the money?

In his reply to Mayer, dated October 11, 1985, Abrams chose category one: gross negligence. "Therefore, and in conclusion, I must conclude that Dr. Privatera (sic) is currently practicing at extreme departure from the usual standard of medical practice."

It would compound the redundancy to dwell on the literary style of a man who can write, "Therefore, and in conclusion, I must conclude . . . ." But, the fact that Dr. Abrams neglects to take the trouble to spell Dr. Privitera's name right deserves comment, and raises the question of whether he is motivated by unspoken ethnic prejudice.

Why does Dr. Abrams accuse Dr. P. of gross negligence? Early in his letter, he spells the doctor's name right and says this: "It is my opinion after reviewing this material in its entirety, and after a review of the literature regarding commercial hair analysis on the one hand, and dark field microscopy on the other, that Dr. Privitera's use of the medical laboratory technology available, and his treatment of patients is an extreme departure from the standard of medical practice in this community, and indeed an extreme departure from the standard of medical practice in any community in this country. . . ."

Abrams thereby tries to create the impression that Dr. Privitera is using bizarre techniques unknown to medicine, from the annals of black magic. On the contrary, hair analysis, like darkfield microscopy, is a recognized diagnostic tool. In fact, *in the very next paragraph*, Dr. Abrams says this: "Hair analysis with the intent of determining the nutritional and/or health status of an individual as opposed to its use in determining toxic states is not unheard of in this country. *Indeed, it is rather widely practiced.* There is, however, no scientific evidence whatsoever as to its efficacy in determining nutritional status or health status, *with the exception of a very few deficiency or toxic states. . . .*" (Italics added)

So, first, Dr. Abrams says hair analysis is not in use. Then, he says it is widely used to determine nutritional and/or health status, but there's no proof it's any good for the purpose. He says it's of no use in determining toxic states. Then, he says it is efficacious in "a very few deficiency or toxic states."

In our practice, we have found hair analysis to be a very helpful diagnostic tool. We respect Dr. Abrams's opinion that it is less helpful. Even if he is right and we are wrong, doesn't the fact that it is as helpful as he says it is make it useful, in those "very few deficiency or toxic states?" If hair analysis helps one patient, shouldn't doctors use it? Should the doctor who uses it be condemned for gross negligence? People who come to holistic physicians are often suffering from deficiencies and toxicity. That is why they come. Should the medics kick them out to avoid gross negligence? If doctors refuse to use a diagnostic tool Dr. Abrams admits is helpful for the purpose, wouldn't they be committing gross negligence?

Now, let's see what Dr. Abrams has to say about darkfield: "Dark field examination is but one of many microscopical methods used for examining tissue. *Its advantage over usual bright field analysis is that it reveals cellular contours and borders more clearly than bright field examination, and hence may be used to study cellular contours without immobilization and staining of the elements to be examined.* It is thus a variation of 'vital' cellular examination. As such it is inferior to phase microscopy. *Insofar as its ability to detect platelet aggregates (or even red cell or white cell aggregates) in blood is concerned, dark field examination would be superior to the usual form of right field examination*; however, by merely closing the bright field diaphragm or racking down the condensor, bright field examination is equally efficacious at this task. Furthermore, there is no evidence whatsoever that platelet aggregation in vitro (as practiced by Dr. Privatera) (sic) bears any relation whatsoever to the individual's cardiovascular status or susceptibility to atherosclerotic disease. *The articles submitted in support of such a correlation are indeed interesting, largely valid* (though there is some question regarding the article from the University of Austria), but unfortunately bear no relevance at all regarding Dr. Privatera's (sic) claim." (italics added)

So, according to Dr. Abrams, darkfield examination is not only useful; in at least a couple of ways it offers an "advantage" and is "superior." Dr. Abrams clearly prefers bright field examination, so we have here a professional disagreement. Isn't this why patients get second opinions--because doctors may honestly disagree? Does such a disagreement constitute gross negligence, especially when the accuser makes admissions against interest sufficiently gargantuan to choke a hippopotamus?

Along these lines, notice that, according to Dr. Abrams, "there is no evidence whatsoever" that clotting "bears any relation whatsoever" to possible heart problems, but the articles submitted in support of such a correlation are "indeed interesting" and "largely valid."

Incredibly, on page 3 of the accusation against Dr. P., the Medical Board states that darkfield microscopy is unproven, useless, in a “clinical setting,” hinting that something evil or at least negative occurs to a microscope in the transition from laboratory setting to clinical setting; implying that the microscope won’t provide the accurate images in the doctor’s office that it gave in the laboratory.

We are sure you will agree that Dr. Abrams earned his $50 an hour, and we hope he enjoyed spending whatever he was paid. The trouble is that his artful report is a symptom of quackery. CABOMQUA used it as "evidence" in a scheme to revoke Dr. Privitera’s license--thereby denying these techniques to patients who want them--and throw the doctor in jail. The only reason we are able to show you Arnold Abrams's pathogenic literary effort is that Dr. P. refused to genuflect before the (false) god of consensus. He fought back and won. "Consensus medicine" says that if a big enough group of doctors says we should bleed you with leeches, or give you a radical mastectomy, or deliver babies without washing our hands, or give you a cesarean when you don't need one, or ream out your prostate and make you impotent for no good reason, we should, and that any doctors who disagree should be thrown into jail.

There is clearly something immensely evil behind this, something far worse than the obvious fact that it quacks like a quack, and when you finish this book, you will know what it is.

Meanwhile, let's move along to the story of Chrystyne Jackson, who has been Dr. Privitera’s patient for many years. In 1984, he treated her, but her insurance company refused to pay. Mrs. Jackson considered this frivolous, so she called on the California Insurance Commissioner for help. In the spring of 1985, a man called her and said: "I am Robert Caldwell. I work for the Insurance Commissioner of the State of California. I'm doing follow-up work in processing your complaint against your insurance carrier. I know Jim Privitera. He's a good doctor and a nice guy. I'm a good friend of his. We go to the deli together. I'm sure that I can help get your claim paid by your insurance carrier. I just need for you to sign an authorization for our department to review your records. I'm sure we at the Insurance Commissioner's office can get your claim paid."

Shortly thereafter, Mrs. Jackson received an authorization form, which she signed and returned, but she got no help from the Insurance Commissioner with her claim, because Robert Caldwell had lied. Unknown to Mrs. Jackson, Caldwell the liar worked not for the Commissioner but for CABOMQUA. On March 5, 1985, Mrs. Jackson wrote to CABOMQUA, revoking the fraudulently obtained authorization, despite which CABOMQUA used her chart to continue its conspiracy against the doctor.

The fraud against Mrs. Jackson was not the only crime Caldwell committed. In 1975, Dr. P. was convicted of conspiracy for telling a patient where she could buy laetrile. He didn't prescribe it for her, didn't give it to her, and made no profit on the sale, but the fact that he had merely told her where to get it was a "conspiracy," and in California a conspiracy to commit a misdemeanor is a felony. Selling unapproved substances for cancer is a misdemeanor. Laetrile is of course Vitamin B-17; along with other supplements, such as Vitamin A, it is helpful in some cancers, in some patients. At the time, it was "illegal," because the oncologists and radiologists outnumbered the holistic practitioners who used it. There is little profit in the apricot kernels from which laetrile is derived, so lockstep medicine labelled it "quackery." Later, Governor Gerry Brown gave Dr. P. a full and unconditional pardon, which means that, in the eyes of the law, the conviction was totally expunged and never happened.

In 1980, before the pardon, Dr. Privitera entered into a formal settlement with CABOMQUA, in which he was placed on probation for ten years. Robert Caldwell became his "surveillance officer," supposed to report any violations of the settlement. Here is an example of Caldwell's surveillance. In 1983, he asked the doctor to bid on his daughter's 4-H cow. The doctor suspected that the wrong answer could give her daddy an attitude, so he bought the cow for $2,500, and shipped it to a Catholic convent in Nebraska, where the sisters put it to good use.

In 1984, Caldwell asked the doctor to bid on another bovine, but by now Dr. P. felt that he was sufficiently invested in bull poop and declined. Sure enough, a special investigator showed up at his office. Just as Caldwell had lied about whom he represented, so, now, the CABOMQUA investigator lied about who she was, giving a false name and posing as a patient. Before he examined her, Dr. Privitera required her to sign a standard form that stated she was not an agent of any government. She signed it, thereby committing fraud. She also signed a "Binding Physician-Patient Arbitration Agreement," which CABOMQUA routinely ignored. In his naiveté, Dr. P. examined her and recommended treatment.

Later, CABOMQUA accused him of three things: first, testing for "platelet clumping" via darkfield. Of course, he was "guilty," but the phony patient showed no excess clumping, which Dr. P. reported. And, by the way, why is testing for platelet clumping so bad, especially since the literature shows it can reveal clinical conditions not uncovered in the lab? The medical totalitarians have yet to reply, which proves again that quackery goes CABOMQUA in the night!

The second thing CABOMQUA accused Dr. P of was a urine analysis of "bowel toxemia." *Der* CABOMQUA *doktors* say this with a hiss, as if there is no such thing. Yet, the literature talks about a test called urine indican, or the "Obermayer" test. Should a doctor lose his license because another doctor doesn't use it?

The third thing CABOMQUA didn't like was a "diagnosis" of hypothyroidism. The trouble is that the "patient's" chart shows no such diagnosis, because this charge is another lie. The CABOMQUA agent posing as a patient complained of headaches and a history of anemia and fatigue. We know she was a liar and a fraud. Was she also lying about this rendition of her symptoms? It really doesn't matter if she was, because patients with such symptoms should be suspected of hypothyroidism, and prominent physicians who have written on the subject say, according to the

1988 edition of (Conns) *CURRENT THERAPY*, by Rakel (page 507) that "the physician must depend primarily on the bedside assessment of the patient and institute thyroid hormone therapy on clinical suspicion." Here, Dr. Privitera told the "patient" to do the axillary temperature test, which has never been disproved as a test for low thyroid. The doctor made no "diagnosis" and gave no impression of hypothyroidism, and the fake "patient" never returned.

Remember that CABOMQUA sent the fraud to Dr. P's office in 1984--two years *after* Governor Gerry Brown granted a full and unconditional pardon in the laetrile matter. Again, the pardon had expunged the conviction as if it never had occurred. Yet, CABOMQUA persisted in keeping the doctor on perpetual probation for the conviction that never had occurred, and then sent an impostor gunning for him, an impostor who committed perjury in a legal document.

The reader will recall that, under color of law, CABOMQUA'S Robert Caldwell had extorted $2,500 from Doctor P in payment of his daughter's cow. So, in 1988, the doctor wrote to California Deputy Attorney General Charles J. Post, who represents CABOMQUA in court, and told him that, if his client did not drop the charges just described, he would convene a press conference and tell the world the shocking story. Soon after the press conference, the doctor was arrested and charged with the crime. That's right! The victim of the extortion was arrested and charged with it.

At the preliminary hearing in May, 1989, Superior Court Judge Alban Niles dismissed the charge against the victim because of insufficient evidence. The court also suggested that Caldwell was guilty of official wrongdoing, that he should be investigated, and that the doctor had been the victim of discriminatory prosecution.

During the hearing, there was testimony that still another doctor on CABOMQUA probation had bought steers from Caldwell's daughter. How many other victims Caldwell nicked with this sleazy racket into which he thrust his daughter, we don't know.

In May, 1989, Dr. P sued CABOMQUA in federal court to defeat its phony charges. In August, 1991, he agreed to drop his suit in exchange for CABOMQUA'S representation that it would dismiss all pending license revocation charges against him. There the matter stands at this writing. The haunting question remains: How many other doctors succumbed to CABOMQUA'S terror/extortion campaign because they were not in position, as Dr. Privitera was, to fight it, and how many patients suffered intolerable pain, disfigurement and death as a result?

With the departure of CABOMQUA, the Internal Revenue Service took up the cudgels against Dr. P in behalf of the medical monopolists. In 1993, federal judge William D. Keller signed an order authorizing I.R.S. to enter clinic premises to effect a levy. His honor's order states in part as follows: "3. That in making this seizure the revenue officer(s) shall not seize the patient medical files of the taxpayer, his employees or his patients, nor shall the revenue officer(s) cause said files to be placed beyond the reach of the taxpayer's employees at any time.

"4. That such officer(s) shall make a detailed inventory as to the property seized, leaving a copy thereof at the premises . . . ."

The inventory they left said in its entirety as follows: "All rights, title, interest including lease hold. Completed list to be issued at a later date."

The I.R.S. did sequester his medical files, in direct violation of court order. Until the doctor got them back, patients would ask him what to do; he couldn't tell them with certainty, because he had no records and histories to review. No doctor could render the best treatment without histories, except possibly in a terminal emergency. Dr. Privitera has no way of knowing how much suffering this caused.

Chapter Twelve
Monopoly Medicine

Medicine is inextricably tied to religion. This has always been true, since before Jesus healed the woman who had an issue of blood, exorcised the Gadarene swine and others. The question is: what kind of religion is it tied to? In the jungle, many witch doctors build thriving practices on tea leaves and entrails. Rivals with less magic and fewer spears often wind up in the tribal cooking pots.

In the United States, we are nowhere near so crass. Because of our humanity, when a doctor threatens our lucrative monopoly, we simply call him a "quack," seize his property and throw him into jail; often destroy his family and drive him to suicide. We have nothing personal against him. It's business.

In surgery, orthopedics or other mechanical therapies, American medicine has no peer. In chronic, degenerative diseases, American medicine with some exceptions has been floundering like a flounder out of water. Patients are not abandoning American surgery in droves; on the contrary, they come here from other nations to enjoy it.

However, more and more of them--still a minority, but a growing minority--are deserting American oncology, American radical mastectomy, American cardiology, American quadruple bypass, American diabetic amputation, American arthritis, American impotence and diapers via prostatectomy and others. The defection from these therapies is becoming an embarrassing sequel to the "Great Escape," and orthodox practitioners are searching in desperation for ways to stanch the hemorrhage. *Why* are the patients escaping? Because they are dissatisfied. Because the orthodox therapies aren't working. If they were, why would so many patients abandon them? If they were, "alternative medicine" would not have become the colossus it is today. Because in so many cases orthodox medicine doesn't work, and because so many patients have shunned it, its champions have been conducting a literal reign of terror.

On February 26, 1987, agents of the Food and Drug Administration, accompanied by armed U.S. marshals, smashed in the doors of the Florida offices of the non-profit Life Extension Foundation, which offers the power of group vitamin buying to its few thousand members. The warrant was good for only 12 hours, during which the invaders seized every file, every vitamin and newsletter they were able to load on a rental truck. They were in such a hurry, they tore the computer and telephone wiring out of the walls.

Four years later, in Tempe, Arizona, they did it again, to Life Extension's distribution center. This time, the raid took three days to complete, and the invaders hit the foundation with an embargo on 42 of its best-selling products.

On January 24, 1991, attorneys for Life Extension showed the Arizona Attorney General proof that F.D.A.'s actions were illegal. Hours later, he ordered the Board of Pharmacy to lift the embargo.

It was spring, 1988. So lovely. But a cloud appeared, no bigger than a man's hand. An F.D.A. agent appeared at Highland Labs, in Mt. Angel, Oregon, population 2,000 and complained about the product literature, so Highland stopped distributing it. Other agents posed as clients and convinced company telemarketers to send copies of the literature in the mail.

In the fall of 1990, 9 F.D.A. agents, accompanied by 11 U.S. marshals and 8 Oregon state policemen, arrived in 13 cars. They surrounded the building, kicked the door in and the employees out.

The raiders confiscated $37,000 worth of property, but to date no charges have been filed. The owner says he has to pay F.D.A. each time he wants a copy of any of his records.

Highland Labs tried to appease F.D.A., by hiring a mailing service in Portland to send information to its clients. The Food and Drug Administration raided the home and office of the owner, and held her at gun point while they searched her belongings.

On August 27, 1990, Mrs. Sissy Harrington-McGill was sentenced to six months in maximum security prison for telling customers that her vitamin-enriched pet food "was a healthier diet for animals."

On October 24, 1990, the Century Clinic in Reno was full of patients when F.D.A. arrived, and told patients taking I.V.s to unhook them and leave. Paradoxically, F.D.A. wouldn't let them leave without identifying themselves, and they were interrogated about their illnesses and the therapies they were taking. The agents physically searched the doctors running the clinic, and stole 95 patient charts along with cash and checks totaling more than $10,000.

In 1991, Jonathan Wright, M.D., sued F.D.A. for seizing his stock of L-tryptophan, an amino acid. Thoroughly trained in orthodox medicine at Harvard and the University of Michigan Medical School, Dr. Wright had discovered the efficacy of nutrition therapy, and the medical establishment considered him a traitor.

At 8:45 on the morning of May 6, 1992, F.D.A. agents accompanied by sheriff's deputies surrounded his Tahoma Clinic in Kent, Washington. Kicking in the doors and storming in with guns drawn, they shouted that the receptionists should, "Get your hands up in the air where we can see them." Needless to say, the receptionists stopped typing, talking on the phone (since they usually did those things with their hands), and recepting. The invaders stayed for 11 hours, and finally left with vitamins, medical equipment, computers, bank records, $50 worth of postage stamps and almost 100 patient records. The King County Council called for an investigation of the raid. The F.D.A. district director wrote the Council that the reason for the invasion was "the manufacture and distribution of injectable drugs under conditions which were not approved by the Food and Drug Administration." Yet, neither F.D.A.'s affidavit to the judge nor the search warrant said anything at all about the manufacture of drugs.

At a press conference at F.D.A. headquarters, an official showed reporters a vial of an injectable vitamin that had been contaminated by mold. "No one would want to be injected with a drug like this found in the clinic's dispensary that day." Shouldn't he have added that F.D.A. had found that vial *not* in the clinic's dispensary, but in the garbage, where the Clinic had tossed it precisely because it was contaminated?

In the months following the invasion, F.D.A. interrogated clinic employees and patients at their homes. The *Seattle Times* quoted an F.D.A. memo made public as part of a civil suit Wright filed against the government in 1992. The memo revealed that "local F.D.A. agents were coached to tell the press that Wright was smuggling foreign drugs into the country, the clinic was manufacturing medicines using improper procedures, and Wright was 'trying to defraud the government.'"

In 1995, after investigating him for four years, the federal government abandoned the case with no charges being filed and most of the seized medicine and equipment slated to be returned, the *Times* reported. The newspaper said "the decision ends an investigation that outraged thousands of followers of alternative medicine. They saw the crackdown on Wright as part of a government-led effort to snuff out a growing sector of the health-care industry devoted to vitamins and other natural healing therapies instead of drugs or surgery."

For months in 1992, the Texas F.D.A., guided by its big brother in Washington, and the Texas Department of Health, raided health food stores across the state. The highwaymen stole more than 300 products, including aloe vera, zinc tabs, flaxseed oil, herb teas and vitamin C. The health food stores have not filed claims in fear of reprisal.

Of course, every dictator known to history has trumpeted the "welfare" of his subjects as the "selfless" reason for his crimes, from ancient Rome (bread and circuses), to Mussolini (punctual trains) to Hitler (peaceful streets, gun control, national health insurance and boat rides); and now to the Food and Drug Administration (raids, confiscations and delays). As you will see, behind F.D.A.'s reign of terror are the sleazy quacks of orthodox medicine and some of the pharmaceutical houses, who will commission major felonies under color of law to preserve their lucrative monopoly. Author and private investigator Peter J. Lisa reports that "the medical establishment has used the tactic of forming 'front groups' to go after their economic competitors. They have hired outside professional writers to publish their own materials about given targets, and then promoting these published works as being 'independent' of the 'house of medicine.' They have even advocated one writer doing a breaking-and-entering burglary of a chiropractic school to obtain data from chiropractic files for his book against chiropractic. The A.M.A. even went so far as to buy 250,000 copies of this book and distribute it."

Peter Lisa reports that the Food and Drug Administration's so-called Health Fraud Task Force has tapped phones, broken into homes and offices at night--even into attorney's offices--stolen mailing lists and records. They have used threats and intimidation to convince patients to testify against their doctors.

Notice that next to nothing of all this appears in the nation's mass media, which slavishly print F.D.A. handouts as if they were gospel.

Chapter Thirteen
The Secret Combine

In 1963, the American Medical Association formed the Committee on Quackery, whose basic purpose was to destroy chiropractic. In 1965, A.M.A. formed the Coordinating Conference on Health Information (C.C.H.I.), whose members included government agencies and private groups. The main difference between these two fronts was that the Committee on Quackery worked in the open (later it would be forced to disband), while C.C.H.I. worked in secret. Indeed, H. Doyl Taylor, director of A.M.A.'s Department of Investigation, told C.C.H.I. participants to work as a conference, not as a committee, because the government people involved would catch less flak as conferees than they would as committee members. The scheme included F.D.A., the Federal Trade Commission and the Post Office. In our time, Hillary Clinton applied the same hi-jinx to her secret committee to seize control of a monster chunk of our economy via the nonexistent "health care crisis."

Eventually, disclosure did for C.C.H.I. what it had done for the Committee on Quackery, and it disbanded. Apparently realizing that A.M.A. could no longer conduct its own dirty tricks, even through front groups, the conspirators passed the scalpel to Stephen Barrett, M.D., a Pennsylvania psychiatrist, which recalls humorist Tom Anderson's aphorism: "I never met a psychiatrist who didn't need one." Armed with A.M.A.'s files, Barrett incorporated a group called the Lehigh Valley Committee Against Health Fraud. Soon, another bizarre extrusion appeared, originally called the Southern California Council Against Health Fraud, now known as the National Council Against Health Fraud. Founded by Dr. William Jarvis, of Loma Linda, California, who is not a physician, its board includes the same Dr. Barrett, which means that the two groups are legs on the same bug.

According to investigator Peter J. Lisa, Dr. Barrett says his group is "a bunch of guerrillas." In an article, he explained: "By working 'undercover,' using assumed names and box numbers, we've gotten all sorts of information and publications that other groups, like the medical societies, haven't been able to lay their hands on."

In June, 1978, the American Council on Science and Health incorporated in New York. Run by Elizabeth Whelan, A.C.S.H. is a front group and mouthpiece for the food, chemical, sugar and drug industries. Its board includes Barrett, Jarvis and Victor Herbert, M.D. (not the composer), all members of Jarvis's N.C.A.H.F. For the incredible story of *this* Victor Herbert, see P.J. Lisa, *The Great Medical Monopoly Wars* (International Institute of Natural Health Sciences, Inc., 1986, P.O. Box 5550, Huntington Beach, CA 92615).

As part of their continuing scheme to destroy chiropractic, but not to be blamed, the A.M.A.'s conspirators encouraged the formation of the National Association for Chiropractic Medicine (N.A.C.M.) to take control of it. The N.A.C.M. board included Barrett and Grace Monaco Powers, an attorney, who is president of a group called Emprise, and is a board member of N.C.A.H.F. So is John Renner, M.D., who helped Grace found Emprise, is on the N.A.C.M. board, and is president of the Kansas City Committee on Health and Nutritional Abuse.

Another leg of the conspiracy against competition is the alliance between the drug companies and F.D.A. In 1983, the Pharmaceutical Advertising Council (P.A.C.) signed an agreement with F.D.A. for the purpose, and launched a "Public Service Anti-Quackery Campaign," under the imprimatur of a group called PAC/FDA (Pharmaceutical Advertising Council/Food and Drug Administration). The F.D.A. kicked in some money, and so did the companies. The first three were Hoffman-LaRoche, Lederle and Syntex. The agreement they signed said that the campaign wouldn't name specific products, services, treatments or companies, but they did so anyway. Their first victim was a southern California company called Herbalife.

In April, 1985, Herbalife was doing almost $1 billion a year. Among its products was HCG, an anti-arthritic herb. So, the F.D.A. and media launched a *blitzkrieg*.. The PAC/FDA coordinated and financed it. Paul Chusid, President of Grey Medical Advertising, was campaign coordinator, and asked ad agencies and public relations companies for ideas. Herbalife was made to look like a scheme concocted by Charles Ponzi and run by *Cosa Nostra*. Investigator Peter J. Lisa reports that the assault even included illegal electronic surveillance. Federal and state agencies intervened. Herbalife was sued. Soon, its business was down 90%, to $10 million per month. Herbalife lost about $960 million that year, along with millions in legal fees.

Why? Enter Syntex Pharmaceuticals, a client of Grey's. At the time, the most important drug Syntex sold was Naprosyn. Standard & Poor's *Stock Reports* for April, 1985, said as follows: "The single most important Syntex drug is Naprosyn (generically called naproxen), a nonsteroidal antiarthritic with fiscal 1984 sales of $366.5 million. . . ."

And Herbalife's HCG was competing nose-to-nose with Naprosyn. Syntex's way of competing with HCG was secretly to finance the PAC/FDA "Anti-Quackery" assault on Herbalife, hiding behind a spurious cloak of "public interest" for the purpose. The ostensible reason for the assault on Herbalife was "mislabeling." It is interesting to note that Syntex was also nailed for mislabeling of Naprosyn; yet, F.D.A. simply got Syntex's agreement "to correct misleading promotion of their arthritis drug

(Naprosyn)." In short, F.D.A. slapped Syntex's hand, but cut Herbalife's off.

Of course, Syntex is just one example of the many drug companies that participated in this illicit scheme. They actually had an "enemies list," the same thing the Nixon Administration was denounced for. So, it is perfectly accurate to call the thing we are talking about a conspiracy; and since it is in bed with the government it is a conspiracy that is fascist. Remember that F.D.A. is acting as a front group for the companies.

Among other drug companies financing the campaign--according to Paul Chusid, in a letter dated November 15, 1985--were Bristol-Myers, Burroughs Wellcome, Carter Wallace, Merck Sharp & Dome, Sandoz, etc.

An example that underlines the fraud of the present campaign against "quackery" is the issue of fluoridation. This is not the right place to voice our opinion of fluoridation, although we have one. The only point we want to make here is that fluoridation of the water supply is a legitimate issue in the scientific community. All over Europe, countries have banned it. Many American dentists swear by it, but many others don't, along with many physicians and other scientists. They don't because, they say, a critical examination of the scientific evidence raises serious doubts as to whether fluoridation really does prevent tooth decay, ostensibly the altruistic reason for forcibly introducing it into the water supply. The scientific evidence also raises serious questions regarding carcinogenicity and harmful effects on enzyme and immune function in the body. Many scientists say fluoridation is dangerous, forced, mass medical treatment, with all the efficacy of the swine flu fiasco. To which we add, wasn't forced, mass medical treatment one of the main horrors that earned Hitler the opprobrium of the civilized world?

Yet, fluoridation hasn't been considered, isn't even mentioned, by the "anti-quackery" police. It isn't an issue. Why not? Because fluoridation doesn't emanate from alternative medicine, or alternative dentistry, if you will. Fluoride is a poisonous, industrial waste, some of it used in rat and insect poison, that is expensive to dispose of, and used to be considered garbage. It should be treated as hazardous waste, but much of it now is profitably dumped into the public water supply with the endorsement of the American Dental Association. It may not be possible to turn a sow's ear into a silk purse, but A.D.A. certainly has turned poisonous garbage into profitable treatment.

The fact that the campaign against quackery has seven kinds of conniptions about Vitamin C, but doesn't say a word about fluoridation, proves all by itself that the campaign is a total fraud.

Still along these lines, consider the present mortal struggle over abortion. As in the case of fluoridation, we have an opinion, but shall not intrude it here. Suffice it to note now that the battle cry of the medical practitioners who champion abortion--we're not talking about the relative innocents who man and woman the barricades in the streets, but about the abortion strategists at the top who do the thinking--is "freedom," and "freedom of choice." We are told that a woman has the unalienable right to "control her own body." These terms are trumpeted no less fervently than the name of Allah in the present holy war conducted by fundamentalist Islam. Yet, the abortionists have not a word to say in defense of the parallel right to the medical treatment of one's choice. One has the unalienable right to control one one's own body only in abortion. Why? What is the unifying element? Simple. Both its friends and enemies agree that abortion is a multi-billion dollar industry. Abortionists have wives and families like everyone else, along with mistresses who need apartments, ensembles, automobiles and manicures.

The big insurance companies constitute another important element in the conspiracy. Especially in health care, insurance companies are in the business of collecting premiums, paying dividends, making money, and denying and delaying claims. The more premiums a company collects, and the more claims it denies and delays, the more money it makes. The insurance companies have happily been selling health insurance, but because of government collusion millions of patients believe medical care is "free," with the predictable result that the prices of surgery, testing, pharmaceuticals, services and fees, some of them unnecessary, some of them designed solely to protect the doctor and hospital from litigation designed to benefit the lawyers, are going through the roof.

Of course, alternative medicine is almost always tens of thousands of dollars less expensive than orthodox therapies. That is the main thing the "anti-quackery" conspiracy has against it. Because alternative therapies are so much less expensive than orthodox medicine, they are much less profitable. Yet, the conspiracy constantly complains even about the modest prices alternative practitioners charge. The insurance industry could save considerable money by paying those modest charges for policy holders who prefer alternative therapy rather than orthodox treatments. The fact that, on the contrary, the industry elected to participate in the illegal scheme to squelch helpful therapies like darkfield, live cell analysis and chelation, is another proof of conspiracy.

James Garcia, of Aetna, led the way. By the end of 1985, most major health insurance companies formed the National Health Care Anti-Fraud Association, which launched a computer tracking system designed to monitor every liberated physician who ever filed a claim. The system is housed at the massive Blue Cross/Blue Shield computer facility just outside Harrisburg, Pennsylvania. Proof that N.H.C.A.A. knows perfectly well that what it is doing is illegal, appears in a "confidential memorandum" dated August 8, 1990, composed by Thomas Brunner, its attorney. Brunner told the Board this: "As you know, The Pennsylvania Project has been carefully structured to minimize any threats of civil liability from information sharing. With this goal in mind, we have arranged a system where the disclosure of information is strictly limited, based on agreements by all participating companies on how information can be used." Barrister Brunner explained: "We are concerned about N.H.C.A.A. operations in unauthorized states.

Any information sharing outside the boundaries of the current guidelines presents potential liability issues."

The problem is that one of the main purposes of the computer tracking system is to reduce competition, and Timothy J. Muris, of the Federal Trade Commission, explained as follows in Senate testimony, on June 24, 1984: "Sharing information is lawful, *unless it reduces competition.*" (emphasis added)

And the purpose of the conspiracy is *precisely* to reduce competition. So, the conspiracy is clearly illegal because it violates the anti-trust laws of the United States. The four legs of the conspiracy are totalitarian medicine and its front groups; the insurance industry; the government; and the drug companies.

By no means do we say that all drug companies are bad. Doctors have prescribed and will continue to prescribe pharmaceuticals for those patients who need them. Some such products are immensely beneficial. What holistic doctors do say is that, despite the good things they do, many of the nation's largest drug companies are illegally conspiring in restraint of trade.

Samuel Hopkins Adams wrote as follows in *Collier's* magazine: "Gullible America will spend this year some . . . millions in the pursuit of patent medicines. In consideration of this sum it will swallow . . . a wide assortment of varied drugs ranging from powerful and dangerous heart depressants to insidious liver stimulants and, far in excess of all other ingredients, undiluted fraud. For fraud exploited by the skillfullest of advertising bunco men is the basis of the trade. Should the newspapers, the magazines and the medical journals refuse their pages of this class of advertisement, the patent medicine business in five years would be scandalously historic as the South Sea Bubble, and the nation would be richer . . . ." Of course, Sam Adams wrote this in *Collier's* in *October, 1905*, when such sentiments could still be voiced in a national magazine, before patent medicine billions had subverted the media, the medical journals and the medical schools; before totalitarian medicine threw doctors who disagreed into jail.

In June, 1992, U.C.L.A. researchers published a study in the *Annals of Internal Medicine*. They examined 109 prescription drug ads in 10 medical journals and found that a staggering 92% of them violated federal rules. Yet, those misleading ads are one of the main sources of physician knowledge about the patent medicines they regularly prescribe.

However, the incest between the drug companies and government officials is so pervasive the companies are not even slapped on the wrist. We've seen how one company, Syntex, secretly financed a media-government campaign to destroy its chief competitor. Go down the line, and you will see one company after another doing the same thing.

As of November, 1985, there were 25 drug companies that had contributed to PAC/FDA's illegal, anti-competitive conspiracy. Among them are Smith, Kline & Beecham and Hoffman-La Roche. These companies make Thorazine, Valium and Librium, which are hawked as sedatives, helpful for insomnia--and they apparently believe it's well worth the deductible expense to squelch anyone who uses chiropractic or vitamins to compete.

Of course, Thorazine is extremely dangerous and addictive, and has caused uncounted deaths. The same is true of Valium and Librium, which are addictive psychotropics produced by Hoffman-La Roche. Perhaps the most destructive aspect of these dangerous, addictive "feel-good" products has been the promotion of the psychology that fermented the so-called "drug culture." How serious can any "war on drugs" be where the "ethical" drug pushers are legally turning users into zombies and corpses? Were a vitamin company, or some other alternative enterprise or practitioner to amass such a horrific record, he would be closed down by F.D.A. and thrown into jail, but the "ethical" drug houses get away with it because they pay well. They already do billions of dollars in volume, but they want it all.

One of the biggest “feel good” drugs is Prozac®. A patient in her thirties with melanoma of the ear came to see me. The only drug she was taking was Prozac, for depression, which, of course, many cancer patients experience. I am wary of the use of this drug as there is some evidence that it promotes cancer in animals and may suppress the immune system. (See *Science*, 3 July 1992, p. 22).

The conspiracy we are talking about began early in the Twentieth Century, when medical schools were converted from homeopathic to allopathic curricula; from prevention to treatment; from vitamins, minerals and enzymes to drugs--prescription drugs manufactured by the frauds Sam Adams wrote about in *Collier's.* They bought expensive ads in the medical journals and contributed liberally to the schools. Today, it is no exaggeration to say that, with some exceptions, the only thing your doctor knows about the patent medicines he prescribes is often what the drug company "detail man" tells him. Of course, the detail man is not a doctor, and the only thing he in turn knows about it is what his boss said.

In 1988, the conspiracy conducted by the American Medical Association was finally exposed. We don't need to guess about that. U.S. District Judge Susan Getzendanner ordered the *Journal of the American Medical Association* (*JAMA*, v. 259, no. 1, January 1, 1988, page 81) to print her determination as follows: "Under the Sherman Act, every combination or conspiracy in restraint of trade is illegal. *The court has held that the conduct of the A.M.A. and its members constituted a conspiracy* in restraint of trade based on the following facts: the purpose of the boycott was to eliminate chiropractic; chiropractors are in competition with some medical physicians; the boycott had substantial anti-competitive effects; there were no pro-competitive effects of the boycott; and the plaintiffs were injured as a result of the conduct. These facts add up to a violation of the Sherman Act." (italics added)

Among the proofs of conspiracy was a memorandum from A.M.A.'s Committee on Quackery to the A.M.A. Board of Trustees, dated January 4, 1971, which recalled that "your Committee has considered its prime mission to be, first, the containment of chiropractic and, ultimately, the elimination of chiropractic.

"Your Committee believes it is well along in its first mission and is, at the same time, moving toward the ultimate goal. This, then, might be considered a progress report on developments in the past seven years. The Committee has not previously submitted such a report because it believes that *to make public some of its activities would have been and continues to be unwise*. Thus, this report *is intended only for the information of the Board of Trustees*." (italics added)

Incredulous innocents who go to work every day, pay the taxes and visit chiropractors, often ask: "Do you mean that these people--doctors, pill pushers, insurance moguls and government officials--actually sit down around a table and plan these things?" Yes, that's exactly what we mean. These elaborate schemes don't happen by themselves. The expensive crooks at A.M.A. do the same thing cheap crooks do when they sit down around a table and plan a heist.

Farther along in her permanent injunction against A.M.A., Judge Getzendanner says: "Although the conspiracy ended in 1980, there are lingering effects of the illegal boycott and conspiracy which require an injunction. . . ."

Again, the judge forced *JAMA* to print her order. There should have been a firestorm of media coverage, in view of the fact that some of the people who control organized medicine in this country, had now been nailed as participants in this chintzy outrage. The prestige they had paid many deductible millions to enjoy should have been stripped from their tunics. Yet, the coverage was as fleeting and as sparse as the media thought they could get away with. Would you give the story the coverage it deserves if you knew that millions, eventually billions, in advertising contracts were at stake? Again, were alternative practitioners ever caught in such *flagrante delicto*, they would be jailed in conditions that would make the gulag archipelago look like Cancun, and henceforth would be allowed to practice nothing more than the yo-yo.

Notice also that Judge Susan says the conspiracy has "ended," but that there are "lingering effects." Not quite. As we have seen, the conspiracy simply changed hats; the effects today are far worse than they were when the conspirators at A.M.A. were simply trying to destroy chiropractic.

Chapter Fourteen
From the Horse's Mouth

In the previous chapter, we saw that the National Council Against Health Fraud is an important front for the medical monopoly. On October 31, 1985, the Council filed the required Statement By Domestic Nonprofit Corporation, with March Fong Eu, California Secretary of State. The Chief Executive Officer of N.C.A.H.F. was of course William T. Jarvis, who lived at 25015 Tulip Ave. in Loma Linda, 92354. The Secretary was Lynn Caldwell, of 25177 Starr Street, also in Loma Linda.

Who is William Jarvis? As we have seen, he is not a physician. He has been an associate professor of preventive dentistry at Loma Linda University. Confronted with his own quackery on Alan Stang's radio talk show in Los Angeles, he walked out. To see how much he really knows, wouldn't it be helpful to see what he was saying long ago and compare it to what we know today? Thanks to the miracle of modern journalism, we can do that.

The *Los Angeles Times* of August 24, 1978 printed an article by Staff Writer Myrna Oliver, entitled "Medical Quacks Growing Threat Told." Miss Oliver quotes Jarvis as follows: "The health food industry is based on the idea that you can't get safe food in a grocery store. . . . Actually only one food additive has ever been proved detrimental to humans--salt."

Of course, no one with any sense would make such an absurd statement about grocery stores--I have never heard anyone, in or out of the health food industry, make it--but it certainly helps if you are trying to discredit someone and need to concoct fraudulent quotations for the purpose. You *can* get safe food in a grocery store, despite which the health food industry is based on the fact that there are other, important, things you can't get there. As for the Jarvis comment about food additives, tell it to the many Chinese restaurants, for just one example, who now advertise that they use no MSG, because of medical findings on the subject.

Jarvis also says: "You get all the vitamins and minerals you need just by eating the big four--dairy foods, meat, vegetables and fruits--and bread and cereals." Of course, since 1978, when Jarvis said this, the evidence for the efficacy of vitamin and mineral supplementation has mounted so dramatically, that even orthodox medicine has started to admit it. See many recent issues of *Reader's Digest*, for instance.

Since Dr. Jarvis's 1978 comments were so helpful, let's see what else he and his fellow totalitarians have to say. As you will recall, Dr. Barrett used phony names and addresses to collect information. Since such practices presumably are therefore perfectly acceptable, we did the same thing. We wrote to N.C.A.H.F., using a phony name. After our check cleared, Dr. Jarvis, who is not a physician, sent us considerable, dubious material. Thank you, Dr. Jarvis.

For instance, there is the industry propaganda group in New York, called the American Council on Science and Health, run by Elizabeth Whelan, who turns up on countless warped boards. In the March/April, 1985 issue of *A.C.S.H. News & Views* (v.6, No. 2), Densie Hatfield wrote at length about chelation: ". . . Since EDTA binds with metals in the blood and allows them to be excreted, it is an effective treatment in lead poisoning. . . .

"The rationale for the use of this treatment in atherosclerosis is that EDTA binds calcium and removes it from the bloodstream. Because calcium is found in the plaques that block arteries, proponents of chelation claim that lowering blood levels of calcium will cause calcium to dissolve out of the plaques in the artery and allow blood to flow more freely. But in fact, 1) the bulk of material in a plaque is not calcium; 2) EDTA has not been proven to remove the calcium from plaques; and 3) to date, no persuasive evidence from properly controlled studies has established that chelation therapy relieves symptoms of atherosclerosis."

In short, says Hatfield, chelation works on lead, but not on calcium. Yet, in the very next paragraph, Hatfield says this: "The rationale for the use of chelation therapy for the treatment of atherosclerosis sprang from work done in the 1950s, in which a decrease in calcium deposits was observed in several parts of the body after administration of EDTA. When this was seen, it was suggested that EDTA might also promote the removal of calcium from hardened arteries and possibly stop the development of atherosclerosis or even reverse the damage already done."

So, maybe chelation does flush out calcium. Indeed: "There is normally a certain amount of calcium circulating in the blood, which is absolutely essential for heart, nerve, and muscle function. The administration of EDTA can upset this delicate balance by combining rapidly with the calcium and then being excreted via the kidneys. In addition, the removal of calcium from plaques in the arteries can literally be life-threatening in itself if the loosened material that is being carried by the bloodstream lodges elsewhere. The result can be stroke or heart attack; exactly what chelation therapy is supposed to prevent."

So, first Hatfield says chelation won't remove calcium, then Hatfield says chelation removes too much calcium.

In fact, says the same article: "There are some physicians, albeit a minority, who feel that chelation therapy does hold some promise for a certain type of patient and only for a limited number of diseases and feel that it is worthy of a controlled trial study under properly controlled conditions. But no one seems to feel that it is worth the time, money and energy that is necessary to carry out this type of study, not even the chelation therapists and their supporting group, the American Academy of Medical Preventics."

This characterization of A.A.M.P.'s position on chelation studies was absurd. When Hatfield's article was published, the organization had vigorously been calling for such tests for many years. Also, if chelation helps in a "limited number of diseases," which presumably means at least 2 or 3, wouldn't it be immensely beneficial? Wouldn't it be immenscly beneficial if it helped only one disease?

Obviously, this incredible hodgepodge of conflict originates in Hatfield's desire to impugn chelation in the face of so many favorable reports, at the same time covering that desire with a patina of twisted objectivity. Why go to so much trouble? The answer, she says, is that "the chelationists are getting rich. A course of chelation therapy may begin with a battery of tests in order to 'profile' the patient's condition. The costs of these tests may exceed $1,000. The treatment itself typically consists of 30 to 40 sessions in which EDTA is given intravenously (I.V.) over three to four hours on a strictly out-patient basis. The sessions are generally spread out over several weeks or even several months. Each one of these sessions may run $75. The patient may then be left with somewhere in the neighborhood of $4,000 in out-of-pocket expenses for somewhat dubious benefits. Chelation therapy is obviously not a cheap alternative to orthodox medicine, as many of its supporters claim."

So, as always, we arrive at the real point of the phony "war on quackery."

Yes, we chelationists do begin with a battery of tests such as darkfield, to find out whether the patient is a candidate for chelation. If his kidneys don't work properly, for instance, he isn't a candidate, because his kidneys won't flush out the heavy metals the chelation removes (or doesn't remove, or does remove, according to Hatfield), which could be dangerous. Would orthodox medicine prefer that we administer the procedure without taking a history and running the tests? How much do orthodox medicine's tests cost? The answer is: much more, thousands more.

Hatfield says chelation is administered "on a strictly out-patient basis." Yes, it is, because it has proven so simple and safe, so unlike open heart surgery. Would the American Council on Science and Health prefer that we keep patients overnight unnecessarily, and thereby add considerably to the cost?

Finally, the patient may be left "with somewhere in the neighborhood of $4,000 in out-of-pocket expenses . . . ." Yes, that's true. Why? The answer is that the patient may be left with all those out-of-pocket expenses, because, as we have seen, the quackery conspiracy has colluded with the insurance companies to deny insurance coverage for techniques and therapies like chelation and live cell analysis--despite which those therapies are much cheaper than dangerous, often temporary, orthodox procedures like bypass. If a chelation practitioner is "getting rich" from $4,000 in out-of-pocket expenses, is the bypass surgeon getting even richer from a fee of $40,000 and more?

Whenever someone complains about how much someone else is making, it's a good idea to demand that he tell you how much *he* is making.

We do not argue that dangerous, exorbitant, temporary procedures like bypass be banned and their advocates jailed. We favor an even playing field and freedom. If the bypass surgeon gets $40,000 each from patients who are voluntarily willing to pay it, we have no objection. We do, however, demand the same liberty for everyone.

After a while, a compulsive liar trips over his own lies, because he can't remember what he told whom. In like fashion, the May/June, 1984 (v. 5, no. 3) issue of the *A.C.S.H. News & Views* is amusing. The newsletter says it asked Dr. Barrett to interview two professors of pharmacy about vitamins. One was Murray M. Tuckerman, Ph.D., professor of pharmaceutical chemistry at

Temple, whom Barrett asked: "How many of these people [millions of vitamin users] don't need the supplements they are taking because they are getting adequate amounts of vitamins in the food they eat?" Dr. Tuckerman replied:

"Assuming that all of these people are normal and healthy and eating a standard American diet, none of them should require a vitamin supplement..." Elsewhere in the interview, Dr. Tuckerman speaks of the "*Handbook of Nonprescription Drugs*" published by the American Pharmaceutical Association, which "makes clear that vitamins are not usually needed by any age group of normal healthy Americans . . . ." In other words, if you are healthy, you don't need treatment. But, if you're sick . . . .?

The other pharmacist Dr. Barrett interviewed was David B. Roll, Ph.D., professor of medicinal chemistry at the University of Utah. Again Barrett popped the question. Dr. Roll replied: "I have no way of knowing, nor does anyone else. We do know, however, that the results of four major national nutrition surveys have revealed that some segments of our population have vitamin intakes below the recommended levels." Indeed, said Professor Roll, "there is a large body of the population who might benefit from supplementation . . . ."

Dr. Barrett may be stupid, but he's persistent. Still struggling to snooker the answer he wanted, he asked: "Do you think that 'unnecessary vitamins' should be an ethical issue of concern to pharmacy school educators?" Dr. Roll replied: ". . . Frankly, we spend more of our efforts in identifying the unnecessary and improper use of prescription medications than in doing the same for nonprescription products, since there are many physicians who know little about the pharmacology of the drugs they prescribe. The potential for harm from these drugs and their interactions with each other is much greater than that from the daily ingestion of a low-dose multi-vitamin supplement."

Dear me! How embarrassing!

Among the plethora of quack publications is *A.M.A. Insights*, published by *JAMA* (*Journal of the American Medical*

Association). The issue for July 13, 1984 (v. 252, No. 2), says, "MEDICAL QUACKERY continues to thrive in the United States. Harrison L. Rogers, Jr. MD., told the House Subcommittee on Health and Long-term Care. The Association fights health fraud by educating physicians and the public about such nostrums as megavitamins, chelation therapy, and laetrile. Dr. Rogers urged Congress to continue support for federal efforts to stop health fraud, and called for a closer look at vitamin and mineral supplements that are sold over the counter. . . ."

Notice that Dr. Rogers apparently isn't opposed to vitamins and minerals. He's opposed to selling them *over the counter.* Selling them over the counter is a multi-billion dollar business, which Dr. Rogers doesn't have a piece of. If selling them over the counter were banned, which is the goal of the draconian 1994 regulations F.D.A. and the totalitarians behind it have imposed, people who want vitamins and minerals could get them only by paying Dr. Rogers for an office visit. What a remarkable coincidence! And how much do *you* make a year, Dr. Rogers?

Of course, it's difficult to know when to believe the American Medical Association, if at all, now that a federal court has nailed it for running a conspiracy, but, for what it's worth, paragraph 15.002 of Policy Compendium/43, says as follows: "Chelation Therapy: The A.M.A. believes that until proponents of chelation therapy conduct clinical studies, chelation by EDTA and its salts cannot be advocated for diseases and conditions other than acute hypercalcemia, lead poisoning, and intoxications caused by some other heavy metals." (CSA Rep. F, I-84:272-274) You will find a similar statement in *Reader's Guide to Alternative Health Methods* (p. 158), published by A.M.A.

In other words, chelation *can* be advocated for acute hypercalcemia, lead poisoning, and intoxications caused by some other heavy metals. The American Medical Association says so itself, which means the procedure is a considerable boon to mankind. Yet, the conspirators at A.M.A. call it quackery.

By the way, what is hypercalcemia? It's too much calcium in the blood. The A.M.A. says chelation can be advocated for it, which presumably means it isn't quackery, but who could believe an organization that a federal judge has caught running a conspiracy.

Still another A.M.A. publication is *the Journal of the American Medical Association* (JAMA), a reprint from which Dr. Jarvis sent your reporter under another name. Thank you, Dr. Jarvis. The date on the reprint was April 10, 1987 (Vol. 257, No. 14), which contained an article by A.M.A.'s Council on Scientific Affairs. The abstract at the beginning of the article, like the headnotes in a law report, tells the busy doctor what the piece is about: "Healthy adult men and healthy adult nonpregnant, nonlactating women consuming a usual, varied diet do not need vitamin supplements. . . ." Remember that the party line is that supplements are a lucrative hoax.

Now, what does this A.M.A. article actually tell the harried doctor who finds time to read it?: "Since the RDA are established for healthy people, they do not cover special needs for nutrients by persons with specific clinical problems, such as premature birth, inherited metabolic disorders, infections, catabolic states including weight reduction, chronic diseases, and drug therapy, all of which may alter requirements for given vitamins."

For instance, clinicians have noted that victims of leukemia have a voracious tolerance for vitamin C. Ten grams would probably induce diarrhea in a healthy patient. A leukemia patient could ingest that much and more with no such effect.

The A.M.A. piece also says: ". . . If the total energy intake falls below 1200 kcal (5040 kJ), it becomes increasingly difficult to obtain all of the protective nutrients in adequate amounts, and supplements may be needed."

This is an example of the fact that the opposition has to admit some science in their desperate need to maintain credibility. Again: "Healthy adults, 18 years of age and older, receiving adequate diets should have no need for supplementary vitamins. Dietary practices in the United States, however, have changed in ways that may have reduced the overall vitamin delivery from the diet. Since the turn of the century, *consumption of processed foods has increased*, many more meals are eaten away from home, and a greater portion of the diet is consumed as between-meal snacks. . . . Before deciding whether a vitamin supplement should be recommended to an adult, however, a history regarding the adequacy of dietary intake, usual dietary practices, and specific issues of life-style and life situation must be carefully evaluated. . . ." (italics added)

I can easily imagine myself writing every word you just read. In fact, I *have* written it. When I write it, the Establishment doctors call it quackery. When it appears in *JAMA*, it is presumably authentic. The A.M.A. types tell us "you get everything you need from your food," and that processing is good. Now, here, A.M.A. says it is bad. Doesn't that mean the allopaths are wrong? On the other hand, remember, A.M.A. was convicted of conspiracy, and hasn't been pardoned.

JAMA also says: ". . . Vitamin deficiency diseases may occur in association with poor diet and alcoholism in adults." So, alcoholism is still another vitamin deficiency "disease." *JAMA* warns that "assays to monitor the efficacy of vitamin treatment are highly desirable. In cases with the most severe malabsorption, recourse to parenteral sources of all nutrients, including vitamins, may be required." In other words, just because you're taking vitamins, doesn't mean they will be absorbed. Special testing is required. "Any forms of synthetic or semi-synthetic diets used in prolonged parenteral, enterostomy, or tube-feeding regimens must include adequate levels of vitamins. . . ." Does the fact that *JAMA* feels it necessary to say this mean perhaps that some doctors, at least, don't know? ". . . If a single vitamin is excluded from the solutions administered to patients maintained with total parenteral nutrition for long periods, latent or clinical deficiency disease will occur."

Remember that the main purpose of the *JAMA* article is to denigrate vitamin therapy. However, because the positive evidence sustaining supplementation makes Krakatoa look like a firecracker, the conspirators apparently can't decide whether to praise it with faint damns or the opposite. For instance: "Of all the claims for the efficacy of vitamin E in the prevention or treatment of cardiovascular disorders, the only one that has survived controlled clinical investigation is intermittent claudication. The effects of 400 IU/d on intermittent claudication are not noted until after 12 to 18 months of therapy, and the effects are variable. Improvement in blood flow to the extremities has been noted in some patients. Patients with genetic deficiencies of glutathione synthetase and glucose-6-phosphate dehydrogenase, as well as others with prooxidant states such as retrolental fibroplasia and bronchopulmonary dysplasia, may improve with vitamin E therapy." Question: If vitamin E helps some patients, isn't it worth using with those patients? How many therapies help every patient?

Of course, this is just one of many examples. There is the Harvard University study which surveyed 120,000 men and women and found that the incidence of heart disease was 40 percent less among individuals who took the most vitamin E, compared to those who took the least.

How about a recent outcomes study done by Pracon, a hospital analysis firm in Virginia, which found that more vitamin E supplementation could mean shorter hospital stays--and a $7.7 billion saving. Wouldn't that be good for the hospital bottom line as well as for patients?

Medical research on the benefits of supplementation has exploded. The quantity and quality of this continuing research makes Establishment denials ever more blatant. According to monopoly medicine, supplementation is beneficial only in nutritional deficiencies. With so much evidence accumulating, it is astounding that (either out of ignorance or malice) monopoly medicine would continue to insist supplementation does not help prevent and ameliorate serious diseases.

A 1992 symposium sponsored by the New York Academy of Science was called "Beyond Deficiency: New Views on the

Function and Health Effects of Vitamins." At the symposium, researcher after researcher presented new findings on the beneficial effects of vitamins and minerals against cancer, heart disease and other illnesses.

Medical World News, an informative periodical read by many doctors, led off its January, 1993, issue with an article entitled, "Vitamins: Emerging as Disease Fighters, Not Just Supplements." The article said that new studies on the role of vitamins are shifting the foundations of nutrition research, policy and public health in this country. Let's hope so.

Despite monopoly medicine's pusillanimous hems and haws, the typical American diet--unbalanced, processed, devitalized, dead--affects health dramatically. Nutritional surveys conducted periodically by the U.S. Department of Agriculture show that Americans in vast numbers do not consume enough essential nutrients. Harvard nutritional researchers Drs. Meir Stampfer and Walter Willett have commented that the recent scientific evidence "strongly indicates that such low intakes are associated with serious health consequences."

Back to Dr. Jarvis. Another article he sent us after our check cleared appeared in the *Journal of Nutrition Education* (vol. 15, no. 2) undated except for the year, 1983. Dr. Jarvis sent it to us about ten years after it was originally published, long after it became embarrassing. Authors Michael A. Dubick and Robert B. Rucker, of the Department of Nutrition at the University of California-Davis, say this: ". . . That niacin has not been found to be effective except by those who initially proposed its use is worth noting." So, in 1983, the authors were excoriating niacin therapy. Twelve years later, they have egg on their collective face, since niacin lowers cholesterol, at the very least.

Vitamin B-12 fares no better. After the usual excoriation, our distinguished authors say this: ". . . The only established therapeutic role of vitamin B-12 is in the treatment of vitamin B-12 deficiency. . . ." We presume this is sarcasm and we are dutifully amused; but, by the way, have you boys ever heard of the scourge called pernicious anemia? Did you know that the cure is vitamin B-12?

Another Jarvis reprint (N.C.A.H.F. number 510) is an undated issue of the *FDA Consumer* (HEW Publication No. [FDA] 79-2117). It says this: "Vitamin E in humans acts as an antioxidant that helps to prevent oxygen from destroying other substances. In other words, vitamin E is a preservative, protecting the activity of other compounds such as vitamin A. No clinical effects have been associated with very low intake of this vitamin in man. A rather rare form of anemia is (sic) premature infants, however, responds to vitamin E medication. . . ." So, then, is vitamin E helpful, or not? Would the real Dr. Jarvis stand up?

The same F.D.A. publication says this: "Synthetic vitamins, manufactured in the laboratory, are identical to the natural vitamins found in foods. The body cannot tell the difference and gets the same benefits from either source. . .." As we have seen, this isn't true. The reader will recall that natural and synthetic vitamins even look different under the microscope. Indeed, believe it or not, on the very same page, F.D.A. says this: "There are several natural forms of vitamin K, which are essential to cause clotting of the blood. One type, K1, occurs in plants. Another, K2, is formed by bacteria in the intestinal tract. Yet a third is found in some animals and birds. *The synthetic vitamin K, menadione, because of the potential for harm involved in its use, is dispensed only by prescription. . . ."* (italics added) In short, says F.D.A., there is absolutely no difference between natural and synthetic vitamin K, but the synthetic version could be dangerous. Is it any wonder that these charlatans have lost all credibility?

Another reprint Dr. Jarvis sent us (N.C.A.H.F. #90) is "Diet and Cancer," prepared by Elizabeth Whelan's American Council on Science and Health, dated September, 1985. On page 6, it says: "It is readily apparent that considerable difference of opinion continues to exist among scientists on the diet-cancer issue. Qualified experts examining the same data can and do reach very different conclusions. . . ." I agree with this completely. The fact that other doctors disagree with me doesn't prove they are quacks. Yet, as we have seen, some of those doctors also disagree with this A.C.S.H. statement. Indeed, as part of the totalitarian network, A.C.S.H. clearly doesn't believe it.

On page 10, the A.C.S.H. report says, "The great majority of case-control epidemiologic investigations indicate that there is no more than a marginal association between fat consumption and cancers of the breast, colon-rectum, and prostate . . . ." On page 17, it says that a National Cancer Institute meeting found that "the increased cancer risk associated with low fruit and vegetable consumption is not terribly impressive . . . ." We learn that "the risks associated with eating meat and fat have been overstated," and that "the benefits associated with eating fruits and vegetables also have been overstated as regards cancer." On page 20, we are told about a National Research Council finding of "no conclusive evidence to indicate that dietary fiber . . . exerts a protective effect against colon-rectum cancer in humans." Again, the date on the A.C.S.H. report is 1985. We leave it to the reader to decide ten years later whether it holds up or is fat-industry quackery.

Still another article from N.C.A.H.F. appeared in the *Archives of Internal Medicine* in February, 1980 (v. 140, p. 173, cf.). Entitled "The Vitamin Craze," the article is by Victor Herbert, who is both a physician and a lawyer. Again, you will find much more than you want to know about Herbert in Peter J. Lisa's book, *The Great Medical Monopoly Wars* (International Institute of Natural Health Sciences, Huntington Beach, California, 1986). In his article, doctor-lawyer Herbert pays the usual, party-line obeisance to processed food and synthetic vitamins: ". . . Anyone in this country who eats a balanced diet can get enough vitamins in his regular food . . . ." He speaks of "the incorrect belief that synthetic vitamins are different from natural vitamins." Indeed, in this 15-year-old article, Victor Herbert says many people "erroneously believed that many diseases, including arthritis and cancer, are partly caused by a lack of vitamins and minerals; . . . ."

Does the fact that Dr. Jarvis continues to send this completely discredited claptrap out, mean that he needs the services of psychiatrist Stephen Barrett?

Jarvis's *N.C.A.H.F. Newsletter* for May/June, 1985 (vol. 8, no. 3) says as follows: ". . . Humans may have a self-regulating system that renders the infusion of antioxidants useless . . . ." Also: "Some book writers and health food faddists tout the ingestion of large quantities of antioxidants such as superoxide dismutase, vitamin E and carotene as antidotes to aging. But according to studies completed in the last few years, such products may be of little benefit. . . ." Jarvis published this ten years ago. Today we know it is totally wrong, but so full of himself is he, that he still sends it out.

Now, what about the life-saving procedure that is the main subject of this book: live cell analysis by means of the darkfield microscope? James A. Lowell, Ph.D., is a factotum in the totalitarian combine. He is president of the Arizona Council Against Health Fraud. Dr. Jarvis sent us an article by him from the November, 1986, issue of *Nutrition Forum* (v. 3, no. 11), entitled "Live Cell Analysis: High-Tech Hokum." Dr. Lowell begins by covering his gluteus maximus as follows: "Dark-field microscopy is a valid scientific tool in which special lighting is used to examine specimens of cells and tissues. . . . Connecting a television monitor to a microscope for diagnostic purposes is also a legitimate practice. . . ."

There follows a chart of "claims vs. facts." For instance, there is a column of "Blood indicators" like separation of red blood cells, which corresponds to another column headed "Proponents' interpretation." In this case: "Too little separation means oxygen delivery and carbon dioxide removal are reduced, typically caused by too much dietary fat." Presumably, that is what Dr. Privitera says.

Finally, there is a column of "Scientific facts." In this case: ". . . Although extremely high blood levels of fat can cause red cell aggregation, dietary fat does not produce this condition *in normal individuals*." (italics added)

Does this mean the condition can occur in *abnormal* individuals--the ones Dr. Privitera is treating? Not many normal individuals come to see holistic doctors for treatment. The few who do, for preventive purposes, don't complain of symptoms, because they are normal. Dr. Lowell's next blood indicator is the size of red blood cells. The "Proponent's interpretation" is: "They may be too small due to iron deficiency anemia or too big due to B-12 deficiency or rare conditions." The "Scientific fact" is: "Although this interpretation is correct, most people performing live cell analysis have insufficient training to actually identify or treat any conditions they discover."

And if you *do* have sufficient training? Dr. Lowell seems to say that if you do have it you can use live-cell analysis to good effect. Would you have sufficient training if you are the doctor--as is Jim Privitera--who trains other doctors from around the world in the technique? Along these lines, another Lowell blood indicator is "Fat (chylous material) in blood." The corresponding "Proponents' interpretation" says: "Results from a diet high in fats or simple sugars." The "Scientific fact" tells us: "The amount of chylous material . . . in the blood increases after eating. But it is not readily visible under darkfield illumination unless special techniques are used." And if you *do* use those special techniques? Really, Dr. Lowell, is this embarrassing performance the best you can do?

On the next page, he makes light of the problem of food allergies. ". . .Conventional allergists believe that less than 15% of the general population suffers from food allergies." Let's see, the general population numbers more than 250 million. If just 15% of them suffer from food allergies, we're talking about 37 million people. Should we allergists not treat them because 37 million people is too small a number?

Next, Dr. Lowell relates his excursion to a convention in California, where a lady he was with "underwent NutriScreen Live Blood Analysis for the special convention price of only $15."

NutriScreen is of course the company Dr. Privitera founded, so we know something about the procedure.

Dr. Lowell writes that the woman who conducted the test "paid no attention to our patient's medical history or obvious physical problems . . . ." Of course, no real doctor would do anything to a patient without a history, except in a potentially terminal emergency. Indeed, Dr. Lowell says, "Even if live cell analysis were a valid test, I suspect that most practitioners are performing it improperly. The three I have observed so far didn't always clean their microscope slides carefully between patients. (Dirt and dust which show up under the microscope can then be misinterpreted as components of the blood.) No agents were used to prevent dehydration or clotting or to control salinity, pH or temperature. Factors like these can account for variations in rouleau patterns, red-cell clumping and the formation of 'spicules.' Some of the patterns one practitioner saw resulted from his microscope being out of focus and disappeared when I adjusted it properly."

Of course we have no way of knowing whether the incompetent straw men Dr. Lowell destroys here ever existed, or were invented for this juvenile attempt to discredit live cell analysis; we do know that his method would be tantamount to an attempt to discredit open heart surgery by citing the crimes of a back-alley abortionist. No one called us to verify whether we trained this person. We advise against doing live blood analysis at conventions where individuals would be tested without a history and physical examination. Furthermore, we give instructions that clean slides only be used as they come from their container and not previously used slides that are wiped off by alcohol or water. This can cause streaks. We do not want agents added to prevent dehydration or clotting. We are looking for clotting. Changes of pH can cause rouleaux or cause the red cells to stick together or vice versa. We do not want to alter temperature either. As with most medical or scientific tests, good technique is important.

On April 9, 1992, John H. Renner, M.D., testified in Washington before the House Small Business Subcommittee on Regulation. Renner is a member of the board of the National Council Against Health Fraud, run by William Jarvis. Live cell analysis is a "dubious medical device...using a microscope, T.V. projector, T.V. monitor, and an instruction book that can supposedly diagnose almost any illness known to mankind," he told the Subcommittee.

"I have heard practitioners say they saw 'diabetic cells,' 'arthritis cells,' and even an AIDS virus," he testified. "The first two do not exist, and it would take an electron microscope to see a virus. These people fabricate results. Ads run for these gadgets regularly in alternative medical magazines. This gadget generates $60,000 a year per practice."

I have used live cell analysis for some years, and have trained many other practitioners who use it. I have never heard one of them make the absurd statements Dr. Renner attributes to them. Renner's straw men need immediate medical attention. Could that be why he doesn't name names? I wish I had the time and money to fly to Washington to testify and correct Dr. Renner's quackery. I don't. By the way, John, how much does *your* practice generate a year?

All these examples prove that, for many years, Americans have been subjected to chronic medical brainwashing, in which so-called conventional practitioners lie and "anti-quackery" groups tell more lies. They give the term "reliable" a new meaning. Like the woodpecker, constant repetition takes an inevitable toll. If you ask for regular bread in a restaurant, you get white, bleached, refined bread. That presumably makes whole wheat irregular. Likewise, allopathic physicians are called regular doctors, even though what they prescribe is irregular, i.e., it has been around for only 30-50 years (via drugs); while nutrition therapy, which has been around in some form for thousands of years, is called, e.g., "alternative" therapy, or "a departure from the norm." Nutrition therapy is called vitamin quackery, but drug quackery is never called that.

Chapter Fifteen
Bedpan Dictators

Let's look at a book called *The Health Robbers* (Philadelphia, George F. Stickley, 1976), edited by our old pal Stephen Barrett, along with Gilda Knight, of the American Institute of Nutrition. On page 13, it says: "Most cancer patients can be cured if treated properly and in time. . . ." This means "prompt use of *proven* methods of surgery, radiation or chemotherapy." Really? Then why are so many cancer patients dead? Why do so many of them die of those "proven" methods long before they get to holistic doctors' offices?

The 1993 edition of *The Health Robbers* was published in Buffalo by Prometheus, and is edited by Barrett and Jarvis. On page 21, in a list of "misconceptions," they explain: ". . . In fact, the quacks often accuse the AMA of 'conspiring to destroy alternative medicine' even though it is minimally involved. For many years the AMA maintained a department that was active against many types of quackery. But in 1975 it was shut down, and so was the AMA's quackery committee. Quacks cry 'conspiracy' in an attempt to gain support by portraying themselves as underdogs. . . ." Well, who said A.M.A. was running a conspiracy? Wasn't it federal judge Susan Getzendanner? Of course, *Health Robbers* doesn't mention that. The closest it comes is this (p. 188): "In 1987, a federal court judge ruled that the American Medical Association

(AMA) had engaged in an illegal boycott. The AMA appealed, but was unsuccessful. . . ."

On page 406, there is a description of Dr. Privitera's conviction, imprisonment and probation under CABOMQUA. On page 409, the conviction is mentioned again. Remember, however, that all this was expunged, which for legal purposes means it never happened. To cover its gluteus maximus, *The Health Robbers* needs to get this mentioned very quickly, which it does on page 409 in a discussion of the alleged misdeeds of the National Health Federation: "After N.H.F. governor James Privitera, M.D., was charged with a laetrile-related offense, appeals in *Public Scrutiny* raised more than $5,000 to help defend him; and after he was convicted, N.H.F. generated more than 10,000 form letters asking California governor Jerry Brown to pardon him (which he did). . . ." So, now they've said it (in a parenthesis), they've covered their coccyxes, and they never have to mention it again.

On the subject of food processing they make this qualified admission on page 33: "It is true that food processing can change the nutrient content of foods. But the changes are not so drastic as the quack, who wants you to buy supplements, would like you to believe. . . ." It's true. We want you to buy supplements. Barrett, Jarvis & Company want you to buy quadruple bypass and other surgery, chemotherapy and radiation. These things are "approved."

On page 36, we learn that natural vitamins "are identical to those made in the factories of chemical companies."

Later, we are treated to this piece of information: "when sugar is used in moderation as part of a normal, balanced diet, it is a perfectly safe source of calories and eating pleasure. . . ."

The sugar industry no doubt is very happy to hear that. Go ahead and believe it, if you like, and I hope your pancreas holds out. Do the sugar industry and others reward such plugs? If so, how generously? We ask the questions only because the front men for totalitarian quackery constantly worry about how much money we make.

Certainly a good way to expose the mentality of these people who are desperately trying to deny your right to control your own body, would be to look at their conduct in the fluoridation debate. Here we have a form of supplementation that organized medicine fanatically supports.

Because some Americans want fluoridation, while others don't, fluoridation opponents have proposed a solution that the 1993 version of *The Health Robbers* describes as follows (page 300): "Suggesting alternatives is a common tactic. Here the antis propose that the community distribute free fluoride tablets to parents who wish to give them to their children. The suggested program sounds 'democratic,' but it will not be effective from a public health standpoint. Most parents are not motivated to administer the 4,000+ doses needed from birth through age twelve. . . ."

Here is proof that, generally, "democratic" means you do as the non-holistic M.D. says. If you don't, you are not democratic. If "most parents are not motivated," then fluoridation is not important to them--the allopaths admit it--in which case organized medicine says it is perfectly acceptable to force them to comply.

Indeed, on the next page (301), "The Tooth Robbers" says this: "The antis' most persuasive argument, both to legislators and to the general public, is to call for a public vote. On the surface, this appears to be the democratic way to settle the issue. But the antis are dealing from a stacked deck. First, the people who need fluoridation the most--the children--do not vote. Second, it is not difficult to confuse voters by flooding the community with scare propaganda. Average citizens do not have the educational background to sort out claim and counterclaim or to judge which 'authorities' to believe. . . ."

In other words, Big Brother Knows Best. Don't let the people vote. If they don't do what you want, force them to do it. As Franklin Roosevelt's top adviser, Harry Hopkins, put it: "The people are too damn dumb to understand."

"The Tooth Robbers" also undemocratically complains: ". . . If fluoridation wins a referendum, the usual anti response is to work for another one. . . ." Why is this wrong? Don't the totalitarians do exactly this all the time, when they lose?

Among the N.C.A.H.F. reprints Dr. Jarvis sent us was one from the January 1983 issue of *CDA Journal.* On page 64, psychiatrist Stephen Barrett tells fluoridationists this: ". . . Early in your campaign, you should visit newspaper editors to request that they investigate what is sent to them to find out who is lying and who isn't. Your approach should make it clear that many members of the community will admire a firm stand on the part of the newspaper. A meeting with an editor should be attended by several of the most prominent members of your organization, as well as the editor's dentist and personal physician. . . .

"Begin the meeting by stating that you need the paper's help. Ask whether the editor has any doubts about the safety and benefits of fluoridation, whether he or she has any suggestions for your campaign and whether the editor would like to join the citizens' committee. Then point out the nature of anti-fluoridation propaganda and ask whether antifluoridation letters can be followed by editor's notes explaining their fallacies. *Indicate that you realize your request is unusual, but that fluoridation controversies are sufficiently unique to warrant special handling by the media. . . .*" (italics added)

Yes, such a request would be unusual, precisely because it would be an outrageous attempt to manipulate the media. Imagine the self-righteous frenzy from Jarvis, Barrett and their fellow totalitarians, were the forces of medical freedom to attempt such a stunt.

Still in 1983, there were the Proceedings of "Fluoridation: Litigation & Changing Public Policy," a conference conducted at the University of Michigan in Ann Arbor, on August 9-10. Via N.C.A.H.F., Dr. Jarvis sent us his remarkable remarks at the conference, entitled "The Psychology of Antifluoridationism." Dr. Michael W. Easley introduced him at the conference, and said: ". . .

In addition to his major areas of study in health and physical education, he also majored in social studies and sociology. At the University of Oregon, where he earned his doctorate in health education, he specialized in consumer health. His dissertation topic was on chiropractic . . . . He has served as a key defense witness in the antitrust suit brought by chiropractors against 15 scientific medical organizations. . . ."

We knew that Dr. Jarvis is not a physician. Now we learn that one of his majors was gym. Did he specialize in push ups, pull ups or rope climb? He also majored in social studies, which are to genuine history as propaganda is to news; and sociology, the purpose of most of which is to justify collectivism. Notice also that he wrote his dissertation on chiropractic. Imagine winning a doctorate for attacking a healing art. Was the suit in which he was a "key defense witness" the one in which A.M.A. was nailed for running a conspiracy?

Dr. Jarvis begins his remarks as follows (p. 17): "The unifying theme which seems to tie together the exploiters, the promoters, and those who attack public health programs is this concept: that orthodoxy, i.e., science, cannot be trusted. . . ."

So Dr. Jarvis says science equals orthodoxy. Precisely the opposite is true: Science is *not* orthodoxy. Science is the willingness to accept newly discovered facts *in the face* of orthodoxy. That is why science so often *opposes* orthodoxy.

On the next page, Dr. Jarvis complains that "the swine flu immunization program took the brunt of the attack. . . ." Yes, it did, because it was mass medicine, administered without taking patient histories. It was quintessential quackery, later exposed as a deadly fiasco, replete with expensive lawsuits.

On page 19, physical education major Jarvis says that Hippocrates "gave the world the worst system of healing in history." We call him the Father of Medicine only "because he was able to get rid of the supernaturalism principle," says Dr. Jarvis. Hippocrates was of course the author of the Hippocratic Oath to which doctors have sworn allegiance for considerably more than 2,000 years.

On the same page, Dr. Jarvis says, ". . . The essence of antiscience is that the life force is supernatural . . . ." On page 21, he speaks with contempt of "the Hebrew unitary concept that man *is* a living soul. . . ."

At last we find out what Dr. Jarvis's problem is. He's an atheist.

Now, let's look at an issue of the *Journal of Public Health Dentistry.* This is N.C.A.H.F. reprint #298. In 45(3):133-141 (summer, 1985), a Dr. Easley, a dentist, is quoted as follows (page 139): "Fluoridation Referenda: an Exercise in Frustration. Referenda to initiate or retain fluoridation have been defeated more often than they have been won. Antifluoride groups use this trend to great advantage, routinely urging government officials to 'let the people decide.' Social scientists have conducted many studies to determine why fluoridation fares so poorly at the polls. Crain and colleagues analyzed a number of community decision-making variables and determined that the greater the citizen participation in public policy making, the greater the chance that the fluoridation issue would be handled by referenda. On the other hand, a more centralized community power structure (where decisions were most often made by mayors, health officers, or governing councils) yielded limited citizen involvement and resulted in an increased likelihood that fluoridation would be implemented."

As we have seen, that is what the totalitarians want. Would someone please tell us why the only group allowed to denounce the popular will in public and get away with it, time after time, is the fluoridation gang that lusts to impose mass medical treatment by force?

Chapter Sixteen
It Ducks Like a Quack

Since totalitarian medicine and its mouthpieces--groups like the National Council Against Health Fraud and its illegitimate siblings--have slyly, and sometimes blatantly, accused my colleagues and me of such horrific wrongdoing, the obvious questions arise: Does "mainstream" medicine ever do anything wrong? If so, do totalitarian front men like John Renner and Stephen Barrett expose it? If they do, we could at least praise their consistency, however wrongheaded. If they don't, we could logically suspect they are in somebody's pay.

Let's browse through the literature, and see what is happening in the "approved" consensus medicine they say is the antidote to the alternatives my colleagues and I offer. Here are just a few examples.

In *The New Republic* of August 3, 1992, Mark Hosenball writes in an article entitled "Arkansas Gothic," about Susie Deer, 17, who died on the operating table in the emergency room at Ouachita Memorial Hospital in Little Rock. It happened because nurse-anesthetist Virginia Dwire was incompetent and couldn't get a breathing tube down her throat. Hosenball says this wasn't the first time nurse Dwire had slipped up. Could this be one of the reasons?: ". . . The lawyers got her to admit that she often read the racing form and filed her nails while administering anesthesia. . . ."

Of course, I can't speak for any other doctor, but this breathtaking malpractice leaves me aghast. What kind of surgeons would allow nurse Dwire to perpetrate it "often?" Thank God her son was elected governor again and later President of the United States by default, which meant that he would have been embarrassed had his mother been forced to stand trial, and of course, "We can't do anything that would embarrass a young presidency."

In *Good Housekeeping* magazine, for October, 1992, in "A Hidden Epidemic," Paula Dranov tells the story of Muriel Simons, who entered Crouse Irving Memorial Hospital in Syracuse, New York, early in March of that year, to receive chemotherapy for lymphoma. She was dead three weeks later, because the hospital had given her "cisplatin, a drug similar to carboplatin--which her doctor had ordered--but much more powerful." Using the same guidelines the totalitarian front men apply to liberated medicine, I presume we now should call the people who killed Mrs. Simons in Crouse Irving "quacks." And of course we should apply the same guidelines, not just because it's fair, but because, as we have seen, the authoritarians routinely advocate consistent, double-blind studies. Consistency, they tell us, is the key. I should add, however, that, since my colleagues and I no longer practice medieval medicine, I probably would not have prescribed highly toxic immunosuppressive chemotherapy in the first place.

Paula Dranov also tells us that the mortal malpractice committed against Muriel Simons was by no means a fluke:

". . . Each year, the shocking tally amounts to an estimated 1.3 million medical injuries--15 percent of which result in long-term disability--and almost 200,000 deaths, according to Lucian L. Leape, M.D., of the Harvard School of Public Health in Boston."

Only in a major war--a world war--would the casualties be so great, but, without fission bombs or biological weapons, such a war would probably last several years. Remember that the carnage in the hospitals happens every year.

Along these lines, a *New York Times* dispatch from Chicago, printed on June 18, 1995, tells the story of Vincent Gargano, 41, a postal worker with a wife and three young children. On May 26, 1995, he entered the University of Chicago Hospitals for his third and final treatment for germ-cell cancer of the abdomen. He, too, was given cisplatin, which this time was not a mistake, except that, in filling out the prescription, a doctor reversed the dosages of cisplatin and another drug, with the result that for five days, Mr. Gargano received four times the dose of cisplatin he was supposed to get.

According to the Gargano family lawyer, Howard Schaffner, the overdose caused progressive hearing loss, kidney failure, a reduction of body calcium and festering sores, which we believe. There are dozens of people who should have caught that mistake. The whole system just fell apart, says Schaffner. A couple of weeks later, the victim died, another sacrifice on the altar of monopoly medicine. It is interesting to note that the hospital has withheld the identity of the doctor responsible, who is board-certified in oncology and internal medicine. It was a nurse, not a physician, who eventually detected his mistake. Of course, the family will sue.

The *New York Times* comments: "Mr. Gargano's death comes three months after the disclosure that two cancer patients at the Dana-Farber Cancer Institute in Boston had received accidental overdoses of anti-cancer drugs. One patient died and the other was left chronically debilitated."

So, here are three more cancer victims monopoly medicine cured. They no longer have cancer. Again, "approved" cancer therapy is extremely dangerous. Time and again, its cures include a ruined immune system and a panoply of degenerative symptoms. When the victim is hopeless, he finally sees a holistic doctor. Imagine monopoly medicine's outrage were holistic doctors to make such mistakes. They can't of course, because holistic therapies are not poison. Since one of their own was responsible, totalitarian medicine protects him and there is business as usual.

Now let's move along to the *Ladies' Home Journal* of March, 1993, and an article by Andrea Rock entitled "Hospitals: hazardous to your health." There we read the tragedy of Kathleen Gonzalez, 18, a patient, who called her mother from New York Hospital on September 12, 1991, to report that she couldn't breathe, "and they're not doing anything about it."

Her mother, Carmen, rushed to the hospital: "When I arrived, I asked the nurses to call her doctor, but they sent an intern fresh out of medical school who said Kathleen was just having an anxiety attack and didn't need any further medical attention." For more than six hours, Carmen unsuccessfully pleaded with the staff. "Some of them were even laughing at me, saying I was paranoid."

Kathleen died, little more than two weeks later. For five days, the nurses had given her a drug to which she was allergic. They also failed to detect "an alarmingly low level of oxygen in her bloodstream."

New York State Health Department investigators confirmed this. There are many experienced physicians even in a backward area like New York, any of whom could have determined what drugs Kathleen was allergic to, and the oxygen level in her bloodstream.

The fact that none of them was summoned presumably means that the butchers who killed Kathleen Gonzalez were quacks.

Andrea Rock writes that from September 1, 1989, through the end of January 1990, 68 patients at Detroit Receiving Hospital came down with a harmful bacterial infection. William Hall, M.D., chief of disease surveillance at the Michigan Department of Public Health, investigated. ". . . Eventually, Hall and other investigators recommended that the hospital reinforce infection-control standards like hand-washing and sterilization of respiratory equipment."

John Froggatt, M.D., hospital epidemiologist at Johns Hopkins Hospital, in Baltimore also warns: "Hand-washing between patients is the most important action that can be taken to cut down nosocomial infections." In English, that means hospital infections.

Can you believe this? We can't. We are living in the late twentieth century. In the nineteenth century, Dr. Ignaz Philipp Semmelweiss, a Hungarian obstetrician, was driven insane and rejected by a medical establishment refusing to believe his findings that you could sharply decrease deadly maternal childbirth fever in hospitals simply by having physicians wash their hands. Antiseptic practices, of course, eventually became a fundamental of good medicine . . . or so you would think. Yet we learn that modern medicine still doesn't wash its hands! This is the medicine that calls Dr. Privitera and his colleagues quacks!

Still another article in the *Ladies' Home Journal*, this one by Michael J. Weiss, entitled "Licensed to kill," in June, 1993, tells the Boris Karloff story of Los Angeles obstetrician Milos Klvana, who delivered Julie James's baby in his office, because he had lost his hospital privileges. ". . . Klvana tried to speed the birth by incorrectly administering a labor-inducing drug and instructing James' fiancé to push on her stomach. . . ." Rushed to the hospital, the baby girl died. Klvana actually urged the parents to keep her death secret and bury her body in their backyard.

Yes, the monster finally was convicted in 1989 of nine counts of murder, but he was allowed to kill so many for so long by the state licensing board, which took his word for what happened, while it was harassing Dr. Privitera. Medieval medicine is apparently alive and well in California and therefore shares complicity in this serial killer's crimes. Of course, the Klvana monster was just one of many. Laura Wittkin, executive director of the National Center for Patients' Rights, says this: "Too many medical boards are more interested in protecting the practitioner, not the public." Of course, everything depends on the type of practitioner he or she is. If he practices "consensus" allopathic medicine, he will usually be protected.

Now, let's browse through a book entitled *The Truth About Medical Malpractice*, by Ronald E. Gots, M.D., (Stein and Day,

New York, 1975). On page 10, he writes of malpractice "as fatal as an assailant's bullet" that cost a new mother her life.

On page 76, he describes how a cardiologist guided a catheter through a vein toward a young man's heart, and injected the dye to take the necessary pictures. His action dislodged a blood clot which traveled to the brain and caused a stroke. The young man was left with permanent, disabling weakness on the left side. The procedure that caused it was of course part of the orthodox cardiology that establishment medicine wants you to use instead of chelation. Remember, we are applying the same "peer review" to this tragedy that the opposition uses on us.

Another young man, this one a Cuban immigrant, had diabetes and a foot ulcer that became infected. Dr. Gots writes that "many physicians would have waited somewhat longer, for it was not an emergency, and there was an alternative form of therapy available," but the physician recommended surgery, and the young man was horrified when he awoke to find his leg missing. Because his English was poor, he hadn't understood that he was consenting to amputation. He won a malpractice suit (p. 80).

Why has malpractice become the latest epidemic? Dr. Gots explains that "recent social changes and advances in medical technology have eroded the doctor-patient relationship, and doctors are at least partially responsible. Relying more and more on complex technology, doctors have largely forgotten the art of medicine and of dealing with patients. At the same time they have fallen victim to an arrogance of power and prestige, which has infuriated a public just becoming aware of its rights as consumers."

Of course, this could be solved easily if monopoly medicine would just take enough time, but it won't. Dr. Gots says nothing about using any of the modern procedures discussed in this book--darkfield, chelation, live cell analysis, etc.--so I assume that he is not a "quack."

He writes that modern technology helped physicians drive themselves crazy (p. 17): ". . . They became inflexible in their approach to patients, believing themselves to be omniscient. They demanded blind compliance with their recommendations and complete acceptance of their advice. The prevalent feeling in the medical community was that patients, who had no understanding of the complexities of medicine, did not require explanations.

"Thus, modern skills added both a new dimension to medical practice and a sense of arrogance, elitism, and an inflated concept of the capabilities of medicine. The patient, as a person with needs, desires, and problems, as well as a disease, was forgotten. Patients' concerns, fears, and complaints became secondary to their chest X-rays and blood counts.

"Earlier physicians knew their limitations and therefore received complaints sympathetically even if they could detect no abnormalities. The expectations of modern physicians grew more rapidly than their diagnostic capabilities. Reliance on laboratory reports has become so firm that physicians succumb to the temptation of dismissing a complaint that cannot be explained by an X-ray finding or a blood abnormality."

Another book on the subject is *Medical Malpractice*, by Frank John Edwards, M.D., (Henry Holt, New York, 1989), also presumably not a quack. He writes that malpractice suits were a rarity 35 years ago, but "now there are thousands of malpractice suits each year, and tens of thousands of lawyers who do nothing but argue either for the patient or for the doctor. Suing physicians has become an industry. . . .

"Out of a hundred American physicians this year, eight to ten can expect to receive a suit. . . . Sixty-seven percent of all obstetrician/gynecologists have been sued at least once, and the rate is almost as high for neurosurgeons and orthopedists. . . ." (p. 13) Edwards says that many doctors, even many obstetricians, have stopped delivering babies. In some rural areas, women have to travel long distances to find doctors brave enough to do it. In America today, "physicians are more likely to wind up in court than are members of the underworld." (p. 160)

Remember that we're talking here about authoritarian medicine, the medicine the front men are desperately protecting by calling holistic doctors "quacks."

Let's look at another book. This one is called *Lethal Medicine: The Epidemic of Medical Malpractice in America*, by Harvey F. Wachsman, M.D., who is also an attorney, and Steven Alschuler (Henry Holt, New York, 1993).

Dr. Wachsman says he was introduced to medical malpractice early in his career as chief resident in neurosurgery. He saved a child after operating all night, but an anesthesiologist killed him with too much blood (p. xii). On another occasion, he found three patients dead in their beds on a single day, but no one knew how long they had been dead, why they were dead or anything else about them (p. xiii).

Lethal Medicine is a parade of horror that would be envied by Heinrich Himmler. There is Andy Phillips, who went to the emergency room with a stomach ache and wound up with permanent brain damage, which cost him his job, home and wife (p. 3). There is Harold Schneider, crippled for life when the doctors couldn't diagnose a compressed fracture of the vertebrae and a calcified disk--because they wouldn't take X-rays until *ten months* after his automobile accident (pp. 20-21). There is Ann Richards, whose baby was born "irreparably brain-damaged and quadriplegic," because of a doctor who refused to come to the hospital (p. 28). These are just a few examples. Dr. Wachsman would be cross with us if we reprinted his fine book.

Of course, cancer is the disease the Establishment doctors are most jealous of. They consider it their private province. Any doctor who dares to treat cancer must do so exactly as they say, or risk jail. Dr. Wachsman tells us this: ". . . Errors in clinical diagnosis are made in as many as 40 percent of the cases in which cancer patients ultimately die, and mistakes are often made in treating even the most common forms of cancer . . . ." (p. 34)

That's right! In 2 of 5 fatal cases, the diagnosis is wrong. Because of such mistakes, the cancer may have grown and metastasized to the point at which survival is unlikely or impossible. Of course, sometimes such fatal delays are the patient's fault. However, ". . . Many patients undergo examinations during which the physicians have an opportunity to recognize a cancer in its early stage. But either through negligence or incompetence, they fail to note what could be a serious problem. . . ." (p. 35) Wachsman speaks of an insurance company study of malpractice lawsuits in cancer treatment by authors Michael Mittleman and Charles Scholhamer, who report that an incredible 75 percent of the cases involved "an allegation of delay in diagnosis."

One of the hoariest charges the opposition makes against holistic doctors says that cancer patients who come to us waste valuable time, during which early diagnosis could save them. Here we see that as usual this quack charge is a fraud. It is the "cancer specialists" who delay nutritional and immunological treatment in victim after victim, wasting precious time during which the victim could have seen a doctor who offers an alternative to radiation, chemotherapy and surgery. Frequently, when the patient finally does decide to try holistic medicine, he or she has already been discarded by totalitarian medicine, and is so ravaged by its therapy that the prognosis is grim.

Wachsman quotes *Cecil's Textbook of Medicine*, which says "the patient's observations must not be dismissed because they do not happen to fit the pattern of a disease process the physician is entertaining. What a patient says is to be believed and to be understood to the best of the physician's ability. Thus, if a woman tells her physician that she has noted a breast lump, but he is not impressed because of extensive multiple lumps of cystic mastitis, nevertheless, if she has noted one lump above all others, the observation must be believed and acted upon. . . ." (p. 35)

So, according to Dr. Wachsman and *Cecil's*, the mainstream doctors are not always scientific. They contemptuously say the patient's observations aren't proof. No wonder juries nail them for making so many blunders. Wachsman writes: ". . . When a delay in diagnosis or treatment of a treatable cancer occurs because of physician failure to conduct a proper examination or to recognize the seriousness of what the examination reveals, the doctor's actions could be considered the equivalent of sentencing the patient to death."

One patient sentenced to death was Sheila Howard, 42, an executive. She told Dr. Ralph Hawkins she had found a small lump in her breast. He didn't recommend a mammogram, didn't recommend a biopsy, told her it was probably nothing and sent her home, with instructions to see him nine months later. She left in relief, but by the time she returned, she was riddled with cancer and died soon afterward. Wearing his attorney's hat, Dr. Wachsman sued. Hawkins's insurance company agreed to pay Miss Howard's family $1.5 million. Dr. Hawkins kept practicing medicine. His patients never learned anything about the incident (pp. 36-37).

Dr. Wachsman says physicians ignore colon cancer every day, prescribing creams and suppositories for rectal bleeding and iron pills for "tired blood," rather than taking the trouble to investigate. They ignore postmenopausal blood discharges, prescribe lotions and send the patient home to die. They install chest X-ray machinery in their offices. "There's only one problem. A lot of the doctors doing chest X-rays don't know how to read and accurately evaluate the results. Presumably, they are either too arrogant or too cost-conscious to have the X-rays reviewed by a trained radiologist." (p. 38)

Along these lines we saw an article entitled "Why didn't my doctors listen to me?" in the April, 1992, issue of *Good Housekeeping* (p. 103 cf.). In it author Jean L. Block tells the story of Angela Farnum. At Kaiser Permanente, an HMO in southern California, doctors denied Angela a mammogram for five years, despite her pleas. When they finally yielded, she turned up with metastatic breast cancer. Kaiser Permanente settled for a total payout of $800,000. Again, one of the most unfortunate aspects of the type of medicine offered by health maintenance organizations is that it wastes precious time, during which the patient's nutritional therapy is often delayed by treatments that don't enhance his or her immunity.

Now, let's look at what establishment medicine says you should be doing for heart problems instead of trying holistic treatment. Sophie Gross, 71, a victim of osteoporosis, complained to her doctor of pain in her legs when she walked. Her HMO assigned her to Dr. Emil Rani, a vascular surgeon, who diagnosed obstructions to the blood flow and prescribed surgery. Admitted to the hospital, she underwent an angiogram to locate the blockages. Doctors sent her home, despite considerable bleeding from the groin.

A few days later, Dr. Rani saw Mrs. Gross, expressed surprise at the bleeding and bruising, and said she should never have an angiogram in the same hospital again. He then admitted her to the same hospital for surgery to remove the clots. When she awoke the next day, she couldn't feel or move her legs. Almost a full day passed before doctors did a myelogram and found a blood clot causing pressure on her spinal cord. Mrs. Gross needed immediate, emergency surgery, but the hospital lacked the facilities to do it. Nearby was a hospital that could, but her HMO shipped her to another HMO hospital, thereby saving considerable money, which took another four hours. She had now been lying paralyzed in bed for 28 hours.

At the second hospital, doctors did an MRI and a CAT scan, and located the clot. Had they done all this sooner, and removed the clot surgically, Mrs. Gross would have had a good chance to recover. Now, with the passage of so much time, they believed that too much damage had been done and that surgery would be counterproductive. She would be paralyzed, they said, for the rest of her life.

By now, you are probably thinking there wasn't much more that "organized" medicine could do to Mrs. Gross; but you are wrong. She was carted back to the original hospital, where she developed bedsores on her legs. Dr. Wachsman points out rightly that there is only one reason for bedsores: neglect. The bedsores became infected. Doctors eventually amputated almost the entire left leg. She also contracted pneumonia and sustained a collapsed lung. (Pp. 40-42)

None of this incredible malpractice--not any of it--was necessary. Dr. Wachsman agrees the surgery should not have been performed. Before it, she was able to walk up to ten blocks. Of course there is now no way of knowing, but had Mrs. Gross gone to a holistic physician, it is likely that he could have improved her circulation with none of these monstrous side effects.

Dr. Wachsman also writes about Dr. Duc Kwan, chief of surgery, who made the cast on a broken wrist too tight, with the result that the victim, 17, lost almost his entire arm to gangrene (pp. 45-57). Rotting pieces of it fell off in a hospital whirlpool, which Dr. Kwan wrongly prescribed after the horrendous, original malpractice.

There is also Dr. James Burt, an ob/gyn at St. Elizabeth Medical Center in Dayton, Ohio, who specialized in circumcising clitorises without their owners' knowledge or permission, thereby mutilating thousands of women (p. 106 cf.). The deformed victims suffered years of torment. Many doctors knew what this monster was doing--they even made jokes about it--but they were "good Germans" and said nothing. Indeed, Burt served four years on the hospital's quality assurance committee, while he was indulging his psychopathic whim.

Some orthodox physicians who complain about holistic doctors paint themselves as selfless humanitarians a little lower than the angels--an impressive responsibility. Let's look at them in fact.

On page 120 of *Lethal Medicine*, Dr. Wachsman says this: ". . . A 1987 study by Rush-Presbyterian St. Luke's Medical Center in Chicago of a midwestern medical school found that nearly 20 percent of the students had drug or alcohol problems. In a 1989 study published in the *Journal of the American Medical Association*, more than half the members of a third-year medical school class said that they had personally observed classmates abusing alcohol or drugs."

For instance, Stewart and Cyril Marcus were twins and prominent New York gynecologists, practicing at a major hospital. Both of them were addicted to barbiturates. Soon after they were finally exposed, they were found dead in their apartment, one from withdrawal, the other from an overdose.

Yet, after more than 30 years as a doctor, Wachsman doesn't know of one patient who was told that his doctor had a drinking problem. Addiction to other drugs is also concealed. *Modern Healthcare* of July 29, 1991, says that "some operating rooms are staffed with anesthesiologists or anesthesia-related technicians or nurses who are addicted to one of the many potent narcotics readily available to them."

What happens when one of these dangerous junkies is found out? They lie, of course. It's called "peer review." Dr. Wachsman writes about the Cochrane family, whose newborn baby's arms were crippled for life by the doctors during delivery. The Cochranes began to suspect that the doctors had not told them the truth.

"But when they, and later we, questioned the individuals involved--two obstetricians, a pediatrician, and a total of ten nurses who had been involved in the case from labor through pediatrics--they all lied about it. Each swore under oath that nothing unusual had happened during the delivery, that the baby had been normal at birth. The pediatrician testified at trial that during those three months she had treated the child, she had seen nothing wrong. Then she went a step further, suggesting that the cause of the damage to the child must have been parental abuse that had occurred after the Cochranes moved back to Georgia" (p. 141).

The liars didn't know that Mr. Cochrane had taken pictures of mother and child in the hospital. One picture showed the infant, its arms hanging limp. Behind the child you saw a telephone on the stand. Wachsman enlarged the photograph, which showed the hospital's telephone number on the phone. The liars' insurance company settled. Those responsible suffered no penalty. No one knew what they had done. Presumably, they are still maiming and lying, with the licensed blessing of the state.

Remember Dr. Duc Kwan, whose incredible incompetence caused the loss of that teenager's arm? After the disaster, Kwan changed the medical records. Now the records said he had removed the cast much earlier.

"Unfortunately for Dr. Kwan, he was about as skillful a forger as he was a doctor. Rather than destroying the original records and writing out an entirely new version, he tried to erase certain sections and write over them. But his extensive erasures wore through the paper, so he typed up new versions of certain sections on separate pieces of paper, cut them out, and pasted them on top of the handwritten originals. But he did it so sloppily that some of his previous handwritten comments were still visible around the edges of the pasted-on typewritten sections. . . ." (p. 142)

In an earlier chapter, you saw how a liberated physician treats lupus. So, now, let's see how orthodox medicine treats it. In 1988, Harriet Hamlin, a lupus patient, complained to family doctor Sam Lipkin of having difficulty walking. For seven months the situation worsened until she could hardly walk at all. Dr. Lipkin's diagnosis was a blood disorder related to her lupus; he put her in the hospital for transfusions. Later, out of the hospital, she began seeing a hematologist, Dr. Raymond Polonavitz, every other week. During the next two months her right foot turned blue, and she began feeling tingling, numbness and pain in her left foot. In January, 1989, Polonavitz referred the patient to a surgeon, Dr. Richard Vassal, who wrote Polonavitz that he didn't believe Miss Hamlin's problem had anything to do with lupus, but was caused by emboli--blood clots. Vassal recommended tests to see whether they existed. Polonavitz never told Miss Hamlin anything about this.

In February, 1989, more than a year after Miss Hamlin began complaining to Dr. Lipkin, and four months after she first met Dr. Polonavitz, she finally went to the emergency room. There was no pulse in her lower legs, her feet were white, and her toes were blue.

The tests Dr. Vassal had recommended were finally performed, and showed blockages in both legs. But too much time had been wasted. Repeated surgery could not restore the lady's circulation. A week later, both of her legs--now gangrenous--were amputated below the knee.

"A succession of doctors, each relying on mistaken diagnoses, had allowed Ms. Hamlin's legs to be slowly destroyed over a period of thirteen months. She followed their medical advice to the letter. She went for her regular schedule of examinations, and when they mistakenly attributed her vascular problems to a blood disorder, she went to the hospital for her transfusions. During all this time no one thought that a middle-aged patient, complaining of pain and numbness in her toes, might have a circulatory problem--might have blocked blood vessels that need to be cleared or repaired--even though she had been suffering for seventeen years with a disease, lupus, that sometimes causes precisely that type of problem. . . ." (Pp. 178-80)

Darkfield microscopy should have been used here to evaluate for "potential clotting." Instead, Dr. Privitera had to spend about $200,000 defending the use of this excellent, scientific tool. The darkfield test is done on all Dr. Privitera's new patients.

The wreckage of orthodox medicine litters the fields of debate. Remember the swine flu "emergency?" Everyone had to be inoculated by the government, now, if not sooner. Of course, we knew that such mass government medicine was a mistake, and, sure enough, later came the lawsuits that testified to the fiasco. Remember radical mastectomy, absolutely and positively the "only" approved procedure for malignant breast tumor? Now it turns out that in many cases lumpectomy works just as well; it wasn't necessary to mutilate so many sublime women.* Remember

---

* One wonders whether any surgery for breast cancer extends life, since, as reported at the Sixth National Cancer Conference in the late sixties: "The thirty year monotonous plateau of the death rate for breast cancer has persisted despite physicians' awareness of breast cancer, refinements of methods of inspecting and palpating the breast, educating women in self-examination, improvements

breast implants? Despite their certain knowledge of the dangers, plastic surgeons installed them in thousands of women, leading to a gargantuan malpractice payoff of billions.

Prostate cancer is the malignancy most often diagnosed in American men. Radical prostatectomy (removal) is the main treatment surgeons inflict. Between 1984 and 1990, it exploded almost six fold among Medicare patients over 65. It causes incontinence about 50% of the time--which means your patient must wear diapers--and impotence 90% of the time. There are heart complications.

The good news is that you live longer with such radical surgery. Men between 65 and 70 who do absolutely nothing about their prostate cancers average 14.1 more years of life; men who choose removal average 14.2 years; men who choose radiation average 14.3 years. So, you could live an extra 1.2 months, but to get there you have to choose diapers over dalliance for 14 years. In fact, prostate cancer usually grows very slowly, so you would probably die of other causes before it kills you.

Now comes Dr. John Wasson, who states in an article in the *Journal of the American Medical Association*, "We have, in essence, an epidemic of treatment and no scientific proof that it's valid."

Does this amazing horror take your breath away, as it does mine? Here we have an epidemic, not of disease, but of treatment, an epidemic in which surgeons are mutilating thousands of men a year, with no scientific proof that what they are doing is beneficial. Isn't this a good definition of quackery? You will find this shocking revelation in none other than the *Journal of the American Medical Association* (May, 1993). Good medicine would do something so drastic only in the face of an immediate life-threatening emergency. Indeed, the horror is compounded by the

---

in radiotherapy that include supervoltage, use of more extensive surgical procedures, and the use of chemotherapy and hormones. . . ." (*Cancer: A New Breakthrough*, J.B. Lippincott Company, July, 1970, p. 188)

fact that there are non-invasive therapies that have controlled prostate cancer. So, here we have still another example of assembly-line medicine wasting precious time, during which sensible treatment could perhaps have helped the patient.

In short, American medicine is a minefield, riddled with quacks and incompetents. The chance of them killing or maiming you--maybe costing you your job, your spouse and family--is great. Malpractice/quackery is epidemic. What do totalitarian front groups like the National Council Against Health Fraud say about it?

The answer, with a few exceptions, is nothing, not a word, beyond a few obligatory ho-hums. Perusal of their publications shows that they devote the lion's share of their pathological effort to an attempt to put doctors who disagree with them out of business. This fatal omission, this abysmal failure to fight true quackery, this total war against doctors whose malpractice is infinitesimal in comparison, proves that the front groups certainly do not oppose quackery. On the contrary, they protect it, support it, excuse it, encourage it--as we have seen--with the result that the quacks enjoy their would-be monopoly fees, and the drug pushers their would-be monopoly sales, in relative safety. Again, if monopoly medicine worked as well as it claims, patients would not go to holistic doctors. People voluntarily go to them, because holistic therapy often works after monopoly medicine has failed.

Do we recommend that patients stop seeing orthodox doctors? Not at all! Despite the present epidemic of lethal medicine--and despite the fact that the average doctor knows only a tad more about nutrition than does Hillary Clinton--it is also a fact that the overall American accomplishments in surgery, in orthopedics, in trauma, in ophthalmology, etc., represent great advances in modern medicine.

So, what we suggest is that, if you have a difficulty that a practitioner in one of those specialties could help, by all means go to him, if you can establish that he is not a quack. If, on the contrary, you have a chronic, systemic degenerative disease, go to the people who specialize in it, who are not fronts for the pharmaceutical detail men, and who know what they are talking about. Again, this is not to say there is no place for drugs. Drugs should be used last or for emergencies. For our part, we don't need collusion and government interference to compete. In the battle we are talking about, man and synthetics are making war against God and nature, and the latter shall win.

Epilogue

A long time ago, as a new, naive doctor, Jim Privitera believed that competition in the medical economy would determine which treatments succeed. Doctors would use the therapies that work; discard the therapies that don't. The only measure would be the patient. Of course, the doctor has long since realized how egregiously old-fashioned he was. Since then, he has seen "organized" medicine inflict therapies as hopeless and bizarre, as antiquated, as the bleeding that killed Washington, and the surgery that killed Garfield.

Meanwhile, harmless, but helpful, non-invasive tools like darkfield technology, hair mineral analysis and chelation, are savagely assaulted by orthodox medicine and its front groups, as threats to its monopoly and fees. The medical monopolists don't want competition, they want war.

The question arises: Wouldn't the free market medical marketplace we want, in which doctors compete for patients, and the only measurement of success is the patient's health, nevertheless open the door to fraud? Yes, in fact it is a certainty that, despite our best efforts, some patients will be hornswoggled. Freedom is dangerous. But it is less dangerous than the system monopoly medicine wants, in which medical fraud is given *the power of government*. The question isn't whether there is fraud.

There will always be fraud, until the Lord Himself--the greatest physician-- puts a stop to this farce. The question is: what's the best way to contain it? Monopoly medicine's paternalistic "solution" to fraud is to destroy everyone's rights.

However, the solution to fraud isn't dictatorship, but information. Yet, as we have seen, the quacks shrink from the trials of debate. They don't want to compete for your votes. They want totalitarianism. They want the government to force you to take their therapy, or else. If they get their way, the government will control medicine completely, which would mean the usual shortages, interminable waiting for treatment and no choice of doctor.

So, here and now, we declare total war on the quacks. Henceforth, we shall expose the connections and money between them, the proof that their front men are nothing more than that, the quackery they commit, the horrors they conceal, the monopoly-for-profit they conduct. We shall fight them on the talk shows, on television, in print and in the journals. We shall fight them in the courts. We shall fight them everywhere.

We can no longer be passive. They are aggressive. They attack. We must do the same. Since they refuse any middle ground; since they insist on unconditional surrender in which the losing side is completely erased, we say so be it. If you believe in freedom of choice in medicine, if you believe that patients have the unalienable right to control their own bodies and to have all the facts, if you favor medical integrity and oppose medical quackery, get in touch with the National Council For Improved Health, whose Health Freedom Legislative Advocate is the formidable Clinton Ray Miller. Mr. Miller used to do the same thing for the National Health Federation, which we also recommend, and for many years has successfully stood in the breach like Horatius for true medical freedom of choice.

You will find N.C.I.H. at Box 528, Gainesville, Virginia, 22065, telephone: (703) 754-0228; fax: (703) 754-4324. You can find Clinton Ray Miller at 1555 W. Seminole Street, San Marcos,

California, 92069. telephone: (619) 471-5090; fax: (619) 744-9364.

N.H.F. is of course the venerable National Health Federation. Its address is P.O. Box 688, Monrovia, California, 91017, telephone: (818) 357-2181.

Another outfit well worth your time is the American Preventive Medical Association, whose Directors Report, dated February 5, 1995, shows what can be done:

> "We Did It! California Medical Board Decides Not To Decide: On Saturday, Feb. 4 the State Medical Board of California voted down several motions that would have either prohibited the use of EDTA chelation therapy for cardiovascular disease or severely limited its use. Instead, the Board voted only to refer the matter to committee for the possible formulation of regulations. Round Two goes to us. This is an important victory that occurred only because A.P.M.A. and A.C.A.M. rallied doctors and patients around the state to turn back what would have been a precedent-setting action by the Medical Board.
>
> "In a stunning turn-around from the scenario at its November meeting, the Board decided not to pursue Assistant Attorney General Bell's request that they recommend state legislation outlawing the use of chelation for the treatment of cardiovascular disease. They also defeated a motion to limit EDTA chelation's off-label use to the treatment of vascular disease; defeated a motion to limit its use to that described on the package insert; and split 9-9 on a motion to take no action at all. A hearing room packed with an estimated 100 patients and at least twelve doctors from California heard testimony from A.P.M.A. directors Terry Chappell, M.D., and Ralph Miranda, M.D., along with cardiologist and former A.C.A.M. president H.R. Casdorph, M.D., Ph.D. A.C.A.M. attorney Gregory Seeley rebutted testimony by oncologist Wallis Sampson, M.D., and notorious (self-appointed) quack-buster

John Renner, M.D. The board also heard dramatic testimony from A.P.M.A.-member, cardiologist Ralph Lev, M.D., and nearly 20 patients.

"Since November, when we first learned of the Assistant AG's effort to rally support from the Board for outlawing off-label uses of chelation, A.C.A.M. and A.P.M.A. have worked to gather information, prepare testimony, mobilize grassroots participation and generate press coverage of the situation. Greg Seeley coordinated the legal and scientific efforts, while A.P.M.A. contacted nearly 20 organizations to solicit their support. Frank Cuny, Coordinator of the California Chapter of Citizens For Health was of great assistance in alerting Citizens For Health and A.P.M.A. members around the state. Other organizations such as the American Academy of Environmental Medicine, the American and International Boards of Chelation Therapy, the International Academy of Nutritional and Preventive Medicine, and the Great Lakes Association for Clinical Medicine wrote letters to the Board, and motivated dozens of their members to do so as well. The result was an outpouring of support from patients, doctors and supplement companies that helped convince the board that legislation was not the way to go.

"In addition, press releases were sent to every media outlet in California. Channel 9 (TV) unfortunately backed off its original plans to cover the meeting, saying that they couldn't find any patients to complain about chelation! . . .

"Let's not delude ourselves into thinking the battle is over in California. Plenty of people would still like to see anti-chelation legislation introduced, so we will have to keep a trained eye on health committee activities in the legislature there. We will also keep a close watch on the Board's future activities with regard to chelation, and notify everyone if and when hearings are held. In addition, because we really need to focus on the big picture, we will also be working with a broad-based coalition that Cuny is organizing to pass access legislation in that state. Such a bill would prevent this kind of challenge by the Medical Board from occurring in the future and, hopefully, preclude the need to undertake these therapy-by-therapy protection battles."

The American Preventive Medical Association (A.P.M.A.) is located at 459 Walker Road, Great Falls, VA 22066; telephone: (800) 230-2762; fax: (703) 759-6711.

The American College for Advancement in Medicine (A.C.A.M.) is located at 23121 Verdugo Dr., Suite 204, Laguna Hills, CA 92653; telephone: (800) 532-3688.

Appendix A
Why F. D.A. Must Be Abolished

William H. Moore, Jr. is an attorney at law in Savannah, Georgia. What follows is a letter he wrote on March 22, 1995, to Congressman Jack Kingston, in Washington. Your authors are so impressed with it, we include it here, with Mr. Moore's permission.

* * *

When tyranny overtakes America and destroys freedom, it will not be an invasion of foreign troops; it will be through our own government bureaucracy, and that has been occurring with alarming frequency lately--nowhere more than in the FDA.

This has become a criminally corrupt organization under the leadership of David Kessler, who aspires to become America's first Medical Führer. He has already put into place a Fedstapo of FDA Storm Troopers which should be dismantled immediately and irrevocably by Congress--which should, as a matter of fact, dismantle the entire agency as a good idea which went badly wrong, and a mistake our Nation should never repeat. Most of what the agency does could be done much better, at far less cost, by a private sector industry organization much like the Underwriters Laboratory.

The FDA was created to make sure that food, drugs and cosmetics were safe, pure and sanitary. The agency was small but efficient enough; what went wrong was the typical, indeed, irreversible lust of bureaucrats to expand their jurisdiction and meddle into the lives of the citizenry and, by 1962, the agency inveigled a complacent Congress into passing the efficacy requirement for drugs which has been, since its inception, the royal road to disaster for America. Efficacy has nothing to do with safety, purity and sanitation and, indeed, efficacy is and always will be a matter of viewpoint and opinion, unlike safety, purity and sanitation, which are absolutes.

Under the guise of efficacy, the agency has forgotten its safety mandate, driven the cost of drugs and devices to an incredible cost, destroyed the ability of American device manufacturers to compete in international markets and, incredibly, attempted to take over the control of medical practice, over which it was never intended to have any jurisdiction. It has been shot through with corruption, inefficiency and all the other evils of rampant bureaucracy. At this time the FDA has approved several drugs which are unsafe, such as Prozac® (Fluoxetine Hydrochloride) and some common antihistamines which accelerate cancer growth, along with Tylenol® (Acetaminophen) and Advil® (Ibuprofen), which cause end-stage kidney failure and liver damage and although these effects are well known, the FDA has taken no action. In the meanwhile, it has kept off the market many safe drugs and devices while it dawdles its way through efficacy determinations and expends gigantic sums of money harassing people who manufacture, sell or use vitamins, minerals and herbs which are absolutely safe, or seizing large shipments of wholesome orange juice because *Obersturmbannfuhrer* von Kessler didn't like the label.

I and a large number of other Americans feel that the imposition of the efficacy requirement (21 USC 355(d)(5)) in addition to the safety requirement (21 USC 355(d)(1)), was a mistake and one which should be rectified by the repeal of 21 USC .355(d)(5) and the amendment of 21 USC .355(d)(1) to include much more expansive pre-marketing toxicity testing along the lines recommended in the United States General Accounting Office Report (B-235044-GAO PEMD 90 15 FDA Drug Review Postapproval Risks 1976-86), which found severe post-approval risks including heart failure, myocardial infarction, anaphylaxis, respiratory depression and arrest, convulsions, seizures, kidney and liver failure, severe blood disorders, birth defects and fetal toxicity and blindness to have occurred in more than 50% of drugs approved by FDA between 1976 and 1985. The crux of the argument is that where a drug is safe and non-toxic, and a person suffering from a disease wishes to use it, with full knowledge that its effectiveness has not been proven or even is believed by many to be ineffective, the government's intrusion into the individual's choice of treatment is grossly paternalistic and a denial of the individual's right to decide for him or her self.

Approximately one half of Americans now use unorthodox medical services routinely for all or some part of their health care and many Americans have little faith in the Orthodox (allopathic) approach to chronic degenerative diseases such as cancer. This loss of faith is based on the experience of the past 30 years as to the ineffectiveness, toxicity and high cost of FDA approved chemotherapy and now fairly inexpensive demonstration that unorthodox cancer remedies not approved by FDA are frequently effective, produce no side effects and have a far more reasonable cost.

The general belief prevalent in 1962 that allopathic medical treatments were or soon would be universally effective for the treatment of diseases has not stood the test of time, and now, thirty-three years later, is tattered, torn and stained by the failure of allopathic medicine to find acceptable treatments for cancer, arthritis, diabetes, or many other chronic diseases as well as the unacceptable rate of long term harm from the chronic ingestion of drugs approved by the FDA as well as the increasing failure of antibiotics to control infections. The myth of allopathic infallibility has been shown to be precisely that--a myth--nearly half of American citizens now look elsewhere for treatment of chronic diseases--to nutritional, herbal, oriental and homeopathic practitioners to an extent undreamt of in 1962.

In **Regulating the Prescribing of Human Drugs for Non Approved Uses Under the Food, Drug, and Cosmetic Act**, *Harvard Journal on Legislation*, vol. 15:4, pages 708 and 709, Commissioner Kessler stated:

". . . Regulating the uses for which drugs are prescribed is far different from regulating the availability of new drugs. The regulation of uses would broaden the reach of the FDA and would have an added effect on the clinical decisions reached by patient and physician. Under such an expanded role, the FDA would regulate not only 127 drug manufacturers, but also 375,000 physicians. . . ."

This is precisely what Kessler is doing.

Much of the cost of pharmaceuticals is directly attributable to the inordinately high cost of compliance with the efficacy requirements of the 1962 amendments, some three to four hundred million dollars per individual use approval by the FDA--which can amount to several billion dollars a year passed on to consumers as well as two to three billion dollars in expenditures of tax funds for the activity (this year the FDA is requesting an additional $850,000,000 to acquire a new building). These are unnecessary expenses to accomplish governmental purposes which many of us view as inimical to our best interests and to our personal freedoms and liberties as well.

I urge you to initiate, co-sponsor and support legislation to dismantle the rampant out-of-control bureaucracy of the FDA and replace its functions with private sector voluntary testing like the Underwriters laboratory and transfer the FDA's food inspection function to the Department of Agriculture where it has always belonged.

In a recent *New England Journal of Medicine* article (vol. 325:217-220, 1991) entitled **Problems With The FDA**, John K. Inglehart states:

". . .The FDA is charged with regulating products from 90,000 companies that account for 25 cents of every dollar spent by the American consumer--more than $550 billion. Besides regulating the safety and efficacy of new drugs and safeguarding the food supply, the FDA is responsible for a wide array of products affecting all areas of modern life, from the nation's blood supply to vaccines, feed and drugs for animals, cosmetics, medical devices, and microwave ovens.

"As this list of responsibilities suggests, the FDA represents a collection of regulatory authorities thrown together over the years as the consequence of historical accident, legislative fiat, and bureaucratic reorganization. . . ."

This combined with the Commissioner's personal reinforcement and allopathic medical philosophies may be at the root of some of the problems. The efficacy of pharmaceuticals as well as herbs, vitamins and mineral supplements and other nutrients is best left to the consumer and the consumer's advisors of choice--physicians and other health care practitioners. If unwise decisions result and some is wasted, the amount wasted cannot approach in magnitude the present and future costs of the type of regulation we now have under the FDA as it presently exists and operates and at least if Americans make an occasional unwise purchasing decision, it is their decision, not that of an ever expanding bureaucracy. Efficacy, like usefulness of products, is a factor in marketing and purchasing most products--if the products result in consumer satisfaction, they will survive in the market--if they do not, they will disappear from the market. The social costs of Big Brotherism, Lysenkoism and bureaucratic inefficiency should be considered as well as the fiscal costs.

1. The Safety and Efficacy Requirements

The Safety Requirement in FDA premarket approval of drugs is set forth in 21 USC 355 (d) (1), and the Efficacy Requirement is set forth in 21 USC 355(d)(5). These two requirements are separate and distinct and have different purposes. The Safety Requirement comes from the 1938 F.D. & C. Act and it was enacted in response to an incident in which Eli Lilly & Co. marketed an elixir of Sulfonamide, in a base composed of diethylene glycol--now a commonly used antifreeze, which is extremely toxic. There had been no toxicity testing of the substance which was selected by a chemist because it had a sweetish taste.

In the aftermath of this disaster, Congress enacted the 1938 Food, Drug & Cosmetic Act which first set forth the safety requirement. The Efficacy Requirement was enacted as a part of the 1962 Amendment to the 1938 Food, Drug and Cosmetic Act, which was enacted as a consequence of the narrowly averted Thalidomide Disaster and, oddly enough, that was a pure safety issue and did not involve efficacy at all, but the efficacy requirement was included as a part of an overall program to strengthen the enforcement structure of the FDA with regard to drugs.

Much of the current problem between Commissioner Kessler and a large segment of the American public arises from the inclusion in the 1962 Amendment to the Food, Drug and Cosmetic Act of the so called efficacy requirement to the 1938 Act. The pertinent portion of that Amendment reads:

21 USC 355 (d)

"(d) If the secretary finds, after due notice to the applicant in accordance with subsection(c) of this section and giving him the opportunity for a hearing, in accordance with said subsection, that . . . or (5) evaluated on the basis of the information submitted to him as part of the application and any other information before him with such respect to such drug, there is a lack of substantial evidence that the drug will have the effect it purports or is represented to have under the conditions of use prescribed, recommended, or suggested in the proposed labeling thereof: . . . he shall issue an order refusing to approve the application. . . ."

Substantial evidence, as used in 21 USC 355 (d) & (e) (1962) means: "Evidence consisting of adequate and well-controlled investigations, including clinical investigations, by experts qualified by scientific training and experience to evaluate the effectiveness of the drug involved, on the basis of which it could fairly and responsibly be concluded by such experts that the drug will have the effect it purports or is represented to have under the conditions of use prescribed, recommended, or suggested in the labeling or proposed labeling thereof."

Our complaint about safety testing and the FDA approval process is that there is not enough safety testing, and that quite frequently unsafe drugs get through the approval process, i.e., Zomax, Oraflex, etc.

Efficacy, like beauty, ofttimes lies in the eye of the beholder, and certainly is influenced by the medical philosophy of the person who chooses a particular product for a particular purpose. There is no universally acceptable yardstick by which the concept of efficacy can be equitably measured in our country.

Our complaint is that the efficacy requirement has come vastly to overshadow the safety requirement, and it is the efficacy requirement which slows the drug approval process and adds an incredible 2 to 3 hundred million dollars to the cost of approving each use for which an IND is submitted. Safety testing, even more exhaustive safety testing than is now required, could not cost more than 5% of this cost.

Since the 1962 Amendment the efficacy requirement has skewed the drug approval process and has been the basis of widespread anti-competitive activity engaged in by the FDA and the Pharmaceutical Advertising Council. A prime example of lack of attention to safety and overemphasis on efficacy is to be seen in the disastrous clinical trials of Fileuridine (FIAU) at NIH.

FIAU is a DNA chain terminator, akin to AZT, and is extremely toxic--it was being tested as an oral dosage for use in treatment of chronic Hepatitis B. The compound was developed at Memorial Sloan Kettering Institute and licensed to Oclassen Pharmaceuticals, which entered into an agreement with Eli Lilly & Co. to develop the drug. The first three tests were sponsored by Oclassen, the last by Lilly--and were done at the NIH.

Rep. Edolphus Towns (D. NY), at that time Chairman of the House Government Operations/Human Resources and Intragovernment Relations Subcommittee characterized the test thusly: "This is not science--it is lethal science fiction. . . . let's face it, innocent people died and painfully suffered as a result of these misdeeds. It appears this whole tragedy could and should have been prevented."

In all, ten patients died as a result of the toxicity of the drug--five of those during the Phase II Study conducted by NIH. This toxicity could have and should have been anticipated from the results of the earlier tests, in which the five patients who died had also participated as subjects. The upshot is that no one seriously analyzed the potential for toxicity, which was available but not adequately analyzed or reported in a way that might have led to some understanding of the delayed type of toxicity which killed these subjects.

Three of the four deaths in a previous study occurred in patients who had received the drug previously and five of the patients who died in the NIH Study had been treated with a related compound in a previous study. The FDA's analysis of potential toxicity was inadequate.

The determination of the wisdom of continuing the efficacy requirement and whether or not to strengthen the pre-market approval process by requiring more stringent premarketing testing of toxicity is peculiarly that of the Congress, and the courts have consistently refused to substitute their judgment for that of Congress. In the analysis, it is a political question to be determined by this Congress reflecting the will of the people.

2. Cancer Therapies

At the time the efficacy requirement was enacted (1962) there was considerably more reason to believe that allopathic treatments were beneficial than has proven to be the case since then.

In 1962, the efficacy requirement may have seemed a good idea to everyone, as that was a period of limitless faith in drug therapies, and particularly in cancer therapies in which chemotherapy had just begun to be used to treat cancer and everyone expected these drugs to solve the cancer treatment problem in a few years.

In 1974, President Nixon signed a Bill to create the National Cancer Institute and to launch a much publicized war on cancer which was expected to conquer the cancer treatment problems in a decade. Two decades later, it is apparent to everyone that the war on cancer was another Viet Nam, and we lost--the death rate from cancer is much increased due to iatrogenic (drug-induced) diseases and there are still no effective treatments for most cancers, as well as a significant down-side to chemotherapies so that patients who are treated with these drugs frequently die earlier than those who are not treated at all. In 1986, Dr. John Bailer published his classic appraisal of the war on cancer, declaring it had been lost. (John C. Bailar III and Elaine M. Smith, "Progress Against Cancer," *The New England Journal of Medicine*, Special Articles, May 8, 1986).Today, the number of people dying from cancer is exceeded only by the number of people who make a handsome living, mostly at taxpayers' expense, from costly and ineffective research on cancer, all with continuing dismal results.

On the other hand, several essentially non-chemotherapeutic approaches to cancer therapy, none of which has been approved by the FDA, have been developed and thousands of Americans go out of the country to receive these cancer treatments, usually with excellent results, ofttimes with complete cures.

The FDA has waged unrelenting war on these so-called unorthodox cancer therapies; there was an 11-year-long struggle over Laetrile which took place in the Western District of Oklahoma, when the U.S. District Court enjoined the FDA from interfering with patients' access to the drug for years. During that time 26 states passed statutes legalizing the use of Laetrile on an intrastate basis.

The efficacy requirement has been the major weapon used by the FDA to deny approval of and access to many very effective and safe unorthodox cancer remedies and it continues to be used for that purpose.

Whether or not unorthodox cancer therapies should be permitted for those who wish access to them is not a medical or scientific question, it is purely a political question, which must be decided by the Congress and can be decided by the simple expedient of repealing the efficacy requirement.

The toxicity of FDA-approved chemotherapeutic agents for the treatment of cancer is appalling. The FDA claims that the benefits outweigh the risks, but the question remains--benefit to whom?--these benefits are certainly not to patients who die from these treatments rather than their disease, and if they do survive these treatments, frequently develop new, secondary cancers caused by the treatments. If anyone benefits from these treatments it is oncologists, hospitals and the pharmaceutical industry which profit from their sales.

We have developed over the past 50 years a large and, in many cases, government-supported oncology or cancer industry, which remains devoted to highly toxic and frequently ineffective radiation and chemotherapy, both of which are therapeutic disasters which this cancer establishment will not abandon. In desperation, many Americans are turning to other approaches which are non-toxic and more effective but the FDA is intent on suppressing these new approaches in an attempt to force Americans with cancer to take a slow walk through the valley of the shadow of death in the form of allopathic therapy, which usually leaves them in worse condition than they began and exhausts their financial resources as well as hastens their demise.

Meanwhile, safe and effective remedies, such as Dr. Lawrence Burton's Immune Augmentation Therapy, Dr. Stanislaw Burzynsky's antiineoplastins, and Gaston Naessens' 714X are selectively attacked by the FDA. All of these have been shown repeatedly to be effective for a great number of people and absolutely non-toxic--their primary failing being that they do not conform to allopathic theories about cancer and are condemned by the FDA despite their impressive records of success and the thousands of cures they have advanced.

While it is not the task of Congress to weigh the relative benefits of various approaches to cancer and decide which if any is best, it is the task of Congress to ensure that Americans are able to make their own choices and decisions about such matters without bureaucratic interference. This can be accomplished by the repeal of the Efficacy Requirement, thus determining that such matters are not appropriate subjects for government control and should be left up to the people to decide for themselves. This would be one of the most popular Acts this Congress could enact and one which would restore much faith in the political process.

I have no quarrel with the highly toxic chemotherapies being available to those who wish to be treated with them. My quarrel is with the government trying to make these the only treatments available. I don't think that the government has any business in deciding what treatments should be available and not available based on some government official's appraisal of how effective he or she imagines these to be and I particularly object to this being done at the taxpayer's expense.

The repeal of the Efficacy Requirement would not in any way interfere with continuing access to orthodox (allopathic) cancer treatments by those who wish to use them, but it would make unorthodox therapies available to those who do not choose to use the orthodox therapies, and make them available for use by their own physicians at home, so they would not be required to travel to Europe, or Mexico to obtain these treatments. Indeed, the repeal of the FDA Efficacy Requirement may well engender new and more productive research initiatives in cancer research and benefit both the health and economy of America.

Additionally, the manner in which Commissioner Kessler approaches and intends to approach the regulation of drugs has already come closer to Lysenkoism than is tolerable in a free country.

3. Other Disease Treatments

Generally speaking, most pharmaceuticals, particularly those synthesized from petrochemicals, are toxic and their safety for human ingestion needs constant monitoring

Vitamins, trace minerals, amino acids, herbs, herbal extracts, and homeotherapeutic medications are not toxic in appropriate dosages and do not require the level of surveillance necessary for synthetic chemicals, although any substance can be toxic if consumed to excess.

The human race has survived the use of nutrients and herbal medications for thousands of years without any real outbreaks of mass toxic reactions due to these, while the first century for the use of synthetic pharmaceuticals has produced a number of mass toxic deaths and illnesses, attributable to the use of these substances as drugs.

The FDA's surveillance of toxicity, however, is in inverse ratio to the risks involved. Nutrients and herbal products receive extremely vigorous, indeed ofttimes ludicrous surveillance, while highly toxic petrochemical drugs receive inadequate surveillance by the FDA.

Largely due to the efficacy requirement, it costs a minimum of 321 million dollars and takes about 12 years for a new drug to achieve approval by the FDA. This cost is passed on to consumers of the products, adding several billion dollars a year to consumer expenditures for drugs.

Due to its preoccupation with the unnecessary efficacy requirement, the FDA's safety determinations have deteriorated to the extent that over 50% of the drugs approved produce serious and ofttimes fatal toxicity after approval by means not covered in pre-approval testing.

Some classic examples are Chloramphenicol, which produces thousands of fatal blood dyscrasias (aplastic anemia); MER 29, a compound for lowering cholesterol which produced cataracts in thousands of patients; Zomax, a "safe" analgesic which killed thousands of patients after FDA approval; birth control pills that caused strokes and DES, which caused cancer in the daughters of patients.

Many people who still resort to allopathic medical care do so because some one else pays for their care and will only pay for allopathic care. Most people who can afford to pay for their own care get it from non-allopathic practitioners, either here or out of the country.

Commissioner Kessler is trained as a physician and his particular medical philosophy is that of allopathic medicine, one of the five major medical philosophies which have existed in American medicine for the past two hundred years.

The philosophical orientation of allopathic medicine is diametrically opposed to that of the other four major medical philosophies and Kessler and others in the FDA are incorrect in their attempt to establish their medical philosophy, allopathic medicine, as the only true or orthodox philosophy in medicine. Much of their enforcement activity is aimed in this direction, which is a blatant perversion of the enforcement machinery of the FDA, which from its inception was not to have any regulatory function with regard to the practice of medicine, a function reserved to the several states with their police power and the 10th Amendment.

These intentions are contrary to the intent of Congress in enacting both the 1938 Act and the 1962 Amendments and are a stated intention on the part of Commissioner Kessler to attempt to extend the jurisdiction of the FDA to include control over the practice of medicine, which is a matter within the constitutional jurisdiction of the States and not that of the Federal Government through the right and duty of the Congress to control interstate commerce.

A significant number of people no longer repose their trust in allopathic medicine and the exclusive use of highly toxic synthetic pharmaceuticals for the treatment of and prevention of diseases, and in their day-to-day activities regarding their health, they frequently and increasingly look to other philosophies and systems of health care.

Those who wish to continue to use allopathic health care are free to do so; the changes suggested here have no impact on the allopathic health care system other than opening it up to competition by other systems without government interference.

Commissioner Kessler, who of course was trained as an allopathic physician, frequently misuses the FDA's regulatory authority to attack non-allopathic practitioners in an effort to force millions of Americans to utilize allopathic care. This is not a legitimate use of the authority which Congress gave the FDA in 1962; indeed, from its inception, the Food, Drug and Cosmetics Act was held not to have any jurisdiction over the practice of medicine. Commissioner Kessler's intentions in this regard are to be found in his own writings. In **The Basis of The FDA's Decision on Breast Implants**, New England Journal of Medicine, 326:1713-1715 (1992), Commissioner Kessler stated:

"... If members of our society were empowered to make their own decisions about the entire range of products for which the FDA has responsibility, however, then the whole rationale for the agency would cease to exist...."

The regulation of the purity, safety and distribution of foods, food stuffs, and nutritional supplements, including herbs, should not be a concern of the FDA or of any agency resulting from a restructuring of the FDA.

4. Discriminatory Activity By FDA

The FDA has relentlessly misused its regulatory authority to discriminate against non-allopathic health care providers and health food stores. The following is a partial list of Gestapo-type raids conducted by FDA agents to suppress homeopathic clinics (licensed by State law), acupuncture clinics, (licensed by State law), nutritionally-oriented physicians, and physicians whose practices are not in accordance with allopathic philosophy:

Burzynski Research Clinic--Houston, Texas, 7 July, 1985: FDA seized 200,000 medical and research documents, forcing Burzynski to pay to make copies. No charges were filed.

The Life Extension Foundation--Hollywood, Fla., 26 February, 1987: FDA seized US $500,000 worth of vitamins, computers, files, newsletters and personal belongings, ripped phones out of walls, and terrorized employees. The Foundation's leaders, Saul Kent and William Faloon, were indicted on 28 criminal counts with a maximum prison time of 84 years, in November, 1991. Case is still pending.

Traco Labs, Inc., Seymour, IL--November, 1988: FDA seized two drums of black currant oil as well as a large quantity of the capsulized product. On 28 January, 1993, the US Court of Appeals ruled against the FDA. The judge said that the FDA's definition of food additive is too broad--that even water added to food would be considered a food additive.

Highland Labs, Mt. Angel, OR--Autumn, 1990: FDA claimed that product literature (with false claims) was being shipped with products to customers, FDA said these made CoQ10 and GeOxy 132 unapproved drugs. After spending US $250,000 in legal fees, defendant was forced to plead guilty to selling unapproved new drugs. Six months house arrest: US $5,000 fine.

H. A. Lyons Mailing Service, Phoenix, AZ--16 October, 1990: Mailing literature on behalf of vitamin companies. With no advance warning, five armed agents, backed by an armed policeman, raided this home-based business run by a young woman. The owner convinced the agents not to seize her cheque book and cash. They did seize all her business records and literature. No charges were filed.

Nutricology, Inc., San Leandro, CA--9 May, 1991: The FDA raided Nutricology, seized their bank accounts and shut them down for two days, charging them with wire fraud, mail fraud, and selling unapproved drugs, unsafe food additives and misbranded drugs. Twelve armed agents conducted an exhaustive search of the company's offices and warehouse. On 23 May, 1991, Federal Judge D. Lowell Jensen denied the FDA's request for a preliminary injunction. On 10 September, 1991, the FDA appealed to the 9th Circuit Court of Appeals, but was again denied. On 23 September, 1993, Judge Jensen denied the FDA's motion for summary judgment and granted Nutricology's motion to eliminate the wire and mail fraud charges.

Scientific Botanicals, Seattle WA--Autumn, 1991: Alleged labeling violations. FDA seized herbal extract products and literature sent to physicians. FDA forced the company to stop using its patented trade names lest they mislead the consumer. FDA slowly released all seized products, forcing the company to comply with all demands under threat of being shut down.

Thorne Research, Sand Point, ID--12 December, 1991: FDA claimed that vitamin products sold by company were unapproved drugs. FDA agent and three US marshals seized the company's entire stock of US $20,000 worth of products and 11,000 pieces of literature intended for physicians. Thorne initially notified District Court that it would fight, but gave up as the expiration date on the seized products was approaching and it became too expensive to continue. The company no longer publishes any literature.

Tahoma Clinic, Kent, WA--6 May, 1992: After L-tryptophan was banned, Dr. Jonathan Wright continued to prescribe it. The FDA raided him and seized his supply of tryptophan. Dr. Wright filed suit. The FDA retaliated by storming into Wright's clinic with armed sheriffs who terrorized employees and seized vitamins and other natural therapies, allergy screening equipment, computers, bank records, his mailing list and medical records. October, 1992, Wright filed suit in District Court, charging unlawful search and seizure, and demanding his property back. In response, the FDA convened a federal grand jury and subpoenaed Wright's clinic records. No charges have yet been filed.

Ye Seekers, Houston, TX--June, 1992: In February, 1992, Texas health authorities, acting under the direction of the FDA, seized 50 products from several health food stores in Texas including Ye Seekers. Then, in June, they seized more than 250 products including aloe vera, zinc, flax seed oil, herb teas, vitamin C and coenzyme Q-10. Although more than 410 products were seized, the stores haven't filed suit for fear of reprisals. Ye Seekers noted that Ginsana was seized from them at the same time it was being advertised on the Larry King TV show.

Mihai Popescu, 2 June, 1992: The FDA claims that Gerovital (GH-3), which Popescu was selling, is an unapproved drug. Eight FDA and Customs agents raided Popescu's house with guns drawn, holding his eight-months-pregnant wife and 83-year-old grandfather at gunpoint for 10 hours. They seized his computer and business records and US $5,000 worth of GH-3.

Nature's Way, Springville, UT--30 June, 1992: The FDA seized a quantity of evening primrose oil, both encapsulated and in bulk, from this large manufacturer during a routine inspection. They also seized a truckload of primrose oil on the road. The FDA claimed it was an unapproved food additive. Nature's Way filed a lawsuit to get their product back, but was forced to remove the vitamin E from it because the FDA said that vitamin E has not been approved as a food additive for evening primrose oil.

Family Acupuncture Clinic, San Clemente, CA--14 August, 1992: FDA seized US $15,000 worth of Hsaio Yao Tea Pills in an attempt to strike back at acupuncturists who are taking a lot of business away from conventional doctors. The FDA ignored California law, under which acupuncturists are licensed to practice medicine. The seized herbs were shipped back to China by the FDA after they had rotted. Dr. Lee is still in business.

Tierra Marketing, Albuquerque, NM--8 April, 1993: was raided at gunpoint, and had US $20,000 worth of Gerovital-H3 (GH-3) seized along with business records and computers. Employees suffered from post-traumatic stress syndrome after having guns pointed at them. The FDA considers GH-3 an unapproved drug, but could produce no documents indicating they had followed legal administrative procedures to enable them to seize it.

Kirwin Whitnah, Middletown, CA--12 May, 1993: Whitnah was promoting the sale of deprenyl. The FDA considered this selling an unapproved drug. His house was raided at gunpoint when he wasn't home, terrorizing a woman staying at the house. They found no deprenyl. They seized his computer, business records, mailing list, literature and US $4,500 in money orders. No charges were filed, but Whitnah was driven out of business.

Waco Natural Foods, Waco, TX--14 May, 1993: The FDA was looking for deprenyl citrate, a non-toxic supplement. They entered the store with a search warrant wearing plain clothes. They searched for four hours and seemed most interested in possible links to business in the Seattle area. As soon as Mr. Wiggins, the owner, told the FDA his attorney was a well-known defender and prior district attorney in the Waco area, they apologized for the raid and left with some documents. No charges were filed and the store hasn't been raided since.

International Nutrition Inc., Santa Theresa, NM--24 June, 1993 and 3 August, 1993: Alleged misbranding of illegal drugs led five FDA agents, a federal marshal and a PR specialist to enter with video cameras (instead of guns) in an effort to prevent a public backlash. FDA seized US $1,000,000 worth of vitamin raw materials and products formulated by Dr. Hans Nieper of Germany. Also seized were computers and business records; INI has lost 80 percent of its business since the raid and had to lay off 80 per cent of its workforce.

Hospital Santa Monica, Chula Vista, CA--12 May, 1993: Hospital Santa Monica is an alternative cancer hospital in Mexico that competes with mainstream hospitals in the US. They were accused of distributing unapproved drugs. More than 50 federal agents with guns drawn raided the hospital office in San Diego, seizing a tractor trailer of business records, patient charts and computers. They also searched employees' homes and seized US $80,000 found in the owner's safe. Over US $300,000 was taken from the bank accounts of the hospital and two vitamin companies. No charges have been filed.

Most of these raids included the seizure of patient records, computers, data banks, business records and other materials, all of which are retained by the agency. Essentially, there is no follow-up, no criminal prosecution or regulatory action--the business of the targeted practitioner or store is simply destroyed, its own records unavailable to it and it is out of business. These are arbitrary, high-handed and capricious attempts by bureaucrats to destroy businesses without due process of law.

The FDA has further entered into a contract with the Pharmaceutical Advertising Council to conduct a campaign to suppress unorthodox medicine in the United States. This campaign is funded in part by tax funds, by the FDA and in part by contributions from pharmaceutical manufacturers through the PAC--which conducts business on a joint FDA-PAC letterhead.

Homeopathic physicians, licensed to practice homeopathic medicine under state law and acupuncturists licensed to practice oriental medicine under state law are harassed, their clinics subjected to Gestapo-type raids by FDA investigators. An example is the Century Clinic, in Reno, Nevada, which has twice been subjected to such raids because its staff practice homeopathy, which they are specifically licensed to do. This has been ongoing for five years. Apparently one Stephen Kendall of the San Francisco office of the FDA has a years-long ongoing vendetta against the clinic.

Whether this is something personal with Kendall or that sort of activity is the official policy of the Agency set by the Commissioner is irrelevant. The overall purpose of Kendall's years-long harassment is to interfere with patients, including me, being treated at the clinic.

Everything done at the Century Clinic is clearly within the scope of practice of homeopathy as regulated by the Nevada State Board of Homeopathic Medical Examiners, and is in keeping with current standards for the practice of homeopathic medicine.

The FDA Commissioner is an allopathic physician and, as such, probably not an avid fan of homeopathy, but his personal belief in a competitive school of medical practice is no excuse for his misuse of the agency's regulatory process to harass the Clinic and its patients. The choice to seek homeopathic medical care is my personal choice and that of thousands of other Americans who prefer that type of medical care and the Commissioner of the FDA has no legitimate function of directing or allowing his employees to harass the clinic and its patients because he disagrees with the philosophy of homeopathic medicine.

When in exasperation the Clinic agreed to file an IDE on a device it is clearly authorized to use by state law, the harassment continued, papers filed on time are said not to have been received by the FDA, and the general attitude of FDA staffers is one of total non-cooperation with both the Clinic and the Nevada Association of Homeopathic Physicians which acts as the sponsor for the study. This entire affair reflects great discredit on the FDA and its staff.

The people of Nevada, through their legislature, made the decision to separately license and regulate homeopathic medicine and to permit the use of devices and therapies utilized world wide in the practice of homeopathy. It is not the function of a Federal agency to attempt to undo this Act by the Nevada legislature. There surely should be some concept of comity with state governments in the FDA and its staff regardless of their private medical, philosophical orientation. People do have a right to hold differing opinions and beliefs in America, but this point remains lost on the FDA.

I am one of millions of Americans who no longer believe in the efficacy of allopathic medicine and seek health care from practitioners who follow one or more of the other health care philosophies (i.e., Homeopathy, Eclectic Medicine, Nutritional Medicine, Chiropractic, Osteopathic or Oriental Medicine and Acupuncture).

This is my right, and one with which the government should never interfere--one of the important decisions in my life I should be free to make without government interference. There is or should be no official state sponsored medical philosophy in America. All Americans should be free to seek health care from physicians of their choice who follow divergent health philosophies.

I simply no longer believe that is possible to poison a sick man well, and I realize that this is the basis of allopathic medical philosophy, so I no longer rely on allopathic physicians--and I resent efforts by the FDA to interfere with my access to unorthodox non-allopathic care.

I do not wish to impose my own beliefs and ideas about this on other Americans--but by the same token, I do not wish to have their ideas and beliefs imposed upon me by the government in the name of consumer protection.

I should not be required to travel outside of the United States to obtain the type of health care I choose, due to the regulatory activities of the FDA, particularly where its activities in that regard are outside of the regulatory authority given to it by statute.

Voluntary compliance with statutes and administrative regulations is the customary stance of manufacturers; ofttimes they are confronted with a bewildering array of regulations and inadvertent non-compliance occurs from time to time, but this can usually be corrected by merely pointing it out to the company. Gestapo-type raids, confiscation of mechanical equipment and criminal accusations are not necessary or desirable in a civilized regulatory scheme--which we no longer have.

Since 1992, the number of FDA employees assigned full time to the regulation of vitamins and nutritional supplements has increased an incredible four fold, and many of these are new employees whose jobs are to conduct raids and confiscate merchandise.

More than 100 million Americans currently take dietary supplements to balance diets, enhance well being and prevent or treat illness. In 1993, the FDA issued regulations which prevent manufacturers from making truthful health benefit claims for their products, despite the growing consensus of the entire health service community on the benefits of vitamins and other nutrients--based on hundreds of articles in the peer reviewed literature. Yet, the FDA and Kessler are issuing regulations that impede the public's right to access of information about which substances can benefit them the most.

This practice and Kessler's and the FDA's anti-nutritional bias are ubiquitous and rather than attempt to catalogue all of it, I will discuss one nutritional supplement, an amino acid, L-Tryptophan, which is representative, and which has been the source of much public dissatisfaction with Kessler and the FDA.

The L-Tryptophan Scam at FDA

L-tryptophan is an essential amino acid, necessary for human life, which cannot be synthesized by the human body and must be obtained from the diet. It occurs in many foods which are protein rich, such as steak and milk. The average diet contains 1-2 grams per day.

L-tryptophan, as a dietary supplement, has the properties of increasing brain serotonin levels (U.S. Patent #4,687,763) and thusly reducing depression (U.S. Patent #4,377,595) and is non-toxic.

Since the late 1960s L-tryptophan has been sold in this country as a dietary supplement and safely used by millions of people until the fall of 1989, when some batches of L-tryptophan manufactured by the Japanese Showa Denko Company became contaminated during the manufacturing process with two contaminants which produced an outbreak of eosinophilia-myalgia syndrome in some users. In response to this the FDA removed all L-tryptophan from the OTC market, and has forbidden its sale for the past 5 years, despite the fact that there were never any impurities in any commercially prepared L-tryptophan manufactured by any other company and the manufacturing error at Showa Denko was rapidly identified and corrected.

L-tryptophan, while not available OTC continues to be used in total parenteral nutrition solutions, which are administered intravenously, where purity is much more critical than for oral supplements.

The reason for continuing the OTC ban becomes clear when one considers that L-tryptophan is competitive with Prozac®, a major antidepressant which like L-tryptophan raises brain serotonin levels and decreases depression. There, however, the similarity ends. Prozac causes several severe side effects and has recently been demonstrated to accelerate cancer growth.

Prior to this outbreak caused by contaminated L-tryptophan manufactured by Showa Denko, the annual sales of L-tryptophan amounted to 180 million dollars, and the product was widely distributed and sold in tablet, capsule and powder form as a nutritional supplement by vitamin companies, health food stores and other retail outlets.

Investigation revealed that during the time the contaminated batches of L-tryptophan were produced at Showa Denko, that company had simultaneously altered three separate elements of its manufacturing process, which for decades had produced safe L-tryptophan:

(1) They had instituted the partial bypass of a reverse osmosis filter,

(2) a significant reduction in amount of activated carbon used in a filtration process, and

(3) introduced an entirely new strain of a biotech (genetically engineered) microorganism used in L-tryptophan fermentation.

It has now been shown, since 1992, that the outbreak of EMS was entirely due to these defects in batches of L-tryptophan produced by Showa Denko between October, 1987 and June, 1989.

Despite this, the FDA has banned the sale of all L-tryptophan as a nutritional supplement for oral use, although its use in infant formulas and in intravenous feedings of hospital patients is allowed to continue and it continues to be available as an animal feed.

In 1990, the FDA held closed door-closed record meetings with Showa Denko with regard to the EMS outbreak and refuses to release information concerning these meetings.

The other half of the story is simple--L-tryptophan has the property of safely raising serotonin levels in the brain which produces a calming effect and produces an anti-depressant effect when taken orally without side effects.

Far more expensive and toxic pharmaceuticals regulated by FDA have the same principal mode of action--that of raising serotonin levels in the brain--but with side effects.

Prozac® is a chemical antidepressant drug marketed by Eli Lilly & Co., which retails for $1.60 per tablet, and this year sales are expected to top one billion dollars. This drug has produced more adverse reaction reports than any other drug in the history of the FDA's overall reaction reporting process (23,000 complaints). Prozac was cleared for marketing by the FDA with little regard for safety and contrary to recommendations of an advisory committee. As noted above, it also has the property of accelerating cancer growth, and is believed to be implicated in causing severely antisocial behavior in those to whom it is administered.

Dr. Sidney Wolfe, director of the Public Citizen Health Research Group, has pointed out, "Most of these awful adverse drug reactions, whether they're shooting someone, falling down, fracturing a hip, getting depressed, are preventable, and that's the biggest tragedy."

While the Food and Drug Administration is entrusted with the vigilant protection of Americans from dangerous drugs, an inspection of the hazardous drugs it has allowed on the market shows the agency to be ineffective. This ineffectiveness is explained in large measure by the staggering conflicts of interests which the FDA has allowed into the drug oversight process. For example, the FDA held a hearing into the charges against Prozac and other psychiatric antidepressants in late 1991, at which it claimed to be unable to find any damning evidence against antidepressants at all. However, subsequent investigation of the panel revealed that five out of the ten panel members had active financial interests with the manufacturers of antidepressants totaling more than $1 million at the time they claimed to be blind to the evidence against Prozac.

The FDA currently serves the interests of the profit-driven drug companies, not the interests of the American people, and thus killer drugs are placed on the market. Had 10% as much concern for safety been shown in the recent NIH study on FIAU, the unnecessary deaths there could and would have been prevented. Here we have the above mentioned inverse level of FDA scrutiny.

Nutrition

Americans have always been responsible for their own nutritional decisions and the average American housewife is probably a better nutritionist than the allopathically trained FDA regulators. Foods serve important cultural, religious and social functions which should not be the concern of regulators; the same is true of herbs which are foodstuffs. We now have the regulation of foods and food advertising spread out over three agencies, the Department of Agriculture, the FDA and the FTC, which promulgate inconsistent policies. We would be better served and also save a lot of tax money if the regulation of food, in its entirety, were to be returned to the Department of Agriculture where it originated, the FDA were taken completely out of the regulation of food, and advertising claims for food were policed, along with other commodities and products, by the FTC.

There is no sound reason for some foods, i.e., meat, eggs and poultry, to be regulated by the Department of Agriculture, while other foods are regulated by the FDA. This is a historical accident. The FDA originated as a part of the Department of Agriculture, and at that time the major concern was adulteration of food stuff; drugs were almost an afterthought. The sponsor and author of the first Food, Drug and Cosmetics Act, Dr. Harvey Wiley, was a chemist employed by the Department of Agriculture. When the agency, due to its emphasis on drugs, was transferred to the Department of Health and Human Services, its regulatory authority over foods should have been left with the Department of Agriculture. They should now be transferred back to the Department of Agriculture, so that foods are all regulated by a single agency, and to end and avoid spillover of drug regulations into food regulation.

One of the features which distinguishes allopathic medical philosophy from other medical philosophies is its clear and unrelenting anti-nutritional bias--people trained exclusively in allopathic medical philosophy are not trained in nutrition. The National Research Council conducted a thorough survey of nutrition in U.S. Medical Schools teaching allopathic medicine and in its report concluded:

"The committee concluded that nutrition education programs in U.S. medical schools are largely inadequate to meet the present and future demands of the medical profession. This perception, reflecting results of prior surveys and conferences, was confirmed by the committee's independent survey and related investigations as outlined above.

". . . The committee recommends that medical schools and their accreditation bodies, federal agencies, private foundations, and the scientific community make a concerted effort to upgrade the standards as detailed below. The committee recognizes the extraordinary demands placed on the medical education system of today. Nevertheless, it believes these changes could be achieved with minimal disruption of existing curricular and administrative structures although in most cases this upgrading may require a major philosophical adjustment. . . ." (Committee on Nutrition in Medical Education, Food and Nutrition Board, Commission on Life Sciences, National Research Council, **Nutrition Education in U.S. Medical Schools,** National Academy Press, Washington D.C., 1985).

Other medical philosophies which are practiced quite extensively in the country and patronized by millions of Americans embrace nutrition as a therapeutic and preventive mainstay of their philosophy, just as they largely avoid the use of the synthetic, chemical drugs which are the linchpin of allopathic therapeutics.

Americans have the option of using either of these approaches, and would benefit from having the synthetic chemical drugs regulated with more emphasis on their safety and foods regulated by a different agency less concerned with promotion of the use of pharmaceuticals to the exclusion of nutrition. Commissioner Kessler, prior to his appointment, wrote a medical journal article in which he stated:

"The laws that govern the labeling of food were written 50 years ago, when there was little demand for the type of nutritional information that is currently available. To some, the food label as we know it is a relic. Others argue that advances in technology are outpacing the FDA's ability to regulate the labeling of food. The laws and regulations governing the disclosure of the identity, ingredients and nutritional aspects of the food on the label need to be reexamined.

"The most important feature of a food label is the name that identifies the product. The Federal, Food, Drug, and Cosmetic Act (referred to in this article as the Act) governs the labeling of most foods. Labeling encompasses not only the label but any promotional material that accompanies a food product. The Department of Agriculture has jurisdiction over the labeling of meat, poultry and eggs; the Bureau of Alcohol, Tobacco, and Firearms, over alcoholic beverages; and the Federal Trade Commission (FTC) over advertising. Congress gave the FDA the authority to create standards of identify for foods. . . .

". . . The original purpose of standards for food was to prevent cheapened products from masquerading as traditional foods. In practice, the standards have also had an anti-competitive effect, stifling the development and introduction of new foods. Under the traditional interpretation of the food-standards provision, a product that looked, tasted, and smelled like a food covered by a standard, but did not meet the standard in other respects, not only was precluded from bearing the name specified in the standard, but could not even be sold. Under the FDA's restrictive-food-standards policy, truthful and informative labeling is no defense against the charge that a product fails to meet a standard.

"The FDA has gradually shifted away from the rigidity of its food standards over the past 20 years, partly because of the enormous resources required to promulgate standards. . . .

". . . The policy helped keep in check misleading and potentially harmful claims, but it also prevented useful and truthful claims from being made. With the benefit of hindsight, it is apparent that some of the FDA's actions under this policy proved detrimental to the public's interest. For example, in 1964 the agency brought charges against Kraft for promoting an egg substitute as low in cholesterol and saturated fats. Although there was no mention of heart disease or control of serum cholesterol levels on the label itself, the FDA charged that the accompanying promotional material represented the product as useful in controlling serum cholesterol levels. By removing it from the supermarket shelves, the FDA effectively denied consumers access to a healthful alternative to eggs.

"A policy that prohibits all health-related claims is easy to implement, because the agency need not analyze the merits of a particular claim. Moreover, the framework of the statute supports the FDA's blanket policy, because foods bearing such health claims can be classified as drugs; and since they have not met the requirements of drugs for preapproval and labeling, their marketing is illegal.

". . . The current set of food-labeling regulations is the result of patchwork regulatory efforts designed to deal with specific problem. Fifty years after the passage of the Act, the statute needs to be amended to provide a more coherent framework for the regulation of food labeling. The FDA can make some necessary changes administratively, without amending the Act, but unless the overall framework is reexamined, the agency will lack any clear set of directions. Different constituencies--Congress, consumers, health professionals, and industry--will have varying expectations of the appropriate role for the agency. . . ." (David A. Kessler, **The**

Federal Regulation of Food Labeling Promoting Foods to Prevent Disease, New England Journal of Medicine, 321:717-725, 1989).

We do not need Big Brother in our kitchens dictating what we may eat or drink for breakfast or at Christmas dinner or the content of the herbal teas we choose to drink or believe may benefit our health. We have strong traditions, many and varied, about foods and herbs derived from the diverse ethnic backgrounds of the many cultures which amalgamate in American culture; these are better left undisturbed by the sort of pervasive regulations espoused by the FDA and Commissioner Kessler or others who are devotees of bureaucratic regulation of every aspect of life. I believe that the Department of Agriculture can and should ensure the purity of our food supply and I like nutritional labels which inform me of the caloric content, fat, carbohydrate and protein content of my foods as well as of the names of all preservatives and chemicals added to processed foods--but I see no reason why the Department of Agriculture cannot adequately control these features as well as or better than the FDA.

Today a substantial number of Americans do not view the FDA as being a benign agency with beneficent purposes but rather as a run-away bureaucracy intent on intruding on their lives and extinguishing their freedoms and liberty by taking away their right to choose the kind of medical care they will pursue either to maintain their health or to treat their illnesses. In addition to that, many of us view it as a bureaucracy which adds an intolerable cost burden to health care without giving us anything worthwhile in return and feel that, on balance, we would be better off if the agency were simply abolished.

We do need a small agency to monitor product standardization, purity and safety of chemical drugs, but nothing like the bureaucratic behemoth that the FDA has become, and I am sure that such an agency could be set up and run by the industry which markets chemical drugs and medical devices if adequate safeguards were established to ensure that small companies and individuals who wish to enter that market are not shut out by the large corporations which occupy most of that market.

If nutrition, food, vitamins, minerals, amino acids and herbs are allowed to be regulated by the Department of Agriculture and the free market without undue regulation of the type we have experienced from the FDA, we are capable of making our own purchasing decisions without any help from Big Brother and a horde of bureaucrats at our expense. The six thousand or so bureaucrats who now are on the FDA payroll can find honest employment elsewhere and we certainly do not need a new 800 million dollar campus for the FDA. The FDA and its activities should be allowed to dwindle rapidly into a footnote in political history exemplifying the type of bureaucracy not needed by a free people. I think it would be best if the FDA as an agency were abolished, and replaced by a small agency charged with monitoring the safety and toxicity of synthetic chemicals used as drugs.

The efficacy requirement should be repealed, and relegated to the trash heap of history. If a manufacturer makes a fraudulent claim for his product, such fraud can and should be addressed by the Federal Trade Commission; additionally most States have laws prohibiting consumer fraud. All regulations of foods, foodstuffs, nutrients, food additives, herbs and herbal extracts should be conducted by the Department of Agriculture. Efficacy of such products as nutrients should be left to consumers without government interference; outright fraud and fraudulent claims should be addressed by the Federal Trade Commission under state law. The safety of devices should be regulated under an organization similar to the Underwriters Laboratory, sponsored by the industries which manufacture such devices. These measures would result in a very considerable reduction in the cost of health care and health care products, an enhancement in their safety and purity, and much needed cutting Federal expenditures.

I would favor retaining or creating federal preemption of state regulation of food, drugs and Devices under the Interstate

Commerce Clause so that we can enjoy the benefits of a national distribution system without 50 different requirements for labeling being imposed upon manufacturers. The regulation of medical and health care practitioners should remain a function of the states so innovation can continue and develop without Federal bureaucratic interference.

I sincerely believe that millions of Americans agree with these ideas. The regulation of health care by governments, both state and federal, is a 20th Century development, the results of which are far from wholly benign. Largely due to government regulation we have unprecedented inflation in the cost of health care, which might well be reversed to a large extent by the restoration of a free market and substantial deregulation, particularly of the type of regulation for which Commissioner Kessler and the FDA have such a voracious appetite.

The repeal of the efficacy requirement could save several billion dollars a year, as well as restore some much needed competition in the health care market leading to still further savings in health care costs, about one third of which are paid for by the taxpayers.

I would like to amplify many of my remarks in this letter; however, I cannot catalogue all of the faults in the FDA and its operations and their deleterious efforts in just a few pages, and rather than try to do so, I have pointed out some highlights and a few examples of the sort of misconduct and rampant bureaucracy which underline my strong feelings that we as a nation would be better off without what this agency has become.

I have available several filing cabinets full of documentary evidence of misconduct by the FDA and its agents, and know of several hundred people who would be more than delighted to testify to any Congressional Committee which wanted to look into these matters. If any of this would be helpful to you, please let me know sufficiently in advance to have them get in touch with the Committee.

Appendix B
Compassion California Style

George W. Kell is a brilliant, compassionate California lawyer, a former Assistant U.S. Attorney and California State Deputy Attorney General. He has, as he says, "personally experienced the threat to life that confronts every Californian who seeks to recover from cancer and is told that State law requires the patient and his doctor to choose either surgery, radiation or chemotherapy, but bars non-toxic choices."

Mr. Kell was once diagnosed with terminal cancer. He survived because he went to Mexico where real therapeutic choices were available, choices that are not permitted in California.In Mexico he personally saw other "severely sick, point-of-death terminal patients who improved, began to thrive, then fully recovered." They were able to "escape California's death sentence for cancer patients."

Mr. Kell has represented Jim Privitera and other California doctors who cured and alleviated cancer by means of so-called "quack" remedies (diet, herbs, non-toxic substances) and who were arrested, sent to jail, and shorn of professional standing because they courageously utilized such unapproved substances for the "alleviation or cure of cancer" in violation of a heinous California state law. Having read the book to this point, you can now well understand the criminal evil of such a law and the massive toll of suffering it continues to generate.

More than 50,000 individuals die of cancer annually in California. Many of those deaths occur because doctors are prevented by the state from prescribing nutritional and non-toxic remedies. These people are dying because the Legislature has refused to rewrite or completely junk this murderous law.

Mr. Kell wrote the following essay:

* * *

"Everyone should know that the 'war on cancer' is largely a fraud."

--Linus Pauling

Of what advantage to society is a California statute (Health & Safety Code Sec. 1707.1) that prohibits the "alleviation or cure of cancer" by any remedy unless the substance has first been approved by a medical bureaucracy? In the minds of most people any "cure" of cancer is reason enough for approval irrespective of Big Brother's ministrations.

It was, of course, never the intent of the Legislature to frustrate any cure for cancer, or for that matter, any alleviation thereof. That the goal of the legislature in enacting this rogue statute was more compassionate than that is borne out by its statutory scheme, which includes creation of a Cancer Advisory Council to advise the Department of Health Services concerning potentially effective remedies (H & S 1701, 1704) that may then be licensed by the Department. (1707.2)

But, unfortunately, the legislative machinery has been dominated from its inception by allopathic practitioners--surgeons, radiation specialists and chemotherapists--whose only remedies have been and continue to be surgery, radiation and chemotherapy. For 36 years, since enactment of 1707.1, that narrow, now largely discredited, field of choice has been forced upon cancer patients and their doctors--even to the extent of court mandated treatment. To the exclusion of all other remedies, irrespective of the preference of the patient, irregardless of the philosophy or school of medicine advocated by the attending physician, allopathy rules!

The patient does not believe in the allopathic way? His doctor is a vitalist, who believes that "you can't poison a sick person well", and therefore shuns radiation and chemotherapy? They want to choose from alternative remedies, including super nutrition, herbs, non-toxic drugs? Too bad! They have a "choice" of surgery, radiation or chemotherapy--or nothing! Added to that is the threat that the doctor goes to jail if he uses alternative remedies.

That cancer is an ever increasing menace to society is no longer debatable. Cancer mortality has increased in the United States year by year, at the inexorable and unforgiving rate of 1% per year, since 1900 when statistics were first gathered. While cancer mortality has progressed arithemetically the incidence, or rate at which new people are contracting cancer, seems to have recently skyrocketed. In the 1960s one in five of us could expect to contract cancer in his or her lifetime. Now it is one in three! One third of us who are living today can look forward to the enjoyment of that legally mandated "choice."

Since this is where Section 1707.1 has brought us in the 36 years since its enactment, is it not time that we allow an examination of some of the natural, nutritional and non-toxic alternatives this legislation has, in practice, unfortunately swept aside? Where this ratio has increased so dramatically in a matter of 25 or 30 years are we to anticipate that the encroachment of cancer will now cease? Only believe this if you believe in the tooth fairy!

Thirty six years ago it was possible for a cancer specialist, including the Medical Director of the Cancer Advisory Council, to testify under oath that: "There is no evidence that diet or nutritional supplementation has anything to do with the cause, prevention, alleviation or cure of cancer." They did so testify in case after case. But in this day no scientist can honestly make that claim, as anyone who reads a newspaper well knows. (See *The Cancer Industry: The Classic Expose on the Cancer Establishment*, by Ralph W. Moss, Paragon House, New York, 1991).

In the legislative findings which purport to support Section 1707.1 the Legislature declared:

"It is established that accurate and early diagnosis of many forms of cancer, followed by prompt application of methods of treatment which are scientifically proven, either materially reduces the likelihood of death from cancer or may materially prolong the useful life of individuals suffering therefrom". (H & S Sec. 1700; emphasis added)

Unfortunately the statement was false when it was enacted by the Legislature in 1959, in its claim that the accepted methods of cancer therapy--surgery, radiation and chemotherapy--had been scientifically proven. And it is false today. In fact, there have never been any controlled studies to prove the efficacy of surgery, not even to this day. Nor has the cancer establishment ever made any honest attempts to compare its "scientifically proven methods" against the non-toxic, and nutritional methodologies of the alternative medical practitioner.

Paradoxically, medical scientists are also admitting that the "war on cancer" has been a failure. Dr. N. Zinder of Rockefeller University confessed to the National Cancer Advisory Board, "We don't know how to attack cancer, much less conquer it, because we don't understand enough about how it works and what causes it." ("The Cancer Ripoff," Science Digest, September, 1974) In 1975, Nobel Laureate Dr. James Watson, declared at a cancer symposium at Massachusetts Institute of Technology that the American public had been sold a "nasty bill of goods about cancer"; that the cancer war was a "soporific orgy" which had produced no "promising leads" as it claimed, but only "delaying actions"; and that the cancer situation was "A bunch of shit!" (*New York Times*, 3-9-75 and 11-25-77)

The National Cancer Institute has never claimed "what millions of people had been led to expect: that the National Cancer

Program had found a cure for even one major type of human cancer." (*The Cancer Industry*, R.W. Moss)

Cancer experts are instead admitting complete defeat in their efforts to find a cure for cancer:

"The exact cause of cancer remains undetermined. . . . Various definitions of cancer have been put forth over the years. None is an all-encompassing or entirely satisfactory conception." (*Clinical Oncology for Medical Students and Physicians: a Multidisciplinary Approach*, 6th Ed., 1983).

"At least a third if not more than half of what we do is of no benefit, or of such marginal benefit that I think we should reach an agreement in society that insurance should not pay for it. (Robert H. Brook, UCLA professor of medicine, *NewYork Times*, 5-15-88).

"Chemotherapy is bottled death." (Vice Presidential Candidate Hubert Humphrey, shortly before his death, from cancer and chemotherapy, *N.Y. Daily News*, 1-14-78).

"There is a lot of evidence that new techniques are indeed able to diagnose cancer earlier on an average of about one-half year. What does this do? It converts what used to be a 4 1/2 year survival rate to a 5 year survival rate. Nothing has changed in the survival graphs except the points they choose to measure from." (Robert Houston, "Statistics, Data & Evidence in Medicine: Tools for Suppression." The Null Report, 4-4-87).

"The main conclusion we draw is that some 35 years of intense effort, focused largely on improving treatment, must be judged a qualified failure. Results have not been what they were intended and expected to be." (Bailar & Smith, "Progress Against Cancer?" New England Journal of Medicine, 5-8-86).

"[Biased Methods of Reporting Cancer Mortality] artifically inflate the amount of 'true' progress." (U.S. General Accounting Office, "Cancer Patient Survival: What Progress Has Been Made?", Washington D.C., March 1987).

Researchers have found, in experimental studies with animals, that surgery per se has a deleterious effect on a patient's immune system and resistance to cancer. Noting that "Most surgeons have encountered the patient whose cancer grows rapidly following operation, resulting in death within a few weeks." Drs. Gerald O. McDonald and Warren H. Cole purposely injected cancer cells into animals that had undergone various types of surgery and compared the results to control animals, similarly injected. They found that the chances of a tumor growing as a result of surgery increased anywhere from 50 to 450%. (Patrick McGrady, *The Savage Cell*, Basic Books, 1964)

Finally, in 1976, the National Cancer Institute, in proceedings before the Select Senate Committee of the U.S. Congress, declared that proper nutrition, including a diet high in fruits and vegetables, is the best prevention against cancer. Its conclusions were well publicized, and were followed by similar pronouncements from the the American Cancer Society and other authorities.

It is now reported that a recent controlled study by the National Cancer Institute resulted in a 13 percent reduction in cancer mortality in 30,000 residents of Hunan province in China who were provided supplemental carotene, Vitamin E, and selenium.

Closer to home, the National Academy of Sciences declares that 60% of men's and 40% of women's cancers may be due to nutritional factors. (*Diet, Nutrition and Cancer*, National Academy Press, 1982) Does this not imply that at least half the problem is being ignored, and in fact suppressed, by this arrogant legislation?

Even today, with thousands of people including the author traveling to Mexico simply in order to exercise real choice in the matter of cancer therapy, the many victories emerging from those alternative therapies are given no consideration. Only the relatively small band of members and adherents of the National Health Federation and the Cancer Control Society, each of whom maintain liaison with the Tijuana clinics and their patients, have knowledge of the fact that cancer, properly treated by natural therapies yields better results generally, and many cures.

Emblematic of this health revolution is little Billy Best, a formerly terminal cancer patient whose parents fled with him from

California to secure alternative therapy in Tijuana, in violation of a court order that had imposed "scientifically proven" chemotherapy "for the good of the patient." Today Billy speaks from the platforms of the Cancer Control Society, telling anyone who cares to listen of his stunning recovery and current good health. We all heard or read about his case in the news media several years ago when his courageous parents fled with him to Mexico. But, newsworthiness notwithstanding, the general public is completely unaware of the successful conclusion of this family's valiant struggle to protect Billy from certain death had conventional wisdom in the form of chemotherapy, as mandated by the California Legislature, had its way.

While alternative therapies have continued to make great strides forward, the allopaths have continued also--stubbornly doing the same things over and over again and expecting a different outcome. Wasn't it President Clinton who cited this as one of the definitions of insanity?

Dr. Hardin Jones, a biophysicist who taught at the Department of Medical Physics, University of California, studied the demographics of cancer for 23 years. He traveled the world, collecting case histories of women who had biopsy-diagnosed cancer of the breast but who refused surgery, radiation or chemotherapy. He then compared their years of survival, from date of diagnosis to date of death, with the known survival statistics of patients in the United States who were treated by established methodologies. He concluded:

"My studies have proved conclusively that untreated cancer victims actually live up to four times longer than treated individuals...

"It is utter nonsense to claim that catching cancer symptoms early enough will increase the patient's chances of survival. Not one medical scientist or study has proven that so in any way.

"Following surgery, unfortunately, it seems to be only a question of time before the disease pops up again all over the body. I attribute this to the traumatic effect of surgery on the body's natural defense mechanisms [the immune system]. Medical treatment seems to interfere with and mess up this natural resistence.

"You see, it is not the cancer that kills the victim. It's the breakdown of the defense mechanism that eventually brings death."

He so testified in three cases in which California doctors were prosecuted for using Laetrile in their treatment of cancer patients: John A. Richardson, M.D., Stewart M. Jones, M.D., and James R. Privitera, Jr., M.D.

In the years intervening since then knowledge of the immune system--the "defense mechanism" against cancer--has quadrupled, and is largely confirmatory of Dr. Jones' position.

His opinion is now buttressed by that of Dr. Alan Levin, M.D. of the U.C. Medical School, who finds that women with breast cancer die faster with chemotherapy than without that added chemical insult. (*The Healing of Cancer*, Marcus Books, 1989)

And Dr. John Cairns, M.D., Harvard School of Public Health, has found that of the half million people who die each year from cancer, only 2 or 3 percent benefited from chemotherapy. (New England Journal of Medicine, March, 1985)

Because of the U.S. Supreme Court's abortion decisions, everyone in this country is now aware that every individual possesses a "right of privacy" that entitles him or her to make certain basic decisions about personal matters. Our California Supreme Court also proudly proclaims the right of privacy--for the abortion decision--but holds that:

"the right to make the kinds of 'important decisions' recognized by the [U. S. Supreme Court] to date as falling within the right of privacy . . . do not include medical treatment". (People vs. Privitera, 1979, 23 Cal 3d 697, 702).

Paradoxically, a pregnant woman has the right to decide whether to wilfully deprive her unborn baby of his or her life, but does not have the right to save her own life by choosing a remedy for the cure of her cancer unless she chooses the State's mandated, take-it-or-leave-it, surgery, radiation or chemotherapy. This, allegedly, because:

"The lesson of Roe vs. Wade for our case is that a requirement that a drug be certified effective for its intended use is a reasonable means to ' insure maximum safety for the patient'." (23 Cal 3d 697,703)

The court's concern, in so finding, was of course that the State has a right to protect its citizens from fraudulent methods of treatment. Ironically, also, the court evidences a solicitous concern for "safety for the patient." Hence, if we can overlook the fact that the establishment methodologies have not solved anything in 36 years; that cancer mortality, for those who contract cancer, has remained essentially unchanged over the years; that the incidence of cancer has increased year by year to a now overwhelming ratio; and that the legislation was initially based upon an erroneous assumption of efficacy in the first place, we can have no quarrel with the conclusions of the court. Unless we happen to question how deprivation of the "cure" for his cancer is best for the patient! (Note, again, and never forget, the statute prohibits "alleviation or cure of cancer" by any unapproved remedy.)

While the factual underpinnings of the case seem at variance with the conclusions of the court, the legal assumptions upon which the court based its decision are equally unsustaining. In fact, Justice Newman accused the majority of the justices of lying about the state of the law, saying: "By selective quotation the majority opinion downgrades the right of privacy in California..." (p.741)

In the course of its opinion the majority said:

"Whether cancer patients--especially advanced cancer patients who have unsuccessfully sought relief from conventional therapy and who are fully informed as to the consensus of scientific opinion concerning the drug--should have access to Laetrile is clearly a question about which reasonable persons may differ." (23 Cal 3d at 708, (Emphasis added)

This language clearly leaves the rational mind with but one conclusion: since "reasonable persons may differ" as to whether to choose alternative therapy or conventional treatment, the patient logically is the one who should have the right to choose. HOW could anyone believe that the State has the right to force a decision in a situation wherein one might as reasonably choose alternative therapy as conventional treatment? If the State has the right to dictate the choice in such life or death circumstances what has happened to the concept of individual libery?

Since the United States Constitution is entirely silent on the question of medical treatment, or the kind or quality thereof, but does stipulate that two of its purposes are to "promote the general Welfare, and secure the Blessings of Liberty to ourselves and our Posterity," was it not the duty of the court to hold that suppression of a substance that will "alleviate or cure cancer," as per the words of Sec. 1707.1, is no blessing?

And, where the court concedes that "reasonable persons may differ" in choosing between alternative medicine and the potentially harmful effects of the mandated surgery, radiation and chemotherapy, is not the Ninth Amendment controlling?

It provides:

"The enumeration in the Constitution of certain rights shall not be construed to deny or disparage others retained by the people."

Nevertheless, the court inexplicibly found that "the asserted right to obtain drugs of unproven efficacy is not encompassed by the right of privacy embodied in either the Federal or the State Constitutions." (p. 702) Having found no right of privacy the court felt itself free to declare that "The appropriate standard of review is the rational basis test, rather than the compelling State interest test." (p.702, emphasis added)

But, notice where this takes us: Having found that the State has a "rational basis" to regulate in the field of cancer health care, the court irrationally upholds, on that ground, a statute that deprives the cancer patient of a cure--i.e. of his very life. There is no room to argue otherwise, since the statute itself prohibits use of remedies which concededly have the capacity to provide "alleviation or cure of cancer." Of course the court was dead certain that nothing like this could possibly happen--but it was also dead wrong.

Contrary to the court's impression, Dr. Privitera was never convicted of "quackery." He was actually charged and convicted of conspiracy "to commit the crime of the Unlawful Sale of Drugs, Compounds or Devices for the Alleviation or Cure of Cancer (H & S 1707.1)...". He was charged, proven guilty of, and convicted, of "alleviating or curing cancer." (See page 1 of the Indictment appended hereto.) And at least five of his previously terminal patients who had been tremendously improved under Laetrile therapy suffered the death penalty when Dr. Privitera was ordered by the court not to administer or provide Laetrile to his patients any longer.

Let us take a page from a different case, that of Dr. Bruce W. Halstead, M.D., Director of World Life Research Institute in Colton CA. Dr. Halstead enjoyed an illustrious career until he was confronted with the "alleviation or cure" provisions of Section 1707.1. He was formerly president of the Loma Linda Medical School, possesses what is probably the largest privately owned medical library in the State of California, has authored hundreds of learned articles on various medical subjects, and is recognized as a world class expert on marine toxicology. He was also a consultant to the World Health Organization of the United Nations, and authored a huge two volume treatise on marine toxicology.

In a 13 page letter, Dr. Halstead recounts some of his experiences during his seven week preliminary hearing and his 3 1/2 month trial on 28 counts alleging various crimes, all of which arose from his insistence upon alleviating or curing cancer. His description of the termination of poor Mrs. Dix, by enforcement of Sec. 1707.1, tells the whole story. This is a lady who had undergone chemotherapy and over 90 radiation treatments, all of which had failed. Her doctors had told her that she had only 30 to 45 days to live.

Please note that this woman, after use of an allegedly "quack" herbal remedy for 10 days “started doing housework, shopping, traveling, and started entertaining again...She was walking, mentally alert, happy and laughing, and stated emphatically that she was feeling great." (Dr. Halstead' s letter)

But Mrs. Dix quickly relapsed and died after the District Attorney seized her herbal remedy. And Dr. Halstead was convicted of 20 felony and misdemeanor counts, and was sentenced to 32 months in prison.

So much for the court's "rational basis" test.

This hideous scenario, while a little more dramatic than most, has been reenacted many times since the enactment of 1707.1. The reason, simply stated, is because allopathy is the rule of Sec. 1707.1, and allopathy talks the talk and walks the walk that is totally foreign to nature and to nature's laws of healing. This point is explicitly and dramatically demonstrated by allopathy's erroneous definition of "cancer," which is written into the law at Section 1705:

"For the purposes of this chapter, 'cancer' means all malignant neoplasms regardless of the tissue of origin, including malignant lymphoma, Hodgkins disease, and leukemia."

Malignant means merely, "life threatening. Neoplasm means, "new" (neo) "tissue," plus (plasm), i.e., a newly formed lump or bump of abnormal tissue. That, says allopathy, is cancer!

Notice that nothing is said about CAUSE. Indisputably, something caused that lump or bump. But the lump or bump--the result -- is, by definition, the sum total of the disease entity. By definition, also, no consideration whatsoever is given to the health status of the patient.

In practice therefore the allopath pays little or no attention to the question of diet or nutritional supplementation except, in some cases, to attempt replacement of some of the nutrients that are destroyed by chemotherapy treatments. This is where the vitalist, or natural practitioner, collides head on with the allopath, and the patient gets shoved into the ditch. Because of bias and self interest, the allopathically dominated Cancer Advisory Council has never approved anything for cancer treatment except surgery, radiation and chemotherapy.

By administrative regulations (17 Cal Admin Code, Sections 10400, 10400.1, 10400.2, 10400.3, 10400.4, 10400.5, 10400.7) they have barred and made criminal all of the natural and non-toxic remedies of the vitalists. They have even barred the use of a very effective urine test for cancer (17 C.A.C. Sec. 10500.6).

Allopathic physicians, in accordance with the doctrines, tenets and standards of allopathic medicine, attempt to treat cancer by removing or destroying the lump or bump--the symptom of the underlying but undiscovered metabolic cause. When surgery fails, or would endanger the life of the patient, radiation or chemotherapy, or both, are administered. Unfortunately, radiation and chemotheraupeutic drugs are invariably destructive of the immune system, which is the patient's best defense against cancer. Non-allopathic physicians--homeopathic, eclectic and naturopathic, and to a lesser extent the osteopaths--place more emphasis upon strengthening the patient's physical and mental condition, thereby strengthening his innate self-healing capacity.

So there we have it. After 36 years of "scientifically proven" remedies--mandatory remedies--mandated by this abhorrent statute, we are confronted by the following indisputable facts:

1. Cancer mortality is irresistibly on the increase. Also, one out of three, instead of one out of five of us, will contract cancer.

2. Nobody is living longer because of the "scientifically proven" remedies mandated by Section 1707.1. No progress has been made in the 36 years since this monopoly legislation was enacted, as is evidenced by the ever increasing incidence of cancer and the upthrusted mortality curve.

3. The statute fails to address the cause of cancer, but instead erroneously identifies its principal symptom, the tumor, as the disease itself.

4. The immune system--an unknown factor 36 years ago -is now known to be the patient's best defense against cancer.

5. Surgery, radiation and chemotherapy--the "scientifically proven" methods mandated by Section 1707.1--all seriously injure the immune system.

6. Death may be hastened by surgery if the surgeon doesn't "get it all." And both chemotherapy and radiation have the disadvantage that they, in and of themselves, are known to cause cancer.

7. It is now a universally accepted medical fact that lack of proper nutrition may play a part in causing cancer, and that adequate nutrition helps to prevent cancer. Whether nutrition will actually "cure" cancer is still debated.

8. Notwithstanding these admitted facts, the doctor who uses nutrition in his treatment of cancer commits a violation of 1707.1, and stands a good chance of going to jail. And, he goes to jail even thouugh he actually cured cancer with the offending unapproved remedy.

The Legislature of the State of California has become the enemy of the people. Seeking to impose error and falsehood upon the practice of medicine in the guise of compassionate concern for the health and welfare of the people the Legislature, backed by an errant judiciary, deprives us not only of our health but of our wealth, in this mandated utilization of expensive, useless and injurious procedures.

Section 1707.1, now fully exposed to the light and properly understood, offers no "rational basis" test. Instead, it irrationally compels innocent, helpless and trusting victims of cancer to accept, from among the "scientifically proven" remedies endorsed by the statute, the alleged remedy by which their physician will administer the final coup de grace.

This, then, is compassion California style.

ADDENDUM: Those who are new to California's unique brand of compassion, as embodied in Section 1707.1, will find it difficult to accept the full impact of the foregoing conclusions, even in the face of the overwhelming uncontradicted evidence. There is a natural reluctance on the part of everyone of us to believe that our government could be guilty of a course of action that, on careful analysis, circumstantially suggests what can only be described as “homicidal intent”, implied by the blatant suppression of a cure for cancer.

The mind simply refuses to accept the outrageous consequences of that dictate. We mentally grope, instead, by such formulas as "Doctor knows best," or "No court would <u>really</u> apply the statute literally," to ease the horrendous impact of this genocidal phraseology. Even I mentally questioned the reality of the nightmare I was a part of as I appeared in court as attorney for doctors and others who had cured cancer by innocent diets, herbal teas and enemas and were prosecuted for doing so. How could this be happening? How could it have come to this?

Our thinking processes are largely determined by what we “know,” and what we know tends to control what we are willing to believe. There is an overwhelming hypnotic power in what we call “conventional wisdom.” Our existing store of knowledge tells us what is relevant, what is “true” and what is “false.” In effect, **we know** what we know what we know.

Regardless of all evidence to the contrary, what we know stands as proof that a new procedure or scientific fact is false and will not work when it contradicts what we "know." Add to this the force of "law," and we have, again, the scenario of the Church Universal enforcing ordained truth vs. Galileo the blasphemer. GOD/LAW has decreed it; for that reason we believe it, and it is not necessary to re-examine the previously ordained facts.

The defendant, in claiming that he is able to cure cancer, admits his own guilt, and is guilty again in asserting that he can do what God himself cannot do.

But prosecuting the doctor for daring to cure cancer would, by itself, be unacceptable. It must be made to appear that the establishment knows what it is doing, and is making progress in the right direction. Therefore, notwithstanding that nobody knew what cancer was, or how to cure it, it was "defined," in Section 1705. According to the conventional wisdom of the day its physical manifestation in the form of a lump or bump--in reality one of the symptoms--became the "disease." This was a totally erroneous assumption, but it was all that was known at the time and has since served as a very useful lie.

First, it put an end to the war of ideas in the scientific arena. Scientific error was legally institutionalized. Manifestly false science became medical truths which were both practiced and enforced. Of necessity, of course, this resulted in a monopoly for the accepted allopathic procedures: surgery, radiation and chemotherapy.

But, in order to fully protect the innocent public from the "non-knowers" the "quacks" who advocate new and different and competing remedies--it was the good fortune of the "knowers" to be entrusted with the legislative apparatus for the "investigation of new drugs." Sections 1701-1704 gave the oncologists complete control of the Cancer Advisory Council (1701), which is permitted to meet in secret (1702), and which is entrusted with the responsibility to "Hold hearings in respect of those matters involving compliance. . . ." The fox was both guardian and judge over the chicken house.

Although the big lie of the cancer "definition" is readily apparent to those of us who now know about the immune system and its function in controlling cancer, it must be kept in mind that it was the conventional wisdom--the accepted fact--of the day in which this legislation was enacted. That conventional wisdom still acts as a drag upon our thinking processes, our communication, our advocacy, and our interpretation of this legislative program.

Today, everybody knows that surgery, radiation and chemotherapy are not protecting us from cancer, but nobody has been willing to honestly examine the reasons why we have made no progress against it. We need to free ourselves of the shackles of conventional wisdom and look at the express language of the statutes, as they candidly speak to us.

We have all been misled by conventional wisdom and respect for the "Law." Like George Orwell's robotized citizens of his novel, "1984," we have all endured 36 years of hypnotic-trance-like existence, relying upon Big Brother to protect us from our common enemy and unaware of the evil being done to us thereby. By this legislation the State has unduly enriched one segment of the medical profession at the expense of all of us. It is time to wake up!

Index

--A--

--B--

--C--

--D--

--E--

--F--

--G--

--H--

--I--

--J--

--K--

--L--

--Q--

--R--

--S--

--T--

--V--

--W--

--Z--

About the Authors

James R. Privitera, M.D., is a 1967 graduate of the Creighton University School of Medicine, in Omaha, Nebraska. He interned at Providence Hospital, Seattle, Washington, and took a residency in internal medicine at Presbyterian Hospital, in San Francisco. Later, he was a Clinical Fellow in Allergy, Immunology and Rheumatology at Scripps Clinic and Research Foundation, in La Jolla, California. In 1970, he began the private practice of allergy and nutrition in Covina, California, where he practices today.

Dr. Privitera has been professionally affiliated with (ACAM) the American College for Advancement in Medicine; the American College of Sports Medicine; the International Academy of Preventive Medicine; the International College of Applied Nutrition; the Northwest Academy of Preventive Medicine; the American Society of Parenteral and Enteral Nutrition; the American Academy of Allergy; and the National Health Federation

He is a consultant to some of the nation's leading supplement manufacturers on their vitamin and mineral formulations. He advises physicians from around the world on the use of darkfield and live cell analysis.

***

Alan Stang has been a member of the working press for almost forty years. He wrote the Tex and Jinx radio show at NBC in New York. He was an original Mike Wallace writer, and is the reason Mike is meaner than a junkyard dog.

He has written hundreds of feature articles in national magazines. Many of those articles have been reprinted in the millions. He has lectured around the world, and was twice an official guest of the Republic of China on Taiwan. He is a daily network radio talk show host, on stations across the country. He went head to head with Larry King in Los Angeles, and, according to Arbitron, had almost twice as many listeners.

The Pennsylvania House of Representatives cited him for journalistic excellence. The American Academy of Public Affairs of Los Angeles, chaired by Loyd Wright, former chairman of the American Bar Association, applauded his scholarship and journalism. He served two terms as a member of the Board of the National Health Federation.

One of his novels, *The Highest Virtue*, won five stars--top rating--from the *West Coast Review of Books,* an accolade won by little more than 1% of the reviews.

More Clots

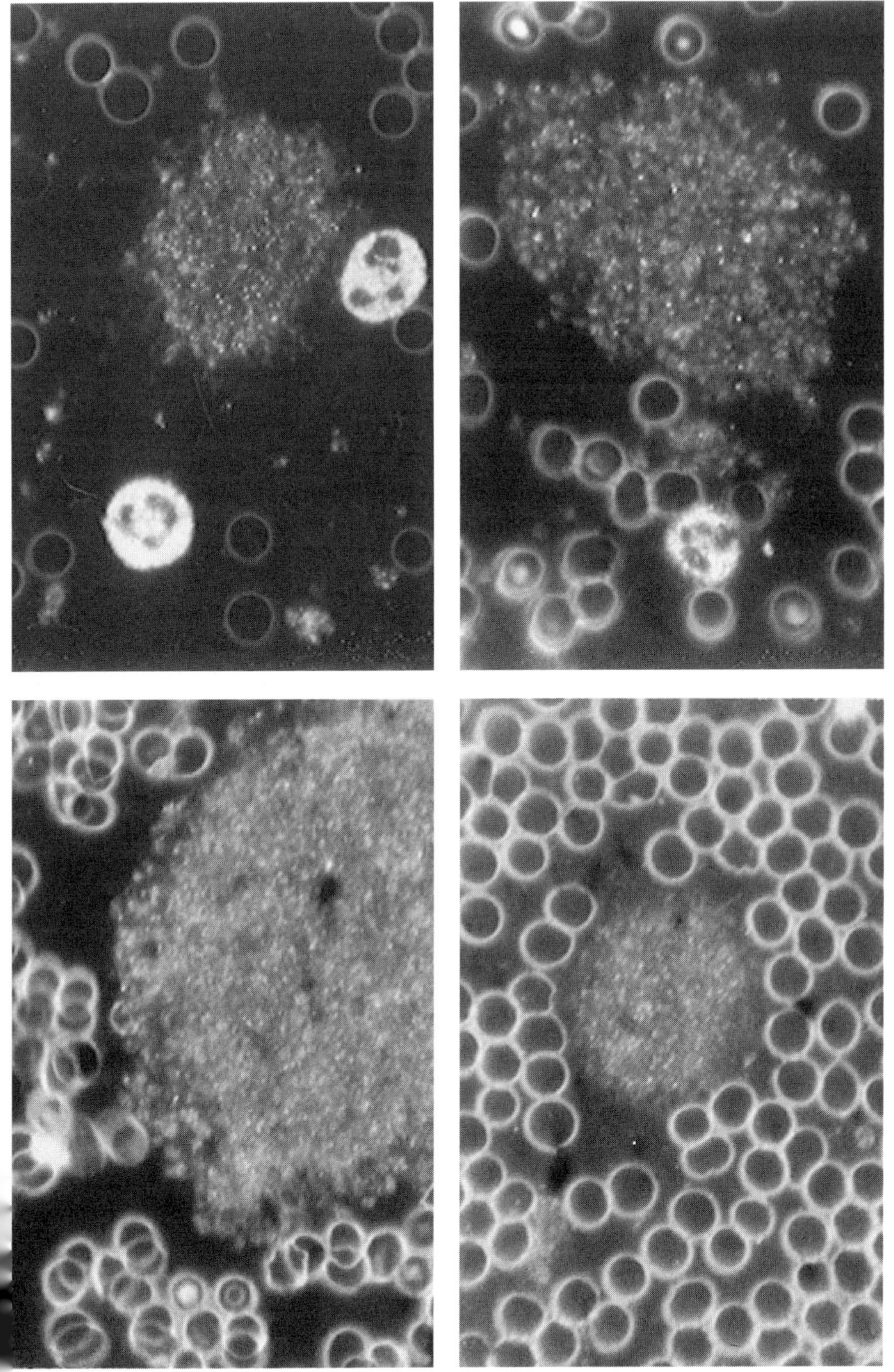

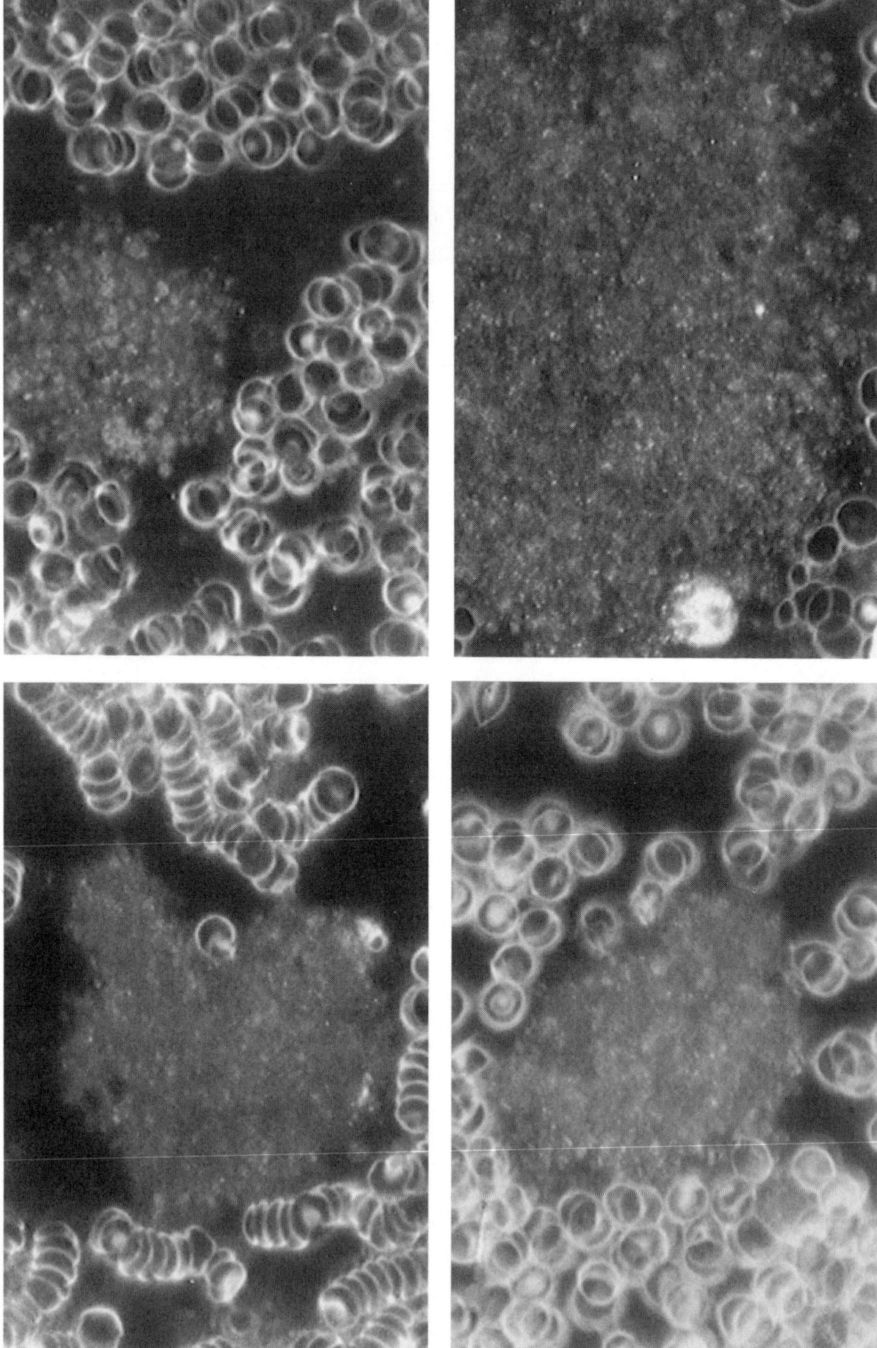